For Shaun, thank you for your support.

PROLOGUE

NOVEMBER 1811

The hard pebbles of the beach dug into her knees and sweat trickled down the girl's forehead, despite the bitterly cold wind blowing fiercely across the shore. With the waves crashing noisily behind her, and the dark menacing Black Ven cliffs in front of her, she pushed the pain aside with steely determination and worked tirelessly on.

Having already been on these shores for hours, out in the harsh elements of Lyme Regis beach, she wouldn't give up now. After all, she was used to this kind of hardship, even though she was barely 12 years old.

As she worked, she remembered the first time she had seen an ammonite and understood it was the remains of an animal not of this world, but from the past. Since then, she had been fascinated by these strange creatures who had lived millions of years before.

Today, the familiar fire inside of her was fuelling her strength and determination to uncover this long-buried creature. It burned like a flame in her heart as she tapped with her hammer and chisel at the rock around it, being careful not to break the skeleton as she worked.

Her hair was a tangled mess around her face, and she could barely feel her fingers they were so frozen with cold, but time was running out. The light was fading fast, and the tide would soon cover this stretch of beach. Hopefully, before that happened, the others would arrive and see this magnificent spectacle for themselves.

At last, taking in a long deep breath of salty sea air, she sat back on her haunches. Her hands were covered in slimy mud and her skirts were soaking wet. The cold wet had seeped into her underdrawers, making her shiver in the bitter cold wind of the late winter afternoon, but joy danced in her chest.

Gazing steadily down at her work, the girl gasped at the sight of what now lay exposed. Even though it was still stuck fast in the solid rocks, she could see the whole skeleton of the strange 'fish-like' creature in front of her.

There was still a lot to be done to release the animal from its resting place, but she could already see the outline of its long body. All the years that her father had searched for a monster like this was now a lead weight in her chest.

"It is somewhere out there on these shores, Mary. It will be found amongst the rocks and cliffs," he had told her firmly. "We just have to keep looking for it."

Now, her pa would never see this monster in all its glory, and this thought brought regret to her heart and tears to her eyes. Her father was greatly missed in the year since he had died.

Brushing her tears aside, she focused on the creature and tried to determine how big it was. At a rough guess it seemed to be about 16 or 17 feet in length, with a long backbone and four paddle feet. It was hard to take her eyes off its huge head and long snout. The large, saucer-shaped eye socket was staring out at her unnervingly from where it had lain for perhaps two hundred million years.

It had been a waiting game, and taken a whole year for the storms to expose the surface of the beach and the cliffs before the foreshore was rearranged by the corrosive action of the sea. Only then was the creature exposed enough to be seen and ready to be excavated. Even now, it would take a huge amount of work and effort to prise the monster from its solid, rocky bed at the bottom of Black Ven cliffs.

"Mary! We are coming to help!"

Mary's head came up at the sound of her brother's voice, and she saw Joseph and her friend Miss Philpott hurrying towards her on the beach. She lifted her hand and pushed her wet, matted hair out of her eyes, before quickly scrabbling to her feet.

Miss Philpott would know what to do next, Mary was certain, as she heaved a sigh of relief that help had at last arrived. She took one last look at the mysterious creature.

"You're quite a monster, aren't you? A gift from another world, but you also be stuff of nightmares," Mary told its black gaze rather fondly. "My father would be proud we found you. But I believe you are not a crocodile, nor a fish lizard. Whatever you be, I'll find out," she promised, before tearing her gaze away from the creature and greeting her brother and Miss Philpott.

CHAPTER 1

PRESENT DAY, ELIZA

"Whoa! What the heck?!"

The words came tumbling out of my mouth on a breathless gasp, as my feet shot out from under me and my bottom met the hard stones of Lyme Regis beach with a loud thump.

As my hands tingled with pain and my head throbbed, I tried to make sense of what had just happened. Embarrassingly, and for reasons unknown, I'd been knocked clean off my feet and was now lying sprawled in an ungainly position on the beach.

I lay there stunned for a moment as the sound of the waves washing to shore, along with the noise of people chattering, seagulls crying, and dogs barking, was suddenly magnified in my ears. I must have been winded in the fall, because my chest ached, and I was finding it hard to breathe.

Forcing air into my lungs, I became aware of a man standing over me. But blinded by the overhead sun, all I could see was his dark-shadow-like figure. I lifted one hand to shield my eyes, but as the sun disappeared behind a cloud, the man's features became clearer, and my heart missed a beat at the astonishing sight in front of me.

Good grief! How could I be looking into the face of a man who lived two hundred years ago? It just wasn't possible. Those amber coloured eyes and that dark hair flopping across his forehead looked so familiar to me, and as thoughts tumbled clumsily through my brain, I tried to make sense of what I was seeing.

With the man now looking at me with a puzzled expression, I suddenly realised I had been staring up at him rudely. I shook that other image from my head and tore my gaze away from the man, while trying to dislodge the eerie feeling that was slowly creeping through my bones. My limbs were now frozen with something other than the tumble I'd just taken, and my confusion grew.

"Oh, Lord, I'm so sorry! Are you okay?" said the man, a concerned frown etched between his dark brows. "Harry really needs to look where he's going. I've told him a million times about racing around the beach like that."

I gulped but no words came out. The long-ago memories had been coming thick and fast a minute ago as I had gazed out to sea before Harry, whoever he was, had slammed straight into me and knocked me for six.

"I think I'm alright…" I murmured at last, still feeling stunned from the fall while mentally checking myself over for any injuries. The man was still staring at me and was annoyingly persistent in his concern.

"Hmmm… are you sure? You don't look alright, to be honest. Can I help you up?" He held out his hand to me while pushing a strand of black hair out of his eyes.

Under his intense scrutiny, my face suddenly flooded with heat, this often happened when I was embarrassed, I was used to it. It went with my fair complexion and auburn hair.

He was so damned handsome I just wished he'd go away and leave me alone to salvage my pride. However, he continued to stare at me, obviously waiting for me to confirm that nothing was broken.

I waved his hand away. "No really, thanks, but I'm cool," I told him, hearing the shakiness in my own voice.

That was an out and out lie but, hey, I was trying to put a brave face on the physical bruises I could feel already forming in my backside area, and the emotional turmoil of only a few moments before which I could still feel in the tightness of my chest and the throbbing of my head.

To show the man that I *was* fine, I hauled myself up quickly from my sitting position, lifted my chin, and then proceeded to give my jeans a quick brush down.

"See I'm okay," I confirmed, lifting my eyes to his amber gaze before glancing around to see a small boy standing awkwardly next to the man.

The child's large brown eyes were wide with worry, as if he was about to be punished for his misdemeanour. This must be Harry, the guilty party, who looked like a miniature version of the man (apart from the eye colour), and the reason I ended up flat on my backside on the beach.

"Don't worry, I'm fine." I offered the boy a shaky smile and tried to put him at ease. Harry looked about six or seven years old, and he had the cutest little face, which was all dark hair and freckles.

"Actually, it was more than likely my fault," I admitted into the silence, swallowing hard while forcing myself to look at Harry. "I was miles away in my head and was prob-ably in the way of your game." I gave a little shrug, hoping this would reassure the lad.

Harry's dad stared at me and then he lifted one eyebrow at me as if to say, 'Are you for real?' "Even so, Harry will be apologising to you, won't you, Harry?" he said, giving his son an extremely stern look.

The boy glanced anxiously from his dad to me. "Sorry," he said quietly. "Didn't mean to knock you over. I was playing tag with my friend Lucas," he explained, indicating another small boy who was standing nearby.

"Well done, Harry," his dad said, sounding relieved and stepping forwards to ruffle his son's hair affectionately. "I'm sure you haven't done *too* much harm to the lady. At least I hope not?" he said, looking across at me steadily with a questioning gaze.

The expression in the man's startling amber eyes made my stomach flutter, not unlike the feeling I got looking into that other intense gaze. Again, that feeling of *déjà vu* came upon me, causing a shiver to run up my spine.

"Course not." I tore my eyes away from the man's penetrating gaze and addressed the child again. "I hope you have a nice day with your friend," I told the boy, while at the same time wondering if it was my imagination, or worse, my state of mind, which was making me have these weird thoughts about Harry's dad.

Harry gave me a wide grin and then ran over to his friend waiting patiently for his return. Relief flooded the man's face as the two boys chattered excitedly together.

"Thanks, I appreciate it. Not everyone would have been so understanding," he said with a tilt of his head.

"Oh well, these things happen, and I'm alright, that's the main thing," I reassured him with a resigned shrug.

Harry's dad shot me an appreciative glance and then turned to the children. "Come on now, boys, and for goodness' sake, be more careful next time," he warned, with a wag of his finger as he shepherded them away.

I was graced with a cursory glance by all three before they made their way across the beach. Maybe they were checking I'd definitely survived the fall intact and wouldn't be suing anyone for damages anytime soon.

Turning away from the trio, I rubbed hard at my sore hand, which had an indent of pebbles from the fall, then I quickly made my way back to work and the teashop. There was something pressing I had to do.

CHAPTER 2

FEBRUARY 1824, MARY

*S*moke grey clouds scudded across the sky above Mary Anning as she searched the Lyme Regis shores in an attempt at rootling out a fossil. The wind was gusting along the shore, the salty sea air filled her lungs, and she shivered while pulling her heavy cloak tighter around her body in an effort to keep warm.

The waves on the beach were high today and were crashing to the shore with a fury often seen at this time of year. Mary always kept track of what the sea was doing. It was dangerous not to. For the sea could be quick to cover the shore when a person wasn't paying enough attention.

Today was one of those days when she found herself longing for the bright sunlight of summer, instead of this dark and cold winter's day, especially as she had been searching for hours but had found nothing of any consequence. However, it was not time to give up yet. As she well knew, perseverance often paid off, and she refused to go home without a good-sized ammonite or belemnite to sell in the shop.

It was just as she had her gaze riveted to the shoreline,

searching for the right size stones, that the sound of pebbles crunching beneath feet reached her ears. Mary glanced across the beach and saw a man striding quickly towards her. Her heart sank. Turning away from him, she hoped he would disappear into thin air and leave her alone, but it was not to be.

As the man came closer, Mary was determined to ignore him, so kept her back turned away. Some days were more difficult than others when it came to facing the visiting geologists, and today, when finding the fossils was harder than usual, was one of those days.

"How do you do?" the man yelled above the roar of the sea. "I apologise for being presumptuous, but are you by any chance Miss Mary Anning?"

Mary could feel him standing right behind her, but she kept her gaze averted, even though she knew this was rude. However, the man was persistent, and he hovered next to her, unwilling it seemed to depart without her at least acknowledging his presence.

Letting out a long sigh, Mary at last turned around and tried to gather her patience. She wasn't in the mood to impart any hard-earned knowledge today.

"I am Miss Anning, that be true, sir," she said with a lift of her jaw. "But I've never seen you afore, although I certainly know your type," she added abruptly.

Hoping he would get the message now, Mary lowered her gaze and began brushing sand from a small vertebra she had picked up earlier. The man shifted uncomfortably on his feet, and she was aware he was still reluctant to leave.

"Mary, you must remember me?" he persisted. "It's me, Mr Hansome," he continued, widening his amber coloured eyes at her.

Mr Hansome? Mary became aware that the name was known to her, but she couldn't place who he was. When she turned around to look at him properly, she was surprised to see his unusual attire.

The man wasn't dressed in the normal clothes for outside work at this time of the year, when the inclement weather was prone to being so cold and wet. Instead of a greatcoat and hessian boots, he had on a dark blue velvet tailcoat and top hat, which was completely unsuitable for the purpose of fossil hunting.

However, underneath that top-hat his eyes looked familiar. They were an unusual colour and reminded her of an amber coloured stone she had found in amongst the fossils recently.

She shook her head. He might look familiar, but he was probably a geologist who had been to see her about buying one of her discoveries recently, and that was how they knew each other. Mary had seen so many geologists recently that she had no idea who this one was. But one thing was certain: he would do what most of the men did, and attempt to take recognition for one of her finds.

She wrinkled her nose in disgust at him. "I be sorry, Mr Hansome, but I'm very busy today," she said, again rather rudely. "If you want to buy a fossil from my shop, it be located at Cockmoile Square, at the top of the hill." She pointed in the direction of the square. "My mother be in the shop and would be happy to serve you."

Then Mary turned her back on the man before adjusting her bonnet, replacing the vertebra in her basket, and calling to her little dog Tray to follow her along the beach.

As she strode away, to her dismay, she could hear the gentleman was still following her. Would he never give up? Mary usually made herself highly approachable to the men of science, because they often bought her finds, and she and her mother had to eat.

But some days she would rather not waste her time

listening to their so-called knowledge, when if the truth be told, she often knew more about the fossils than they did.

"Miss Anning, please don't go. Miss Anning, it's me!"

Mary was determined not to be forestalled by the man as she moved quickly along the shore with her long dark skirts brushing the pebbles behind her. She had often found that if she chose to ignore the visiting geologists, they would go away and leave her alone.

Intent on getting away from the man, Mary hurried, but as always, her gaze was not directed on the horizon in front of her but on the pebbles underneath her feet. This had been her way since she was a tiny girl when her pa had taught her how to search and find the fossils.

Mary's mind was always on what she could find amongst the shells and stones; this was her lifeblood and her very soul. 'You have the eye, Mary,' Richard Anning had told her when he had first started his teachings on these shores. "Not all of us have that ability, but you are blessed."

Mary squinted at the sea creature which was lying between two rather large pebbles; its star shape was almost lost in the colour of the rock, it was so securely entombed. But her keen eye had spotted it. Uncaring now of the man who was still pursuing her, she stopped abruptly, gathered up her skirts, and stooped low to pick it up.

The fossil came out easily, and Mary stood up and stared down at it lying in her palm. Her heart was gladdened that on this day of futile searching, she had found something of a good size that would sell well in the shop, and all before darkness had descended to leave her empty-handed.

The treasures she found never ceased to amaze Mary, and despite the years she had spent doing this, they still seemed to her to be magical beings from another world. As she brushed at the mud encrusted on the rock, Mary became aware that the man had now caught up with her.

"What have you there, Miss Anning? Is it a belemnite perhaps, or is it one of those brittle star fossils?" the man asked.

Mary could feel him waiting for her response to this, and a brief memory surfaced in her mind from long ago. She pushed her bonnet further back on her head and met the man's gaze.

"It is a brittle star," she answered, tilting her head to one side and holding out the fossil to show him the star-fish shape. "What be your name again?" she asked. An image swam in her mind of a dark-haired boy, with unusual coloured eyes, she had known a long time ago.

"My name's George Hansome. You must remember how I used to come to this beach with my father William many years ago. That day, Mary, we searched for fossils, and I found two and you only found one? We particularly loved finding those fossils that were star-shaped as children, didn't we?" His face lit up as he smiled at this memory.

Mary's heart lurched, and she suddenly realised who this man was. As he waited for her response, it came back to her how she had pouted her lips at him that day as a child and demanded he give her his fossil.

"George! I mean, Mr Hansome. Goodness, it's been so long." Her hand flew to her chest. This was George, the boy she had spent many a happy hour with on these shores.

"Sorry for being rude to you just now, but if I be honest, it were hard to recognise you." Mary stared at him for a moment, hardly able to believe he was here, and trying not to remember the times she had thought about George over the years.

"You be dressed strangely for fossil hunting, Mr Hansome, if that's what you be doing here," she ventured, always one to speak plainly.

George let out a long sigh and smiled good-naturedly

back at her, then he looked down at his clothes. "I came straight from the stagecoach and forgot to change before coming to the beach," he explained.

Then he looked around at the gathering darkness of the late afternoon. "I wanted to see you before you finished your fossil hunting for the day," he added, with a lift of those dark eyebrows.

As George spoke, he tipped his hat to Mary, and she saw those familiar black curls springing loose from his head. This was definitely George, the young lad she had loved like a brother so long ago. She attempted to still her beating heart as she straightened her back and took in his appearance, which she tried to reconcile with the boy she had once known.

"How have you been?" Mary couldn't help feeling this was a silly question, and something you would ask if you had not seen each other for a week, not years.

"Life has treated me well, Mary," George answered, holding her gaze.

She was feeling guilty for treating George rudely earlier, and instinctively she held out the fossil to him, even though it was valuable to her. Especially today when it was all she had found of value on these shores.

"I think I owe *you* a few fossils, after all those that I took from you long ago," she said, trying not to stare at his handsome face and remembering how generous he had been back then. But George shook his head vigorously at the gift.

The very first time Mary met George had been on this same stretch of beach when they were children. They had bumped into each other while out hunting for fossils with their respective fathers, and struck up a friendship. George's father William was a doctor, but also a naturalist, and William's passion for nature had rubbed off on his son from a young age.

Even though George and his family lived in Exeter, William had brought George to this beach as often as he could, to comb this Jurassic coast for relics of the past and to see the wonders of the earth they lived on.

Mary's father Richard was a cabinet-maker, but he also earned money from fossil hunting. He had been teaching her and her brother Joseph how to rootle out fossils, learning the best places to find these unknown creatures from earlier mysterious worlds, when they came upon George and his father.

George and Mary were a similar age, with only one year between them, so they had quickly formed a bond in those early days.

"It's been a long time since we met, Mary, but I have never forgotten you showing me how to find the fossils on these shores as children," George explained, looking relieved that she knew who he was at last.

Mary blushed slightly, remembering how George had openly admired her when they were children and was looking at her now with an approving look. He had never hidden how he felt about her, and on the day that he found more brittle star fossils than her, he had not hesitated in sharing them out between them.

"You always found fossils when you were with me, Mr Hansome," Mary said now, remembering how it was back then and reverting to formality.

"That's true enough," George replied. "Especially belemnites and brittle stars."

Mary studied his handsome face and again spoke plainly. "I mistook you for a dandy just now," she admitted. "And I have no time for those kinds of men, having seen far too many of them these past years," she said, recalling how some of these men had slighted her.

George seemed shocked at this observation. "Really? But

I'm no Beau Brummell, Miss Anning," he told her firmly, also reverting to formality. "I'm a qualified geologist," he boasted, giving her a steady look.

Mary sat down on a nearby rock and placed her basket with its precious few fossils onto the ground. As George hovered beside her, she let out a long sigh and lifted her gaze to his.

"Of course you are," she replied simply, seeing how her sarcasm was lost on him. It occurred to Mary then why George had not returned to these shores to see her over the years. It was because he had another life, one he had built since he had grown into a man, but she was curious as to why he had come back to Lyme now.

"What brings you here after so long away, Mr Hansome?" she asked evenly. Even though as children she had known him as George, it was unseemly to address him as thus now he was a man.

"I am working for the South Exmouth mine," George said in answer to her question. "The owner of the mine, Oliver Tyrell, requested that I come to Lyme Regis for research purposes and to look into the rocks here," he explained steadily.

George turned around, surveyed the beach, and then looked back at Mary. "I was more than happy to comply with Oliver's wishes, as I love walking along this beach where I remember how the discovery of something exciting was always a possibility," he told her. "It makes a nice change from poring over William Smith's maps all day."

Mary stood up and brushed off her skirts, swallowing down her envy. "Are you staying on this shore long today?" she asked, when what she really wanted to say was: 'I always knew you would be a geologist one day, George.'

Before he had time to answer her, Mary carried on as if they had only just met. "Be careful how far you go along this stretch of beach, especially Black Ven cliffs. Otherwise, the tide will be in, and you'll get cut off," she warned with a shrug of her shoulders. "You may have forgotten how treacherous it is round here, Mr Hansome."

"Thank you for the warning, Miss Anning. I haven't forgotten," George said with a confused look on his face.

Again, guilt assailed Mary, this time for dismissing George. But she couldn't help it. She breathed in deeply and regarded him. "Perhaps we will see each other again on these shores while you be in Lyme Regis?" she said with a soft shake of her head.

Mary's little dog Tray had been sitting beside her while she chatted to George, and he now followed his mistress as she turned in the direction of Cockmoile Square, and home.

"I will look forward to it, Miss Anning," George called after her, sounding hopeful this would be the case. "I will be here for a whole week," he added.

Mary walked quickly, wanting to get away from George now, feeling the regret in her heart. When they were children and they had searched these shores together, it had seemed that her and George were on an equal footing. After all, they had both learnt everything they knew from their respective fathers at the time.

However, since those early days, George had enjoyed opportunities as an adult that Mary could never have. As a woman of a certain class, or just as a woman, Mary would never get the same chance as George to become a professional in the world of geology.

And this was despite knowing more about the creatures, buried deep beneath the earth, than most of the men at the Geological Society.

CHAPTER 3

ELIZA

The man's handsome features stared back at me from the oil painting, those familiar amber eyes the colour of burnished brandy stirring long-dead memories deep inside me. Waves of black hair framed the man's face, and underneath his chin he wore a white neck tie, which accentuated his dark features and full, wide lips.

He wore a pale blue waistcoat with black buttons down the front, and a deep blue velvet jacket over the top. There was a slight frown between the man's brows, but this detracted nothing from the painting; instead, it added depth to his features, which the clever artist had captured to perfection.

His face had an air of impatience about it, as if he had somewhere he wanted to be other than sitting in front of an artist's easel. Or maybe someone else he longed to be with, because in those beautiful eyes the soft light of love burned brightly.

Even though I had avoided looking at the portrait since my return to Lyme, now that it was in front of me, I suddenly realised that every single detail of the paint strokes on the canvas was imprinted on my mind.

I closed my eyes, seeing again the day Liam bought the picture for me in the local antique shop. I felt again the warm glow of love as he paid for the painting, even though it was way over-priced for such an old portrait. That magical day was etched on my memory forever, but it was the lull before the storm, before everything went horribly wrong between us.

Long dead memories washed over me as thoughts of Liam flooded my mind, just as they had on the beach before Harry had knocked me over. I closed my eyes and reflected on how I lost everything the day Liam died. The sea had claimed it all.

Returning to Lyme meant returning to the memories. It's why I'd stayed away for ten years. The reminders of that time were everywhere here, in the air I breathed and the sadness in my heart for what could have been.

No wonder I hadn't seen Harry approaching earlier. I'd been gazing across at the waves crashing towards the shore, the sounds around me receding into the background. Through that tunnel vision, I'd relived the familiar sight of Liam on a warm summer's day, with his long, sun-bleached hair lifting in the sea breeze.

In that memory he was riding the waves in Old Ned's sightseeing boat, with the sun glinting on the water, the sky cloudless and azure. The tourists were relaxed and listening to his rich tones as he explained all about the history of this incredible Jurassic coast, and his pale blue eyes were full of passion for his subject.

That had been Liam at his best, doing what he loved the most, holding court, out in the fresh air, free from the constraints of life on shore. He had been a free spirit who lived life to the full.

Slowly, I opened my eyes again and rested my gaze on the painting. "Hello, George," I whispered, feeling my eyes prick with tears. I remembered how after Liam had bought the painting for me, I'd turned it over to see the name *George Hansome* written in black ink on the side of the canvas.

I had been surprised on my recent return to Lyme to find that the portrait was still in my mother Chloe's possession. Over the years of trying to forget what had happened here, I had wrongly assumed that she would have sold it or given it away. Finding the portrait tucked away in her spare room had been quite a shock.

My first thought had been to sell it. But somehow, I couldn't do that now that I had found it again. Instead, I had chosen to ignore the portrait by pushing it to the back of my mind and putting it out of sight. It was strange how I was unable to part with it, yet equally unable to acknowledge its presence in my life any more.

With the lighting in the basement dim, and those penetrating eyes looking deep into my soul, my face grew warm under the man's gaze. An odd feeling came upon me. Instead of the sad memories I had been reflecting on in the past weeks, I found that looking at this man's pleasing features was lifting my spirits.

"Hey, 'liza, what you want me to do now?"

The sound of Jessica's voice caused my racing heart to miss a beat, and I whirled around to see her looking somewhat guilty.

"Hi. Gosh! You almost gave me a heart attack, what're you doing here?"

It was a silly question, especially as Jessica worked here, but it was all I could think of to say while I gathered my wits about me. For a moment I had been lost in another time and place.

I had rushed back to the teashop after my encounter with

Harry and his dad on the beach and, leaving my head waitress Pat in charge, had retreated into the back room to look at the painting of George. *Was* there a likeness between Harry's dad and this handsome Regency man? I shook these thoughts from my head as Jessica openly stared at me.

"Jus' standing here," she replied. "You look like you seen a ghost," she added, giving me a funny look.

I gazed back at Jessica for a moment and watched her mood as it suddenly changed. She had obviously taken my silence for accusation, as she lifted her chin in a defiant way while chewing gum noisily.

"Soz, 'liza," she said, fixing me with her vivid blue eyes. "Pat told me off for disappearing, then sent me down here to find you." She shrugged and then ran her fingers through her short fair hair in a resigned fashion.

I smiled at the girl encouragingly. "No worries at all, Jessica. You're here now, that's the main thing," I reassured. "But remember what I told you? No gum in the teashop," I warned, resisting the urge to tell her that chewing gum contained a form of plastic and was bad for the environment. I was acutely aware that teenagers like Jessica hated being told what to do.

She rolled her eyes then obediently took the gum out of her mouth and placed it in a tissue. I reflected on how, despite her un-motivated ways, I quite liked the girl.

Taking a deep breath, I put on my best teacher voice. "Right, Jessica, Pat needs you in the teashop, as it's coming up to lunchtime now," I told her firmly.

Jessica grinned widely and nodded back at me. "Yeah, that's cool," she said before turning away to go back to work.

As I watched her disappear through the door, I heard my mother's recent words of wisdom echo in my head. 'Too much time spent hiding from the truth, that's why it still hurts and why the nightmares come back,' she told me only last year.

The therapist's words had reinforced my mother's sentiment.

'You've bottled too much up in the ten years since it happened, Eliza,' she had said. 'You need to go back to Lyme and open up about your feelings.

'Only then will the memory come back to you of the last hours before your rescue on the boat. And when the memories return, go with them; whatever you do, don't push them away. We need you to remember, to help you to grieve and to heal.'

However, finding the courage to return had been hard. In the end, it had taken Chloe's plaintive request that I run the teashop for her to convince me to set foot on Lyme Regis soil again.

It was time to face the past. This portrait would fit perfectly with the teashop décor, now that I had transformed the shop into Vintage. And that's where it would now be displayed, I decided. I took a long, deep breath. Even though there were many more hurdles to overcome, I had taken one small step in the right direction today.

With one last look at the man's face, I pushed away the niggling doubt that my imagination was playing tricks on me, and I hoped that returning to Lyme was not one step closer to me losing my mind.

CHAPTER 4

MARY

The last time Mary had seen George Hansome was the day after she had found the first complete skeleton of the so-called 'fish lizard' on the exposed fallen rocks on the foreshore between Lyme Regis and Charmouth.

Mary had been 12 years old. Her brother Joseph, who was 15 at the time, had found the head of the creature the year before. The animal was still stuck fast but uncovered enough to see its whole body, and was later identified as an Ichthyosaurus.

The memories had come flooding back this morning as she searched the shores, and she recalled how George and his father came upon Mary, and her brother Joseph, at the site of the creature. Mary saw again how he had gazed in wonder at the creature at her feet, making her realise that George's passion matched her own when it came to fossil hunting.

All those years ago George and his father would search for fossils for their own pleasure and enjoyment, unlike Mary's family, who had to live off the income their discoveries brought. And even more so after her father died. She had never resented this of her young friend, but rather she had been drawn to George's kind eyes and ready smile.

On a dull winter's day, when the hard grind of looking for fossils and not finding them made Mary's heart heavy, the sight of George appearing on the shore had often helped to brighten her day. She had loved him a little bit then, despite the fact that they were merely children.

It was only with George's reappearance all those years later that Mary realised she had missed the camaraderie they had shared all that time ago. Those had been precious times, when George dared Mary to take time out of the serious business of looking for fossils, and race with him along the water's edge, or some other childish game.

Once George had explained who he was to her yesterday, and she looked at him more closely (it being hard to recognise him in that top hat and velvet coat), she was pleased to see him. More pleased than she should have been, for he had grown into a very handsome man. She could only hope that he had not come to steal her hard-earned knowledge to pass off as his own, as so many other geologists had done before him.

"Good day to you, Mary!"

A familiar voice cut into Mary's thoughts, and she looked across at young Fanny Albright walking quickly towards her. The girl was a welcome distraction.

"How good to see you, Fanny," Mary said, and she quickly hugged the younger woman warmly while pushing away persistent thoughts of George.

Mary stood back to look Fanny over. "How be the arm now?" she asked, concerned to see that one sleeve was dangling loose of the long winter coat her friend was wearing, which might mean her badly swollen arm was no better than the last time Mary had seen her.

Fanny pushed back her bonnet and sighed heavily. "I

regret to say that it is worse, dear Mary. But it is early days yet, as I haven't been in Lyme Regis very long," she explained, while raising her face to the clear blue sky overhead.

"I hope the fresh air here in Lyme will make a difference, as it's so much better than smoky old London," Fanny continued, meeting Mary's gaze before putting her good hand over her mouth to indicate suffocating under thick smog.

Fifteen-year-old Fanny had been brought to Lyme for her health by her aunt and her mother two weeks ago. Noticing she was lonely, Mary had befriended the girl while she was wandering aimlessly on the beach one day.

Mary felt sorry for Fanny, who had nothing to do while here in Lyme Regis, so she taught her about the fossil hunting, and let the girl follow her on her searches.

Within a short time, Fanny found her passion and enthusiasm when it came to searching for the long dead creatures buried on these shores with Mary. And it was good for Mary to have a like-minded person to share the long hours of searching with, aside from her dear friend Elizabeth Philpot.

"What will you be teaching me today, Mary? Have you found anything yet?" Fanny fired questions at Mary excitedly. "I'm hoping to find something to add to my growing collection of shells and fossils," she added.

Before Mary had the chance to answer her, Fanny lifted her chin and grinned. "Maybe you'll find another Plesiosaurus, although that might be too much work for me with this useless old arm," she said, tipping back her head and laughing at this idea.

Mary couldn't help smiling at her observation. "It was indeed lots of work, young Fanny," she told her. She remembered how, after finding the creature's skull last year, she had worked through the night in freezing conditions to release the vertebrae, ribs, pelvic bones, and the fine cartilage of its four paddles.

It had been hard not to damage the animal, and Mary's hands had ached for days afterwards. Her fingers had remained stiff, as if they were still cold and frozen from holding the hammer for so many hours.

There were occasions like these when Mary wondered where she got the endless energy to carry out the excavations needed when she made a large find such as the Plesiosaurus. Out of nowhere it seemed to appear, and at these times her whole body would be filled with a strength (she never knew she had) and determination to uncover the creature.

Her mother always told her she was strong because of the lightning strike which happened when Mary was a baby. Up until then, she had been a very sickly child who was constantly unwell. Thinking of this terrible occurrence always made Mary shiver.

Fanny was still looking at Mary expectantly, so she thought quickly. "Did you know ammonites belonged to a group of predators known as cephalopods, all related to the squid and cuttlefish, Fanny?" she asked, hoping her young friend remembered this.

"I do remember that. You told me about the squid last time I was here," Fanny replied, then she looked around her and set her gaze on the shoreline. "What's the best place to start today, Mary?" she asked enthusiastically, always eager to hear her friend's valued advice.

Shaking the memories of her mother's account of the lightning strike from her head, Mary glanced across at Fanny. "Over there looks a good place," she said, pointing over to the cliffs where the tide had exposed the rocks underneath.

Then, after leading Fanny over to the area, the pair began their search for the day. After a while, Mary gave Fanny a sideways glance when her friend was preoccupied, and took in Fanny's fair youthful features.

Whenever she looked at herself in the mirror, Mary saw a face ravished by the elements, a complexion tanned from being outdoors every day. Her dark hair was always trying to escape from the large bonnet she wore, and her brown eyes looked out at the world with interest.

Mary's face was one which had weathered many storms in life, with many more to come, she was sure. Her life was not easy, although certainly it was an interesting one. Even so, she found it hard not to compare young Fanny's looks to her own.

As Fanny looked her way and smiled, Mary scolded herself for envying the girl, who was an invalid and only in Lyme for health reasons. She told herself she was lucky that, despite the poverty she endured, she had her health and strength, in mind and in body.

Counting her blessings included the appearance of the Plesiosaurus recently. This discovery indicated a comfortable winter ahead for Mary and her mother, and matched the feeling of happiness she had experienced when she and Joseph found the Ichthyosaur all those years ago.

Mary put these thoughts aside and worked on the shore. The hours passed quickly as she searched with Fanny, and for once and unusually, Mary hadn't noticed the tide was coming in. Suddenly, she looked down to see that the water was lapping around her feet and was now advancing fast on them both.

She never normally allowed this to happen, as she was always aware of what the sea was doing. Mary scolded herself for becoming so lost in her thoughts and failing to keep her eye on the tide.

Mary stopped what she was doing and looked behind her at the advancing tide and then back at Fanny, who was still lost in her magical world of fossil hunting. She was blatantly aware that Fanny was an invalid and was therefore incapable of clambering over the boggy slopes of Black Ven cliffs. Nor of negotiating the crumbling and sliding of the cliffs, the way Mary was, which was the only way of escape now.

CHAPTER 5

ELIZA

It was a cloudy day with rain threatening, and bluish grey storm clouds were gathering overhead, which matched my mood as I walked quickly back from the supermarket towards the teashop with my bag of shopping.

Last night I had fallen asleep quickly, but was soon awake as thoughts of Liam crowded my head. I had tossed and turned in the darkness and agonised over how to escape this spiral of guilt. My mind went round and round, like a hamster on a wheel, leaving me red-eyed and tired this morning.

I pushed open the teashop door to the familiar smell of homemade cakes and coffee, and glanced briefly around to see it was almost empty. There was only one customer and a child seated at a table at the far end, their heads down studying a menu.

Jessica was standing beside them, notebook and pen in hand, taking down their order. She was smiling as she served them, and I hesitated for a moment and watched her.

As I observed this 'different' Jessica from the doorway, I

hardly recognised the 'teen with attitude'. But as she looked up and caught my eye, her expression changed, and I could see the shutters had gone up again. I nodded hello to her, but as I walked past them, the child's voice rang loud and clear through the teashop.

"Dad, it's that lady what fell over. You remember, on the beach?"

A male voice corrected the child's English. "The lady *that* fell over, Harry."

I stopped in my tracks and whirled around to see little Harry staring across the room at me. Putting down the shopping, I made my way back to their table.

"Hiya, how're you doing, Harry?" I asked, looking at the boy while trying not to stare at his father's dark good looks.

Harry smiled widely and his dad gave me a lopsided grin. "Hello there, we can't keep meeting like this," he quipped. "I hope you haven't got any lasting injuries from your fall the other day?" he added.

"Thanks for asking, but apart from the odd bruise, I'm absolutely fine," I returned, feeling myself being drawn into that amber gaze.

"Look over there, Dad! That man looks just like you!"

We both jumped and looked at Harry, who was staring excitedly at my nineteenth century portrait where it adorned the wall of the teashop over by the counter.

For a moment there was a stunned silence as Jessica appeared behind me, and we all gazed at the portrait. *So, I was right.* Looking at the portrait *was* like seeing a mirror image of this man, who had the same unusual coloured eyes, and the same dark hair and full lips.

Except that one man was simply brush strokes on a canvas, while the other was flesh and blood sitting right here in front of me.

"Good grief. How did I not notice *that* when I walked in?"

Harry's dad declared, shaking his head slightly in disbelief with his gaze on the portrait.

His face had completely drained of colour, his eyes had widened, and his mouth had fallen open. And poor Harry had a worried frown on his little face again. You could cut the atmosphere with a knife as a heavy silence hung in the air.

"You're right there, Harry," I ventured uneasily, addressing the child. "There's a definite similarity between your dad and that portrait."

My voice sounded a little high-pitched, and in the continuing silence I tried to diffuse the tension in the room. "I noticed it when I met you on the beach... except I thought I was imagining it." I looked straight at Harry's dad this time, and was acutely aware the man did *not* look happy.

Eventually he tore his gaze away from the painting and our eyes met. "Sorry..." he began, obviously trying to gather himself together. "It's just so odd seeing that picture again, it's been so long," he explained, letting out a long sigh.

Questions spun in my head. *Why did the two men look so alike? And why was Harry's dad so shocked at seeing the portrait?* Just then I noticed there was a customer waiting to be served at the counter, but as I turned to walk away, he caught my arm.

"Do you mind me asking where you got the old portrait from?" he said uneasily.

My mind immediately went blank, and I tried to remember in which antique shop Liam had bought it for me, all those years ago.

"No worries. The portrait was bought for me by my boyfriend quite a long time ago," I said vaguely, while he continued to gaze at me. "I can't actually remember the name of the antiques shop, off the top of my head." I was feeling uneasy about the situation although I wasn't sure why; after all, the painting belonged to me.

"Liza, where do you want me to put these?"

I was almost relieved to see Jessica standing behind me with a tray of freshly baked cakes, and realised that Pat had served the customer who had been waiting patiently at the counter.

"Look, I'm sorry, but I really haven't got time to talk about this right now," I told the man firmly, before turning back to the counter to instruct Jessica where to put the cakes. Then, without looking back, I picked up the abandoned shopping bags and made my way to the kitchen to unpack the supplies.

As the teashop filled up, my attention was taken up by customers, and the incident with the painting was temporarily forgotten. A while later there was a lull in footfall, and I was busy tidying the counter when Harry's dad approached me.

"Hey there, can I pay the bill, please?" he said politely, while at the same time eyeing me strangely.

"Of course, no problem," I replied, and I totted up how much he owed and then handed him the bill. "Was everything alright for you and young Harry?" I was filled with curiosity, but also determined not to ask any questions about the portrait.

"Yeah, great thanks, the cake was excellent," he said. Then he hesitated before glancing at the painting and then back at me. "In case you're wondering, I was asking about the portrait because once upon a time, it used to be in my family," he explained awkwardly. "But I'd really like to know if your boyfriend bought it locally?"

"Well, as it happens, he did buy it locally, and timing-wise it was about ten years ago..." I began, feeling my chest tighten once again at the memory of that day. It wouldn't do any harm to tell this man where the painting came from, I reasoned, as it came back to me which shop it had been bought in.

I took a deep breath in. "The portrait was bought from the antiques shop at the top of Broad Street," I admitted, feeling as if I was giving away a trade secret.

The man shook his head in a resigned way before giving me a searching look. "Ah, okay, thanks for that. That's interesting, but it doesn't surprise me that's where he bought it – not at all. In fact, it makes sense."

I was about to ask him why it had been for sale in the antiques shop if it belonged in his family, when Harry called over from the table where he had been waiting patiently for his father to return.

"Stay cool, Harry, I'm just coming," the man reassured the lad before turning back to me. "Look, I hope you don't mind me asking you this, but if you find yourself in The Royal Standard tonight, I'll be having a drink there. And I'd love to have the chance to discuss the picture further..." he said. His voice trailed off as he looked at me uneasily and arched one dark eyebrow dramatically.

Meet in the pub with a strange man? I don't think so. Anyway, what was there to discuss? My hackles rose. It was *my* picture, not his. Perhaps he wanted to buy it back from me, and if that were the case, he was out of luck. I would never sell the portrait – not now I'd found it again.

I shook my head. "Sorry, but I'm busy tonight," I told him, looking pointedly past him at the customers patiently queuing to pay their bills. He followed my gaze and then gave a little nod before hurrying back towards Harry.

For the rest of that day, the man's invitation made me feel quite uneasy, especially as I had only met him and Harry a few days earlier. It was all a bit strange. Harry seemed a sweet kid, but I didn't see what there was to discuss with his father about the portrait.

Selling the painting was the last thing I wanted to do right now, if that's what he was angling for. Before I had gone off to Portsmouth University ten years ago, I would have sold it in a trice. But now, I was beginning to realise that the portrait represented Liam and the grief I was desperately trying to come to terms with, and which would hopefully help me find the lost memories.

Those memories could aid my healing process while I was here in Lyme. Harry's dad might resemble the man in my portrait, and it may once have belonged in his family, but the painting well and truly belonged to me now. It was part and parcel of my precious time spent with Liam, and I would never give it up.

CHAPTER 6

MARY

*M*ary had been keen not to frighten young Fanny on Charmouth beach that day, aware that if the girl panicked, it would make the situation even worse. But time was short, as the water got deeper and the waves advanced on them.

In the few minutes since Mary had perceived that the tide was coming in fast while they had been fossil hunting, it was already nearly on top of them. And, despite Fanny not noticing it happening behind and around them, Mary understood that there was only one way of escape now. And it was not an easy way.

"Fanny dear, don't be alarmed, but we have to leave the beach now," she warned, trying not to allow her voice to reveal her anxious thoughts, but aware that time was running out fast for them both. As she waded towards the girl, Fanny's head shot up at Mary's words.

"What's the matter, Mary?" Fanny looked behind her at the depth of the sea and gasped. "Oh, Mary. Lord above, what do we do now?" she exclaimed. Her eyes were wide, and her hand had flown to her chest as she clutched at her bodice nervously.

Mary remained calm and hoped this would rub off on her friend. "There be only one way off the beach now, Fanny," she said, taking in a deep breath.

Before the girl had time to digest this information, Mary swiftly lifted her up and strode with Fanny in her arms towards a ridge in the cliffs, which led to the top. It was a rough path, but it was a path nonetheless. It was also slippery and fraught with danger, especially carrying another person bodily up the slope.

However, Mary knew these cliffs like the back of her hand, and she moved quickly, holding firmly onto the girl, who was thankfully light in weight.

When they both reached the top of the cliffs, Fanny looked down at the sea which had almost covered the shore now. Tears rolled unheeded down her face.

"Oh, Mary, you saved my life," she wailed, throwing herself bodily into her friend's arms.

Mary hugged Fanny, then reassured her that she always knew a way of getting off the beach when the sea came in. There had been nothing to worry about, she told the girl with her fingers crossed firmly behind her back.

As she walked Fanny back to her lodgings, Mary told herself she would have to be more careful next time when Fanny was with her. Not everyone could climb the cliffs the way Mary was able to.

Now, out on the shores again, but this time alone, Mary watched the water washing onto the beach and sorting the stones of similar sizes into bands. A memory came back from years ago, of her pa teaching her this one simple thing to look out for when fossil hunting. This had enabled her to know exactly which bands to find which fossils in – something she had put into practice many times over the years.

While she observed this never-ending process, she thought about Fanny and hoped her frightening experience hadn't put the girl off fossil hunting altogether.

As she bent down on the shoreline to retrieve a fossil, she heard a noise behind her and looked around to see George advancing on her.

"Good morning, Mary," he said with a tip of his hat as he neared her.

"The hour be early for you, Mr Hansome," she said, looking up at the sky where the light was trying to break through the sea mist. George was rarely out at this hour.

He replaced his hat on his head and smiled. "I thought I'd start early today," he said, looking at Mary. "The day promises to be a good one."

As Mary greeted him, she noticed he was dressed more appropriately for his work today, in hessian boots and a greatcoat. The last few days he had become a familiar sight along the Lyme Regis and Charmouth shores, and she had found herself looking forward to seeing him every day.

She could understand why he had been sent here. The appropriately named Blue Lias on this beach comprised the sequence of rocks in which many of the entombed fossils at Lyme Regis occurred.

In some lights the rocks appeared to be blueish in colour, due to the blue-grey hue of the limestone. The Lias was composed of layers, alternating in various degrees, of marls, clays, and limestone. It was an ideal place for a geologist to study the dark shale rock.

As he got closer to her, she could see that he was troubled. "What be the matter this morning, Mr Hansome?" Mary asked with concern.

George shrugged. "It's my wife, Eleanor," he began hesitantly. "She's disgruntled about me being sent on this assignment."

Mary tried not to show how she felt when he mentioned his wife. Hadn't she known he would be married? Curiosity about whether he had a wife had plagued her recently, even though Mary had always known that George, being the son of a doctor, was never destined for the likes of her.

"Eleanor wanted to come to Lyme with me," he explained. "And I have promised her that we will come here for a holiday this summer, as she loves going to the assembly rooms and the bathing machines you have now here at Lyme Regis," George told Mary.

"Lyme Regis is becoming good for tourists," Mary said, brushing sand from a small round belemnite as she spoke. "Your wife will enjoy her visit, I be sure."

"I got a letter from her this morning." George continued shuffling on his feet awkwardly. "She would rather I was at home with her, even though I work for her father."

"Is she interested in geology?" Mary asked, wondering why George's wife wanted him by her side all the time.

George shook his head. "Eleanor has no interest in anything, except dances and pretty dresses, I'm afraid. She claims we are wealthy enough for me to give up work," he explained dismally. He took a step towards Mary and frowned. "But I could never give up being a geologist; it's my passion. I know you will understand that, Miss Anning."

Mary nodded, because she did understand. When she was deep in her studies, there was nothing more satisfying than learning about the minerals, rocks, and gems, and the long dead creatures that she searched for daily.

"I'm only here for a few more days," George explained. "Eleanor doesn't have long to wait until I'm home again," he added, before glancing out towards the ocean.

Mary nodded, not really knowing what to reply. Surely if George was here in Lyme working, his wife should not be complaining?

"I hope your studies be going well, Mr Hansome?" she said, for want of something to say. But before he could answer, Mary found herself asking something else which had been on her mind recently.

"Do you have any children at home, Mr Hansome?" A blush came to her cheeks, and she immediately wished she had not asked this question, but it was too late to retract it now.

George hesitated for a moment before answering. "I have a young son called Frederick," he told her evenly, then he shook his head regretfully. "I always miss him when I go away."

Mary swallowed down her disappointment that George was not only married but also had a child. She was being daft, she scolded herself, for he was never destined for her.

"How fare you since we last met, Mary?" George asked, lifting his eyebrows. "Have you had any visitors recently?"

Mary was glad to be on safer ground and never tired of talking about her work. "William Buckland came to see me yesterday, and we discussed my latest find and his recent studies on the Plesiosaurus," she replied. "It was good to see Mr Buckland."

William Buckland was a larger-than-life character and a pioneering geologist and scholar. He had come into Mary's life after her first big find, the Ichthyosaurus, and had been a frequent visitor to Mary's shop ever since.

"I know Buckland well and often see him at the Geological Society," George replied. "Along with William Conybeare and Henry De Beche, of course."

"Henry be currently away in Jamaica, overseeing his sugar plantation," Mary explained wistfully. She missed seeing Henry and the many discussions they had about what new fossils had been found in the world recently.

Henry De Beche was a good man, who was pulled in

different directions when it came to the sugar plantation he had inherited. It was said he cared for his slaves, and they were content in his employ.

He was also the founder of the Geological Society and, like William Buckland, treated Mary like a colleague or a friend. It was good to be on an equal footing with these eminent gentlemen, and Mary could only wish that all the geologists treated her this way.

"In answer to your earlier question, Miss Anning, my studies are going very well. I do love this coast, as Lyme Regis is such a good area for my work," George said, and his eyes lit up with enthusiasm as he looked across at the cliffs. "The Blue Lias on the rocks is second to none for finding the fossils."

Mary agreed. "Even more fossils can be found after a landslide, although o' course it can also be a dangerous time to be searching," she told him, remembering how her father had fallen on these cliffs the year before she had found the monster 'fish lizard', later named as the Ichthyosaurus.

Richard Anning's fall had been a bad one, which was to affect the family for years to come. The fall had weakened him, and he passed away with tuberculosis the following year.

After he died, her mother Molly had encouraged Mary to search for fossils so that they could sell them to tourists.

The hard times they had endured when her father was alive suddenly became even harder. Her ma had been pregnant when her pa died, and they were virtually penniless.

Molly Anning had been forced to apply to the parish for support, and the family received a paltry amount from the overseers of the Parish Poor for several years. It was humiliating, but they had no choice.

However, her father had trained Mary and her brother

Joseph well, and they knew what to do. She never returned to school, and spent her days fossil hunting instead.

Mary shook her head to dispel the bad memories and looked out at the sea, watching for a moment as the waves washed to the shore. "Imagine what this beach would have looked like millions of years ago," she said to George, wistfully. "It be full of creatures not of this world, the wonders of which we are constantly learning."

In her mind's eye Mary could see the sea monsters swimming around in the sea, the pointed head and large snout of the Ichthyosaur raised out of the water as it searched for its prey. She had learnt through her studies that the sheer size of it was terrifying and stuff of nightmares, and that the creature was likely to have been one of the top predators of the ocean in its lifetime.

George said nothing for a moment then he came to stand beside Mary. "Fossils are gifts from another world," he said, glancing towards the basket she had over her arm. There were only a few curies nestled in the bottom, as it was still early for her to have collected many fossils.

"Are you wishing you could keep the Plesiosaurus for yourself?" George asked suddenly, surprising her with his frankness.

Mary gave an ironic smile. "The Plesiosaurus? I wish for something better, Mr Hansome, much better," she said truthfully.

George looked puzzled. "What could be better than keeping that magnificent specimen yourself, something you have worked so hard to uncover?" he asked, rubbing at his chin. "Payment, perhaps, for all your hard work in finding the whole creature for the first time ever?" he ventured.

Mary hesitated as she regarded him thoughtfully. "Naturally, as payment is why I do this work, otherwise my ma and me would surely starve to death. The truth be that we have no other means of surviving."

She didn't tell him how, when times were particularly bad, there was no money for coal to heat their tiny house, nor tallow candles to burn for light. This made it much harder for Mary to study as she so often did in the long winter evenings.

The thin blankets in bed didn't afford much heat, and Mary often shivered into the night before she could eventually drop off to sleep. But despite these hardships, Mary enjoyed searching for and finding the fossils, and even after all this time of doing it, the work continued to excite her.

Pulling her thoughts back to George's question, Mary admitted, "The fossil hunting be hard, but I love it. Finding the creatures buried beneath the earth, just waiting to be discovered, is my true passion, and you'll be pleased to hear that I have a buyer for the Plesiosaurus. So, payment is coming my way."

She carried on wistfully, "What I really wish for is proper recognition for my work, the reward that I deserve. That would be beyond my wildest dreams." She had worked so hard since she was a child, but was only too aware of how visiting geologists would often take what she had worked for and pass the specimens off as their own.

Whenever she thought about this unfairness, Mary once again remembered when she and her brother found the Ichthyosaur in 1811. Later, they had learnt through visiting geologists that the first ever scientific paper had been written about *their creature*. The papers were published in 1814 but Mary and Joseph were not credited in them, because they were not 'Gentlemen of Science'.

Despite this injustice, their find had come at just the right time, soon after Richard Anning had died, leaving the family with considerable debts.

George nodded his understanding at Mary, and she could see the sympathy in his amber eyes.

"Miss Anning, your recent find of the Plesiosaurus was amazing, and you should be very proud. I can only hope that this time you'll get the recognition for it, too. Otherwise, it is a complete injustice," he said passionately.

Mary had no words. She appreciated George's kind sentiment, but she truly believed she would never get the proper recognition she deserved while she lived and breathed.

"Do you not think that at last with this find, the acknowledgement will be there for you?" George persisted. "Surely the geologists *cannot* deny it, because the evidence is there for them all to see?"

Mary shook her head. "I've heard mutterings of disbelief among the geologists already," she said, feeling downcast. "Can you believe it? Ernest Holmes was already re-naming it. Declaring publicly how it were a cross between a Proteus and a lizard."

She shook her head as she gazed behind George at the muddy cliffs, and marvelled at the abhorrent stupidity that some of these men displayed.

Meeting George's eyes, she shrugged, knowing things would never change but that she could never give up trying. "However, my work is done on the creature now. It be on the way to the Geological Society, to be examined by them all," she told him.

Even to her own ears Mary's voice sounded flat, which was how she felt when she talked about her discoveries sometimes. It always followed the same pattern. She had the rush of red-hot energy coming from somewhere deep inside her while she dug out the creatures, but it was always followed by the disappointment that after all her hard work she hadn't been named as its finder.

"Hopefully they will understand and know it be a

Plesiosaurus, which lived alongside the Ichthyosaurus and is a marine reptile," she said, knowing she was right in this assumption.

She knew this because the Reverend William Conybeare, another eminent geologist, had written a paper on the creature back in 1821, and Mary's find matched his description.

George pursed his lips together and frowned. "Ernest Holmes is a buffoon, despite his eminent connections to the scientific world," he said through clenched teeth.

Mary exhaled deeply. "You're not wrong there, Mr Hansome," she said, feeling gratitude to George. "But there's nothing to be done about that." She was resigned to the Plesiosaurus being misunderstood.

"I heard that this is the second Plesiosaurus you have found, is that correct?" George enquired with a lift of his brows.

"That's right, back in the winter of 1821. It was in the soft marl by the cliff, and was not complete like this one. There be no skull, and the brittle skeleton was in pieces by the time I got it back to my workroom. Even so, I sold it to a Reverend Conybeare for a good price."

George was nodding, but his mind was obviously still on a much-disliked geologist. "I heard Ernest Holmes caused chaos when you discovered the Ichthyosaurus years ago. Sounds like the man has no idea what he's talking about," his words emphasised his disgust at the man's behaviour.

"Holmes confused everyone with his wild guesses that year. He first claimed our Ichthyosaur were a crocodile, then a new amphibian, among other names, not understanding what it really was. A reptile, of course."

Mary was almost amused at the stupidity of Holmes, but she was used to this kind of ignorance from that particular geologist. He was like an errant child who needed a good scolding.

"Surely, the truth will come out about this latest find of the Plesiosaur at the meeting scheduled in two weeks' time?" George sounded hopeful.

Mary was flattered that he seemed to care so much, but she felt more philosophical about it. "There's nothing more to be done now, Mr Hansome. I've given a pen and ink sketch of it to William Buckland, so hopefully they will all see from that what the creature be."

"I wish you could go to the meeting, Mary," George said. "You really ought to be allowed, considering that you found the specimen," he added regretfully.

Mary nodded dismally. She longed to follow the Plesiosaurus to the Geological Society in London, but she couldn't see a way of doing so. It was a closed group where only men could attend.

George's eyes lit up. "I'm going to the meeting!" he declared. "Shall I take notes and report back to you, Miss Anning?" he asked excitedly.

Mary was surprised that George would have time to go to the meeting with his work commitments. "If you're going, I'd love to hear back about what be discussed," she told him. "Especially as Henry's not here to report back to me in his usual way."

"That's settled then, after the meeting I'll write and enlighten you on the conversation and what was decided."

"Thank you, George," Mary said, pleased that someone would be there who would report back exactly what was said.

"However, the truth be that I cannot afford to receive letters from you," she added regretfully. She hated to admit this to George, who was wealthy, but life had taught her that pride did no good if you could not eat and pay the rent.

"I apologise for suggesting such a thing, Mary, I was not thinking this through." George removed his hat and ran a hand through his dark hair. "I've got it!" His eyes lit up again. "I'll make sure that I pay for you to receive the letters before they are posted. Would that be in order?"

Mary told him that would be perfectly in order, and George looked pleased with himself. "Let's hope that this latest find will at last earn you some recognition, Mary."

Just then Tray appeared from where he had been wandering by the water's edge. The dog barked loudly at his mistress, as if nudging her to take notice of him, and Mary bent down to pat his head affectionately.

"Good day to you, Mary!"

At the sound of her name being called across the beach, Mary pushed her bonnet further back on her head and looked up to see Elizabeth Philpott striding across the pebbles towards her.

As the middle-aged lady reached them, her wide face broke into a smile, and Mary introduced George to her friend. "Mr Hansome, meet Miss Philpot," she said, feeling a warm glow, because she was always happy to see Elizabeth.

"Pleased to meet you, I'm sure, Miss Philpot," George said, shaking the lady's hand.

"Good day to you, too, Mr Hansome," Miss Philpot returned. "Pray, will you be fossil hunting with us today?"

George explained that he was on a research trip in Lyme, studying the rocks for the South Exmouth mine. "That's not to say I won't be looking for fossils while I am here," he added, looking affectionately across at Mary.

Miss Philpot nodded. Her gaze darted between the two of them, and Mary didn't miss the knowing look she shot in her direction.

"It's an opportunity not to be missed on these shores, Mr Hansome," Elizabeth returned, her face back to its normal expression. "I hope you find some good fossils here."

George frowned, pulled a pocket watch out of his waistcoat, and looked at the time. "It is getting late, ladies, and I must be going," he said, tipping his hat to them both. "I'll leave you to your searching and say good day to you both." He looked a little flushed as he addressed Mary.

Even though she enjoyed Elizabeth's company and was eager to chat to her friend, Mary watched George walk away, wishing he could stay longer.

"Be careful, Mary," Elizabeth warned from beside her.

Mary could feel her friend's intense gaze on her, and she lifted her chin and turned to meet her eyes. "I know not what you mean," she said. "George be an old friend," she added, swallowing down the fact she knew exactly what Elizabeth Philpott meant.

CHAPTER 7

ELIZA

*H*arry's dad turned up in the teashop the next day, and I was serving at the counter when he walked in. It was hard not to notice him as he strode through the shop in faded cut-off jeans and a short-sleeved shirt. Out of the corner of my eye, I saw him sit down in the corner of the room and spread his paperwork across the table.

"Good afternoon, Harry's dad, how may I help you?" I giggled at my own joke, but what else should I call him as I still didn't know his name? And it seemed he had the same idea.

Harry's dad quirked his head towards me and grinned widely. "Well, in that case, I'd better introduce myself to you properly," he said, with a lift of those dark eyebrows. "Especially as we've met twice now, and I still don't know *your* name. Rafe Hansom," he said quickly, without waiting for my answer, and stretching out his hand towards me.

"Eliza Valentine," I returned, and I was immediately struck by how large and warm his hand felt in mine. "Good to see you again," I said truthfully, because part of me had been wishing that I had met in him in the pub as he had suggested the previous day. "And how's young Harry doing?" I asked, gently removing my hand from his.

"Yeah, Harry's good, thanks," Rafe said, pushing his hair back from his face.

After he had given me his order of black coffee and cake, I saw he was hesitating. "Was there something else you wanted?" I asked, hoping he wasn't going to mention the portrait again.

I had to raise my voice to be heard over the low murmur of customers' chatter, the clinking of cutlery echoing through the teashop, and Buddy Holly singing *Peggy Sue* from a modernised gramophone tucked away in the corner of the teashop.

Rafe immediately shook his head at me, but I sensed he wanted to chat further. However, a customer was waiting to pay, so I turned to go, at the same time hoping he would stay a bit longer.

When at last the teashop quietened down again, I glanced up from the counter to see that he was still here. The coffee had been drunk and the cake eaten, and he had his head bent over the paperwork which was in disarray across the table.

I approached his table and began clearing up the crockery. "Was everything alright for you?" I asked him, as I did every customer who came into the teashop.

Rafe glanced up from his paperwork, looking at little distracted. "Aye, delicious cake, thanks, Eliza," he said, then he looked down at the table. "I brought work with me today, mainly because it needs to be sent off to the Natural History Museum. Sometimes I can work better in a noisy atmosphere," he explained unnecessarily.

My curiosity was now piqued. "The Natural History Museum?"

"Yeah, that's right, I deal with the museum as part of my work," he explained.

"What do you do?" I asked, as I watched him gathering up his paperwork.

Rafe straightened up and met my gaze. "I'm a palaeontologist," he replied, before following me up to the counter.

As he tapped his card on the reader, he looked across at me with a beseeching expression. "I realise you don't know me and all, and I really hope you don't mind me asking again, Eliza…" he began tentatively, as I handed him the receipt. "And say if you'd rather not. But have you got time to meet for a drink later?"

Here it comes again, I thought. I was ready to refuse his invitation for the second time; this thing with the painting, it seemed, was *not* going to go away. But I hesitated for a moment and thought about this second offer.

"Well, actually, I do know who you are, because Jessica told me," I replied, glancing over at the teenager who was wiping down a table in the corner of the teashop.

After Harry and his dad had left the previous day, Jessica had explained that when she had worked in a local children's nursery, the little boy had been a regular there as a baby and toddler.

"Ah yes, Harry does know Jessica, and he told me how much he likes her," Rafe said, looking pleased about this.

Despite the smile which didn't quite reach his eyes, I noticed he was running a hand nervously through his dark hair again, and I began to feel sorry for him. I really hoped that he wasn't expecting me to sell the painting back to him, because if so, I would have to put him straight.

However, it wouldn't hurt to meet up with him and hear how the painting had come to be in his family and, more importantly, whether he was related to the man in the portrait, considering they looked so very much alike.

"As it happens, I'm free tonight, so how about The Royal Standard at seven?" I offered quickly before I could change my mind. "I have to admit that I've always been curious about *my* painting and its origins, so it should be interesting," I added, meeting his gaze; the emphasis making it clear exactly whose painting it was.

CHAPTER 8

MARY

*M*ary pulled her cloak closer around her to keep out the cold wind. Overhead the clouds were building, promising rain to come later. She could not linger in the graveyard here in St Michael's Church long as she had work to do, but right at this moment, she needed this time with her father.

When her pa had died 14 years ago, leaving his family almost destitute, she had sobbed every night, so much so that her mother had scolded her. Her ma had quickly pushed her outside to search for fossils, just as her father had taught her. Mary understood why this was; they needed to eat, and it was one way of earning money. But it was hard.

Mary had made it her business to visit his last resting place once a year, on what would have been his birthday. She had no money for flowers to put on his grave. But this was where she felt close to her pa again and where, year after year on this date, she took a moment to remember him.

Her life from as far back as she could remember had centred around the sea. The ocean provided fish for the family to eat, the waves washed ashore and released fossils from the cliffs, and set them free from the sea bed. Without these two things the Anning family would have struggled to eat or pay the rent on their little house on Cockmoile Square.

"The ocean be part of you," Molly Anning frequently told her daughter. "The sight of the water soothed you when you was but a squalling babe in arms."

Mary remembered Molly telling her how, at only a few days old, she had been beside herself with Mary's screaming. In desperation, Molly had taken Mary onto the beach and held the tiny baby aloft, and within seconds the sound of the waves washing ashore had worked their magic and Mary stopped crying.

The beach was so close to where they lived that the Anning children played on the pebbles as soon as they could walk. Joe was just three years older than Mary, and the two of them spent many hours watching others stroll in Lyme Regis. In the summer months the two children would sit on the sea wall and watch people walking to The Cobb, or going out in the new bathing machines which had just become popular at that time.

Fossil hunting had long been a tradition in Lyme Regis, and when Mary was a child there were a few other collectors – apart from her father Richard – who spent every spare moment out on the shores of Lyme Regis. He much preferred to hunt for fossils than his work as a cabinet maker, but the cabinet making fed the family so the fossil hunting always came second.

One other fossil hunter at the time in the area was William Lock, and as fossils were known as curiosities, he became known as Captain Cury. Mary got the feeling that her pa didn't like Lock, especially as he warned her to avoid him if she came upon him on the shores of Lyme when she was alone.

Another local man was called Mr South, who seemed

pleasant enough, and it was he who taught Richard Anning how to rootle out the fossils. But the one who stood out in Mary's mind the most was a Mr Cruikshanks, who taught her pa how to use a pole to hunt the fossils. The pole was used to poke into the pebbles and turn them over.

Mary couldn't remember exactly when she and Joseph began accompanying their father to rootle out fossils. It seemed to her it was from the moment she had learnt to walk.

Finding these unknown creatures from an earlier mysterious world was what Richard taught them. The children absorbed all the information with enthusiasm, staring in wonder at the fossils as they were uncovered. The learning came naturally, and was part of everyday life, even though it was sometimes dangerous work, even for an adult.

Mary glanced down at the little hammer lying in her basket ready for today's searching – the one her pa had given to her to use as a fossil extractor.

"You'll be able to release the smaller finds with this, Mary," he told her on one of their many walks. And she had been excited to be able to do exactly what he was doing, when she found something of interest.

When she was older, he had shown her how to reveal the jewel-like beauty of ammonites, by slicing them in half to expose the crystalline calcite infilling of their chambers. He had explained what the fossils were called; amongst them were St Hilda's snakes, belamites, curies, sea lilies, and verteberries.

Even though Richard taught Mary and Joe everything they needed to know about finding the fossils, the children developed their own method of uncovering the curies or ammonites. And Mary always found more fossils than her brother Joe.

To her it was like searching for something that looked a

bit different; a stone that stood out from the rest, perhaps. More often than not, this was the one that contained the fossil. And when she found the fossils and cleaned them, to her they were precious, like long lost diamonds in a sea of sand.

When they were old enough, Richard sent his children out searching on their own to supplement the family's income. But Joe was too quick in his searching and often overlooked the ones that Mary found. He didn't enjoy being outdoors the way she did, and was relieved to find an apprenticeship as an upholsterer when he was 19.

Now, Mary reached out and touched the headstone, shivering as the cold stone touched her fingers. "Thank you, Pa," she whispered. "For giving me so much, and showing me the magic of the creatures buried beneath the rocks, which were right on our doorstep," she told him.

Aware she had work to do before the tides covered the beach, Mary brushed the tears from her face before stepping away from the grave, and hurrying down the hill. As she shook off her childhood memories, she hoped a letter awaited her from a certain dark-haired gentleman.

CHAPTER 9

ELIZA

*I*t was seven-thirty in the evening before I arrived at the pub, and as I hurried through the door of The Royal Standard, I asked myself what on earth I was doing meeting Rafe Hansom tonight.

If it was just to tell him that I wouldn't be selling the painting back to him, it would be a total waste of time. But on the other hand, there was also the chance that I might learn something about the portrait.

"Sorry I'm late. I've been looking at the accounts for the teashop and I forgot the time," I told him truthfully.

Rafe stood up when I approached his table. "No worries, I haven't been waiting long," he replied cheerfully. "You've changed your clothes," he said, stating the obvious.

Of course, I had changed. *I could hardly turn up in the pub in the Vintage attire I wore in the teashop, could I?* For a moment our gaze met, and as usual I was struck by the amber colour of his eyes as Rafe stared in open admiration at my casual jeans and striped t-shirt.

My face reddened at this unexpected attention. It had been a long time since a man had looked at me that way, though no doubt that was my own fault for pushing every man away since losing Liam.

"What would you like to drink?" Rafe said at last, breaking eye contact with me.

"Oh, a G&T please." I sat down with a sigh of relief, happy to get the weight off my feet.

As Rafe headed towards the bar, I took off my jacket. And while he waited to be served, I tried not to stare at him intently. He was such an attractive man, but I reminded myself I wasn't in the market for a relationship right now. And, quite simply, I wasn't sure I ever would be.

"I like what you've done in the teashop, Eliza, it looks good," Rafe said on his return. "I mean, the way you've changed things around, it's defo added some flair to the place. Harry and I used to go some time ago, but it was never that busy."

"Thanks. The customers seem to like it. When I arrived in Lyme, I could see that the teashop needed a bit of a revamp, and I love everything Vintage, so I thought it might do the trick. And it has certainly increased footfall," I replied, pleased that he approved.

"So... what's the deal with the portrait then?" I asked, eager to get onto the subject of the painting and the reason for our meeting.

Rafe pressed his lips together, then leaned forwards and laid his hands flat on the table. "Okay, well, here's the thing, as I said before, I haven't seen that painting for years," he explained with a thoughtful look. "So, as you can under-stand, it was a shock seeing it in your teashop after all this time."

"Okay. But what I don't understand is, if it belonged in your family, how come it was for sale in the antiques shop all those years ago?"

Before he could answer, something unsettling occurred

to me. "The portrait wasn't stolen from your family, was it? I mean, I don't think it could have been but..."

I found myself winding a strand of my hair around my fingers nervously. If that was the case, even though Liam had bought the painting for me ten years ago, I might have to return it to Rafe after all. This thought struck dread into my heart.

"Oh God, no. Nothing like that, Eliza," Rafe said quickly to reassure me. "As far back as I remember, the portrait was in my family, and whenever I asked my dad who the man in the painting was, he always told me that the nineteenth century man in the picture was somehow related to us. He loved that portrait."

"So, how come it ended up being sold then?"

"It was always me and dad who loved the painting; my mum actually hated it. She said it was old-fashioned, and while I was growing up, she hid it from view whenever she could. After Dad died, my mother moved to Spain, and in the process of moving she must have sold it," he explained sadly.

"I'm sorry to hear that," I sympathised. "That must have been hard if you were fond of the painting, and it had been in your family for so long."

I thought about how much I loved the portrait, and it wasn't just because Liam had bought it for me. The minute I set eyes on it, I had been drawn to the expression in the man's eyes; they were full of love.

Rafe's voice broke into my thoughts. "Well, I suppose it was my fault, too. At the time that she would've been selling the contents of the house, I was at university. I had other things on my mind and had forgotten all about the painting, so I didn't claim it. And it must have slipped her mind that it was meant to go to me." He sounded philosophical.

"Yeah, well that's understandable. Do you know much about the portrait then? I mean, how the man was related to you, for instance? He looks so much like you that there can't be much doubt your dad was right in his assumption that he was an ancestor."

Rafe leaned back in his chair and sipped at his beer thoughtfully. "Not much, to be honest. I know his name was George Hansome, but that's about it. His surname was the same as mine, but with an 'e' on the end. I read somewhere recently that often happened with an ancestor's surname; over the years the spelling changed slightly."

"That's right, I noticed that his name was written on the back of the portrait," I replied. I quirked my head to one side. "Did you also know that the lovely George came from Devon?"

Rafe looked surprised at this and shook his head. "Nope, that's news to me, Eliza. You know more than me then," he said. "How did you come across that bit of information?"

"When Liam was paying for the portrait, the assistant told us the man was from the Devon area. Of course, she could have made that up," I joked. At the time, I had been hungry for knowledge about this gorgeous Regency man, and full of questions for the poor shop assistant.

I leaned forwards and touched the side of my nose with my finger. "But who exactly was George Hansome?" I said dramatically. "That's what I'd like to know."

If I was honest with myself, I'd always been curious about the man in the portrait. Even when it had been out of my sight and hidden at my mum's flat over the years, I'd often found myself thinking about it.

Rafe gave me a crisp nod. "Oh, me too, Eliza, me too. My father tried to get me interested in who George was when I was young, and he was always banging on about there being a strong resemblance between us."

"There is such a strong resemblance, it's uncanny. Didn't you ever want to look into the portrait's history then? I mean, while your dad was still alive?" Then something else occurred to me. "Do you know how it came to be in your family in the first place?"

"Now, that's one thing I *do* know," Rafe said, meeting my gaze. "The portrait was handed down to my dad from my grandfather Tom. Don't know where he got it from, as he died when I was quite young, and as far as I know, Dad never asked him. If I'm honest here, I was never that curious about it, even though Dad used to talk about looking into our family tree. I was never that interested."

Rafe looked past me as he spoke, as if he were remembering another time and another place, and I was just about to ask if he was okay when he seemed to snap out of it. "God, that was such an awful time," he said, looking across at me with sad eyes. "Dad died when I was 15, still at school, and about to do my exams."

The look on his face tore at my heartstrings, because I knew only too well how grief could tear you apart. I laid a hand gently on his arm. "Perhaps now is the time to do some digging then?" I ventured, hoping I was saying the right thing.

Rafe shrugged then quickly recovered himself. "Sorry, Eliza, it was a long time ago and I should be over it. But yes, I think you're right. Now is a good time to look into who my ancestor was. I'm more interested since having Harry. Having children alters things a bit," he added with a quirk of his brows.

"I'm sure kids are a great leveller," I agreed, feeling the black cloud hovering nearby, and trying not to remember that I could have been a parent if only things had been different. I tried to steer the conversation in a more cheerful direction.

"You've got a lovely little boy, by the way," I said, forcing a smile and remembering how cute Harry was. "He looked very sorry for knocking me over like that."

Rafe grinned widely. "So he should be, the little devil," he quipped. "I must say you did look funny when I was trying to help you up, what with Harry standing there looking like butter wouldn't melt in his mouth."

Suddenly, I found myself warming to Rafe, and it wasn't just that he was so attractive. He seemed like a good guy to me, and so far, he hadn't asked to buy the painting off me, which was a good plus point.

"Well, that's nice, I'm sure," I pretended to be offended. "I bet I did look a bit funny lying on the beach wondering what or who the hell had pushed me over. Although, as I told Harry, it was probably my fault anyway."

Rafe's expression became serious. "What do you mean, your fault? Harry was being naughty and not looking out for other people on the beach as he raced around."

It was then that I realised I'd ventured into painful territory, and my light mood vanished as soon as it appeared, the tightness was back in my chest. I didn't know how to answer Rafe without bringing painful memories back into focus.

"Eliza, are you okay?" Rafe leaned towards me with a concerned frown between his brows. "What on earth is it? You look awful, is everything alright?"

I swallowed hard and tried to smile, but my face just wouldn't curve upwards. "The thing is, I was so lost in thought at the time," I began, feeling shaky. "In fact, I was miles away in my head…" There was a lump growing bigger in my throat.

As I tried to explain, the words got stuck. I attempted to change the subject back to the painting, but I was painfully aware that hot tears were not far away.

Rafe was still staring at me in confusion.

"I'm fine, really, it's nothing," I fibbed, hearing the wobble in my voice as I spoke. I forced a weak smile on my face. "When I saw you on the beach that day, I was shocked at your likeness to George, and I honestly thought I might be going mad."

Rafe had obviously not been fooled by my explanation, as he seemed to be scrutinising my face. But taking my lead, he carried on the conversation as if nothing was wrong.

"Ha, I know what you mean. It's quite spooky, isn't it? When I look at George, I see myself," he said. "In a Regency outfit!"

"But you *are* like two peas in a pod," I agreed, feeling a little better now I'd stopped focusing on memories. "It would be interesting to find out how far back the link goes between you, don't you think?"

"Yes, it would. By the way, I've been meaning to ask, how come you're running the teashop now?" Rafe was looking thoughtful again. "Wasn't there an older woman in there before you?"

"Yep, that was my mum, Chloe," I told him, glad to be on safer ground now. "She moved to Australia for a year, and asked me to manage the teashop for her while she was gone."

"Sounds perfect to me. Have you always worked in Lyme then?" he probed. "I mean, before you took over the teashop? I don't remember seeing you when your mother was there," he continued.

This bit was difficult to explain, particularly when people had no idea of my past or what had gone before. But he was looking at me expectantly, and I felt obliged to explain. Besides, it is what I'd been told to do repeatedly by the therapist – to face my demons.

Here goes. "I worked in Plymouth at the National Marine Aquarium as a marine-biologist diver. But after eight years, I needed a change, and to be honest it seemed the ideal time to leave and return to Lyme when Mum asked me to run the teashop for her."

Again, the tightness in my chest was back, and I wondered why I couldn't talk about coming back to Lyme without welling up.

Rafe's concern was back. "Are you alright, Eliza? Sorry if I'm prying, but something is wrong, I can see that. If you'd rather not say, that's fine."

The sympathy in those amber eyes pulled at my heart, and I struggled to compose myself, but the sadness was suffocating me now and this time I just couldn't hide it.

"Coming back to Lyme has been hard..." I whispered, staring down at my lap. I forced myself to look back up and meet Rafe's gaze. "I'm fine really," I said, lifting my chin and scrubbing at my face with the back of my hand. "I'm sorry, it's just... too difficult."

The words had vanished into thin air, and I had a far off feeling as if I'd had one too many G&T's. Rafe placed his hand on top of mine where it lay on the table. His palm had a few rough areas on it, and in my head, I saw him chipping away at fossils as a palaeontologist would, which was strangely comforting.

"Eliza, please, you need to take a moment," he soothed. "We all find things in life hard at times, there's no need to be embarrassed."

But despite his words of comfort, I was ashamed for letting my guard down to someone I didn't really know. *Get a grip, Eliza.* Taking a deep breath, I lifted my chin and regarded the man sitting opposite me intently.

"Rafe, I'm sorry to put a dampener on things, I really don't know what came over me. But I'm fine." A voice in my head told me I wasn't fine, and that I did need to start talking about this. But not to someone I had only met a few days ago – even if we did have a shared love of a painting.

Forcing myself to look into those beautiful eyes, I tried to explain as simply as I could. "The thing is, I've been advised that to help the grieving process I need to talk about what happened, but it's harder than I thought."

I pursed my lips together to try and stop myself saying any more, then berated myself. Ten long years of saying nothing to anyone, and now I was blabbing to an almost complete stranger about my innermost feelings.

Rafe leaned back in his chair and regarded me with a sympathetic expression. "No problem, Eliza, honestly. But try me, I've been told I'm a good listener," he reassured. "I know we've only just met, but I won't tell anyone else what you say to me, I sincerely promise you that."

I thought hard about his words, then I set my jaw and made a decision. What did it matter if I hardly knew Rafe? He was offering a listening ear, and today was the first day since *it* happened that I had actually felt like talking about the accident. And, if Rafe didn't like what I had to say, then I didn't need to ever see him again.

I took a deep breath and tried to choose my words carefully. "Okay, here goes. You may remember hearing about a boat which sank off the coast of Lyme ten years ago," I began, not taking my eyes off his face. "It was one of the pleasure boats which sailed from The Cobb. At the time, there was a report in the paper about it, and it even made the national news that day."

Rafe nodded hesitantly. "I do remember that because, as you say, it was in the news. Also, I was working at Lyme Regis Museum that day, which meant I saw the RNLI boat go out."

I continued to stare at him for a moment, unable to say any more. With a look of dread on his face, he went on, "I seem to recall that the skipper drowned, but his passenger survived. Is that the accident you are talking about, Eliza?"

I nodded slowly at him. My chest had loosened but it was aching now, and my eyes were bone dry as if there were no more tears left to cry. There was only sadness in my heart and in the deepest recesses of my soul.

"That's the one," I replied miserably. The cloud hovering nearby was getting blacker and making me feel quite morbid with the intense pain of it all. "I was *that* passenger, and the skipper was Liam Sutherland, who was my fiancé."

CHAPTER 10

MARY

*M*ary waited eagerly each day for the post cart to deliver a letter from George. She was desperate to know what had happened at the recent meeting in London about the Plesiosaurus.

She was used to being kept in the dark about her finds, but with George came the hope that she would soon have knowledge of what exactly went on at the society when there was a new discovery.

This thought excited her and brought light back into her life, which she realised had been missing for many years. She admitted to herself secretly how much she had missed his friendship growing up.

As she went about the daily business of searching the shores, she was distracted and thought of George constantly. Today dragged on, and she resisted the urge to rush home and check if a letter had been delivered.

At the end of the day, as soon as she walked back into the shop, Mary saw that not one letter, but two, had arrived. She hurried to open them, eager to hear George's news.

Dear Mary,

On my return home I went straight to Eleanor, and told her I would be going to the Geological Society in London, to attend the meeting about your Plesiosaurus. Unfortunately, her reaction was not favourable.

Eleanor tried again to force me into giving up what she called my interest in rocks. If only she understood what I went through to get my qualification. How hard it was to win the scholarship to Oxford in the first place, being one of five children of a doctor.

I regret to tell you that my wife's jealousy has increased since my return home, and has become intolerable. So much so that I am pleased to be escaping her dark moods and going away again so soon. Although I will miss young Frederick terribly.

Forthwith, I stood my ground with Eleanor and told her I would be going to London, but in the end to appease her, I agreed to go to a local dance with her at The Pavilion. My wife often attends dances there, as they allow lone women so long as they are both upper class and wealthy. She fits in nicely with these requirements.

As soon as I have news from the meeting, I will write to you again.

Yours truly,

George

Mary thought about the kind of life George's wife Eleanor must have, and once again envy rose in her throat and threatened to choke her. Eleanor would no doubt spend her days entertaining her friends, sewing, or painting water-colours, and would have a nanny for their child.

Mary knew she would have been bored with Eleanor's life, but her own was so hard at times. She spent her days working outside in all weathers, sometimes scrabbling on her hands and knees, looking for specimens. Then when she made a discovery, the preparation of the fossils was laborious and exhausting, and involved scraping and cleaning the objects for hours.

When at last they were ready, the fossils would be sold in her little shop. Although Mary loved finding the fossils, and took great pleasure from her studies of geology and anatomy, there were times when she wished there was another way to earn a living.

George's features came to mind as Mary folded up the first letter. She could see again his silky black hair and those expressive amber eyes. She couldn't help thinking they would have made such a good match in marriage, with their shared passion in the discovery of fossils and interest in the natural world.

Mary shook these thoughts from her head and put away the letter. She reminded herself that George had never come looking for her when he was free, before he met Eleanor.

And, she asked herself, *why would he?* Eleanor must have come with a large dowry, and being married to her would be serving George well in his work. Mary would have had nothing to offer him but love and their shared interest. She sighed, reached for the second letter and began to read.

Dear Mary,

As soon as I sat down at the meeting, the controversy over your creature began. In the middle of the room was a large table, which was empty. Your Plesiosaurus should have been laid out for all to see.

Then it was announced that your creature had been delayed in the Channel, and it was not on show at the meeting, as planned. The geologists were disappointed, because they were waiting for it to arrive, and they were eager to see it in all its glory.

These words made Mary's heart lift. These were the same men who came to her door, bought her discoveries, and then claimed them as their own. And the glory which was rightfully Mary's so often became theirs. It was good to know things didn't always go their way, as they waited with bated breath for Mary's creature to arrive at the society.

Sometimes the bitterness inside Mary refused to go away, especially when it stifled her voice and threatened to choke her. It was partly her own fault, because she often gave her time too generously, as her friend Elizabeth Philpott frequently explained.

"We are both guilty of the same thing, Mary,' Elizabeth often said. "But you are more guilty than me. You are too open-handed and generous in sharing your knowledge with those who come to these shores to search for the fossils."

Mary knew it was true, but she found it hard to be mean-spirited with the enthusiastic visitors and professional men when they came calling. Working as their guide was always a pleasurable task for her, and it brought her company in what was often a long solitary search in all weathers.

As Mary continued to read George's letter, she sensed his warm regards coming through the written page. And when he said how proud he was of her, Mary found herself smiling at this endearment.

I am convinced that finding this creature will make you famous at last, Mary, and from now on your name will be treated with respect in the scientific community.

Mary desperately hoped George was right in this, as the recognition had been a long time coming for her. However, the next paragraph was a little worrying.

As the meeting progressed, Ernest Holmes stood up and declared your discovery was a different creature altogether to a Plesiosaurus. I lost my temper and fought him over this stupidity...

This made Mary afraid for George. She had heard from other geologists that Holmes was a nasty character, and someone not to be crossed.

As she came to the end of the letter, George told Mary that he would write again as soon as there was more news on the arrival of the Plesiosaurus. The last line of the note was strange, though. Once again, he hinted how Eleanor's behaviour was spiralling out of control, before saying no more on the subject.

CHAPTER 11

ELIZA

*O*pening up to Rafe last night had been easy. Which doesn't make any sense at all. Maybe it was his relaxed way of listening without interrupting, or his kindness, but being with Rafe brought back those early memories of Liam which had been buried for such a long time. Today, though, I wished I could take back everything I told him.

Despite my misgivings, I felt lighter this morning, as if some of the weight had been lifted from my shoulders. The words had flowed out of me in the pub, and once I started talking, it had been hard to stop.

"When Liam walked into Lyme, I was down on the seafront sitting on the wall outside The Royal Standard," I told Rafe, seeing that day in my mind. "He appeared out of nowhere and I knew at once he wasn't a local boy."

"He had devil-may-care looks and was tall and long-limbed, with shoulder-length fair hair and a handsome, tanned face. As I watched him approach Old Ned, the boat-yard owner, Liam walked past me, and our eyes met for the first time."

The past, which had been bottled up for so long, had poured out of me as I shared those memories with Rafe.

"Liam was unlike anyone else I had ever known," I told him. "Sure, I'd had romances with local boys, but there had never been anyone special in my life before."

"How old were you then, Eliza?" Rafe had asked me kindly.

"JUST TWENTY, and working in the teashop alongside Chloe. I was looking forward to going to Plymouth University in the autumn to study marine biology, and was over the moon at being offered a place on the course."

Rafe gave me an understanding nod. "And what happened to change all that?"

"Meeting Liam." There was a lump in my throat as I remembered how I'd been bowled over by him. "We were deliriously happy for the summer months." Without meaning to, I had fallen head over heels in love with him, and although he never promised me anything from the start, I was ecstatically happy.

'Life is for living, Izzy,' he used to tell me, regarding me with those pale blue eyes which were always so full of life.

Liam was a man of few words, but I didn't mind that because he was also a maverick, whose non-conformist ideas made me feel more alive and freer than I'd ever felt before.

The excitement of leaving home to pursue my ambitions was soon replaced by one thing only – to be with Liam. And as the months flew by, we became inseparable.

Liam had told me he would only be in Lyme for six months, working for Old Ned until the end of September. But I harboured the hope that he would love me far too much to leave me and Lyme Regis behind. Our bond, I told myself, was too strong, and going away to university had lost its appeal.

The next bit had been impossible to explain to Rafe, as tears pooled in my eyes at the memory of the unplanned pregnancy. No wonder I had hidden from the advice to return to Lyme for so long; the memories were too painful to face here.

"Eliza, you don't have to tell me any more," Rafe had soothed when he saw how upset I was getting. He leaned across the table and touched my arm tenderly.

As the salty sea breeze hit my face, I shook last night's memory from my head and stepped onto the pebbles of Lyme beach, taking in a long, deep breath.

The sky was filled with dark velvet blues and greys, and despite the clouds, I could see the promise of sunshine yet to come. It would be a warm day later. But there was a cool breeze, and I shivered as I pulled my fleece tighter around me and walked briskly, hoping the fresh air would clear the throbbing headache I had woken up with this morning.

As I paused for a moment on the beach and gazed at the waves crashing onto the shore, I could see two fishing boats in the distance. They were setting off for their early morning catch from the end of The Cobb.

Chloe had told me recently about The Lyme Bay Fisheries and Conversation Reserve, which was now active in Lyme Regis, and how the organisation was trying to maintain a sustainable Marine Reserve within the bay. This was a subject close to my heart. Since I was a young girl, my dream had been to become a marine biologist, and I had achieved that. But being a marine diver at the National Marine Aquarium in Plymouth was not what I really wanted to do.

However, right now, I told myself my career was on hold. But returning to Lyme had made me realise how much I had missed stepping out of my front door and seeing the ocean, with all its wonders laid out in front of me.

I loved that once again I was living close to the beach and nature, where Liam and I had spent so many happy hours together on Old Ned's boat from the first day we met. He even nicknamed it Izzy and talked about setting up his own business. I used to dream that we were a small happy family, living in Lyme Regis, pushing university firmly to the back of my mind.

Despite Lyme's beautiful surroundings and the recollection of happier times, it was so hard to shake off the bleakness which followed me around daily, and the dark clouds overhead mirrored my feelings.

As I arrived by the steps at the far end of the cliff walk, I descended them, taking care not to slip. Then I gazed across the shore at Black Ven cliffs stretching along the coastline.

This was the first time I'd ventured into this area since my return to Lyme, and it was not easy to be here. This was where Liam's body was found. My heart raced and my legs were decidedly shaky as I forced one foot in front of the other; I didn't want to give up now that I'd got this far.

Suddenly an image of me in hospital, waking up bruised and battered, came into my head. I had opened my eyes to the news that Liam was dead. Not only had I lost Liam, but I had also lost all memory of what had happened in the final hours onboard the boat. As a result, the question of how I managed to survive the tragedy, while Liam perished, had been unanswered ever since.

Reaching the bottom of the steps, I momentarily closed my eyes against the overhead sun. Memories of that other time before the accident, when life was full of possibilities, flooded mercilessly into my head. I had been so sure of what I wanted in life then, when I was young and full of hope for a bright future.

I opened my eyes and shook my head. There was no point in dwelling on the past. I lost myself the year Liam died; a huge part of me departed along with him. But somehow, now I was back in Lyme, where it all happened, I had to find a way of uncovering the truth and finding myself again.

CHAPTER 12

GEORGE

When they were first married, George and Eleanor had been happy enough, although signs of Eleanor's jealousy soon seeped into their relationship.

One evening George went with Eleanor to The Pavilion in Exmouth to watch the dancing. She was expecting their son, and her pregnancy was concealed well, but she was forbidden to dance by the doctors.

At that time, George had been deprived of affection and missed the physical love they had enjoyed in the first months of wedded bliss. While at the dance, one of Eleanor's friends (who was married to a wealthy older man) requested a dance with George, which was difficult to refuse.

This single act of dancing was innocent enough, but later when George took a break outside of the hall for some fresh air, the lady quickly followed him out.

Eleanor noticed this, and when she caught up with them, George was in a passionate embrace with the woman. To this day he could not remember how he came to be in the lady's arms. However, Eleanor's cry of anguish had jolted him back to his senses, and he could only conclude he had got carried away after having too much to drink.

Unfortunately, Eleanor would never forgive this one mistake, despite his pleas that the kiss, and the woman, meant nothing to him. Later, when Frederick was born, Eleanor told George he was just like her father.

"You're a philandering cad and not to be trusted," she had yelled, refusing to allow him near her again. After that, her blue eyes became narrowed when she looked at him and her back ramrod stiff.

George knew it was his own fault that she didn't trust him any more, but it was a mistake he couldn't rectify. If he could turn the clock back to somehow get things back the way they were, he would have done.

After a while, George saw it was fruitless to try, and he gave up trying to make amends. Their marriage had become nothing but an empty shell. Thinking about Eleanor made George wonder what he would have to face on his return. Especially as he had gone against her wishes to come to London for the meeting about Mary's Plesiosaurus.

It was true that Oliver Tyrell had given him leave to attend the meeting in London, and it was also true that he had shown favouritism towards George in the past. But that didn't mean he wouldn't listen to his daughter and dismiss George on his return to Devon and his place of work.

Worse still, now that he was here, he would have to stay longer than he had initially intended. This was due to the re-scheduled meeting, which was a result of Mary's creature's delay in the Channel, meaning it had not reached London yet. But that couldn't be helped, and for now he put Eleanor firmly out of his mind.

George looked around for a nearby carriage in the hustle and bustle of the London street, and after locating one, instructed the driver to go to White's Gentleman's Club in St James Street.

A short while later, he alighted outside the club and, pushing open its dark wooden doors, he headed towards the smoking room where his good friend Thomas was usually to be found. The inside of the club was dark, and George took a moment to adjust to the dimness. When his eyes had adjusted, he spotted Thomas in a chair in the corner of the room.

"Good afternoon, old fellow," Thomas said, standing up to greet George.

"Good to see you, Thomas," he returned, sitting down next to his friend.

George looked forward to seeing Thomas Bailey whenever he was in London. It was Thomas who had made sure that George had been elected into the gentlemen's club and not blackballed, as he could have been.

Just like the Geological Society's membership, for George it was Eleanor's money which smoothed his passage and made working at his profession much easier. But he couldn't help thinking that all he really wanted was to be with Mary.

"A brandy for you?" Thomas offered, as the waiter approached them.

Brandies ordered, the pair settled into high-backed, winged chairs and proceeded to discuss the next meeting of the society, when hopefully Mary's creature would have arrived from the Channel.

"It promises to be an interesting evening," George said. "Except for that buffoon Ernest Holmes, who will make a bally nuisance of himself, no doubt."

George had heard how Ernest Holmes operated, and was convinced the man would use every trick in the book to claim the Plesiosaurus for himself.

Thomas was silent for a moment as he regarded his

friend, and seemed to be deep in thought. "Listen, George, be careful. You would do well not to make an enemy out of Holmes. I heard you confront him at the meeting, and then saw him push you out of the way as you left," he said with a lift of his brows.

Before George could comment, Thomas warned, "Remember, Holmes is a very influential man, but he could also be a very dangerous one."

George nodded, knowing Thomas was right. "I understand, but the man's a complete idiot. Although, having said that, Holmes was not the only one to get it wrong."

He was remembering a second meeting at the society the day before, when Georges Cuvier, a French naturalist, had stepped up to the front of the library, shuffled his notes, and then looked up at the audience.

A hush had fallen over the crowd, only interrupted by someone pushing their way to an empty seat at the front of the room. George had been dismayed to see that 'someone' was Holmes, arriving late and shoving his way rudely past everyone in pursuit of an empty seat.

They had all attended the meeting to see what the so-called experts made of Mary's precious discovery. When Holmes was finally seated, Cuvier acknowledged he had been wrong in his assumption that the creature was a fake.

The man looked slightly embarrassed and had gone quite red, but then declared that even a leading vertebrate palaeontologist like himself was not infallible.

At first the audience had been stunned to hear this admission, then applause rang through the room. George thought it was as much to congratulate Cuvier on admitting he'd been wrong than anything else.

Thomas interrupted George's thoughts now. "Have you heard the latest on what Holmes has been up to?" he asked with a frown.

George shook his head, knowing he wouldn't be surprised at any misdeeds Holmes was involved in.

Thomas touched the side of his nose with his forefinger, as if what he was about to tell George should be kept quiet.

"As you know, my wife Juliette is part of the blue stocking brigade," he began. "She went to a meeting at Annabelle Hadcliffe's house, where the lady told my wife that her brother, Ernest Holmes, has been removing his deceased brother-in-law's unpublished papers from The Royal College of Surgeons, supposedly to catalogue them. *But* what he has actually been doing is publishing them under his own name."

"Oh. Good grief!" George was shocked and disgusted at Holmes's behaviour.

Common knowledge was that Annabelle Hadcliffe had been left in debt after her husband's demise, due to a maintenance order to the Queen and other debts owed. Considering that she was related to Holmes, this confirmed to George that the man was completely heartless and had no scruples whatsoever.

"Why is Lady Hadcliffe letting Holmes get away with this?" he asked, feeling his temper rising at this injustice.

Thomas leaned back in his chair and lifted his brows. "On account of Holmes's

violent temper, so I've heard. Lady Hadcliffe is frightened of her own brother."

Heat flooded through George's body. "It's going to be hard to keep silent about such a dirty deed!" he declared through gritted teeth.

Thomas gave George an incredulous stare. "Good God, man! Don't be a dammed fool or even think about it," he said fiercely. "If you value your life, it would be best to let this one go. I should not have told you about Holmes taking the credit for the papers; it was foolish of me. Especially as I know how you hate injustice."

George sat back in his seat and sighed. "Hell and damnation, Thomas. I'd love to, but I won't say anything to Holmes. It seems as if there would be little point if, as you say, it cannot be proved."

Despite his words, George's mind was running in circles at this latest revelation about someone who was becoming his enemy. He couldn't help thinking that somehow he could use this information to his advantage.

Holmes was fast becoming a nuisance to George, so maybe he could warn him off by telling him he knew exactly what he was up to. After all, Holmes wouldn't want it common knowledge amongst the learned gentlemen in his circle that he was a fraud.

If this came to light, Holmes would be the laughing stock of the Geological Society, and he might have to admit that the scientific research was John Hadcliffe's work and not his own.

Maybe if this happened, Holmes would disappear from the meetings at the society, which would certainly make life a lot easier for George.

CHAPTER 13

ELIZA

I glanced up from the counter of the teashop at the sound of the door opening to let the first customer of the day walk in. And my spirits rose when I saw who it was.

"Hello, Drew, how the devil, are you?" I greeted my friend enthusiastically. "It's good to see you, but why aren't you at home putting your feet up?"

Drew was one of my oldest friends and someone I'd known since primary school. Although she had lived in Lyme Regis all her life, I hadn't seen her much over the past ten years when I was living in Plymouth.

She huffed at me and pulled a face. "Hang on a minute, Liza, so many questions! I had to get out of the house as the sun is shining," she said, rubbing a hand over her extended stomach. "I'm so fed up with doing nothing, and I wanted to come and see you. Besides, I wanted to know how you're doing with the new Vintage teashop?"

She glanced around at the room, then back at me. "It looks great, it really does. I love the pink wallpaper, and you look very nice indeed." She looked me up and down appreciatively. "The green in that spotted dress really brings out the colour of your eyes," she added. "And as always, I'm envious of that lovely hair of yours."

"Thanks, Drew," I said, remembering how she had always admired my auburn hair and bemoaned her own mousy locks.

"When this baby's born, if you need any help in the teashop, I'm your man!" Drew continued. "My mother-in-law has already offered to help out with childcare."

"I'll remember that, thank you. It must be awful being cooped up all the time," I sympathised. "Have a seat over here." I indicated the empty tables around me, then pointed to one over by the window overlooking the beach.

I pulled out a chair and watched as she heaved her great bulk down onto the seat. As Drew settled into the chair, I noticed her blue eyes looked bright and her face was glowing.

"Pregnancy suits you, you're positively blooming," I told her appreciatively.

Drew threw back her head and laughed. "Blooming enormous!" she guffawed. "I don't feel very attractive at the moment."

I swallowed down my envy and headed off to the kitchen to fetch some of her favourite carrot cake. When I returned a few minutes later, Drew was gazing out of the window at the sea beyond.

It was one of those cloudless days where the sea was calm, and the sun was sparkling on the waves. Drew looked relaxed with her white tunic dress stretched tightly over her large bump. She leaned back in her chair and laughed.

"Sorry, I didn't mean to put a dampener on things just now. It's hard at the moment, as I feel as if I'll be pregnant forever," she said with a lift of her eyebrows.

"It's fine, everyone's entitled to a rant every so often," I said.

But listening to Drew bemoaning her pregnancy made my mind wander back to the day I found out I was expecting Liam's baby. I'd gone to the local chemists, bought a pregnancy testing kit, then gone straight home to our flat.

And while Chloe worked in the teashop below me, I did the all-important test. I knew what the result would be, even though I had never been pregnant before. The sickness I was suffering, which I desperately tried to hide from my mother each morning, was a clear indication of my condition.

The next day, Liam and I had gone out in the boat together. The sea was calm, and I was feeling peaceful as I gazed over at him. He was steering the boat out to sea, riding the waves across the beautiful landscape, and I could feel myself relaxing as I always did when we were out on the ocean together.

"Are you okay?" Liam had asked me.

I nodded back at him. Life was exciting, I was so very much in love, and for the time being I was hugging the news about the baby to myself. I didn't want the bubble of happiness to burst, and I hoped Liam would be as happy as me about the news. I pushed away any doubts I had about his reaction.

But when the time eventually came to tell Liam I was pregnant, and I was unable to put it off any longer, I was really nervous. I knew the most important thing to him had always been his freedom, and I was about to take all that away.

In the end, we sat in a quiet corner booth of the pub, and I blurted it out before I lost my nerve. At first, Liam looked shocked, then he stared at me uneasily. When he eventually found his voice, he looked at odds with himself as he spoke.

"If you decide to have the baby, Eliza, it'll be cool," he said. "It's your decision."

I longed to tell him it was not only my baby, but his too, and I desperately hoped he would offer to marry me. It might have seemed old-fashioned, but it was what I wanted. However, that would never happen. Eventually, after much thought, I decided to defer my place at university and stay at home to have the baby.

We agreed I would live with Chloe for the time being, Liam would get a permanent job at the end of the summer, and then together we would rent somewhere to live on our own. He wore that trapped look on his face, but I carried on pretending this was what we both wanted.

Now Drew leaned across and placed a hand tenderly on my arm. "I'm sorry, Liza, I know it must remind you of what you lost," she said with an understanding nod.

Jessica arrived with our tea, which was a welcome distraction, so I changed the subject and filled Drew in on the portrait, until the point where I had met Rafe in the pub to discuss the painting.

"I've seen Rafe Hansom around here, he does fossil walks," Drew said. "He's a good-looking bloke, isn't he?" She raised her eyebrows at me enquiringly.

I wasn't getting into any of that with Drew, who was always a bit of a matchmaker. "Fossil walks are part of his job, as he's a palaeontologist working at Lyme Museum," I told her. "And honestly, Drew, it's uncanny how much he looks like the man in the portrait."

"Interesting stuff, and will you be meeting Rafe again?" Drew asked, looking thoughtful. "I mean, to discuss the painting, of course."

"I'm sure we'll meet up again soon. The last time I saw him, the only information we had was that the man in the painting was called George Hansome," I replied, omitting to tell Drew how the conversation on that first meeting had revolved around Liam more than the portrait. I had already promised myself not to let that happen again.

If truth be told, I was embarrassed that I'd told Rafe so much about me when I barely knew him. The poor guy must think I was a bit strange. And to make matters worse, he hadn't been in touch, despite promising to meet up and discuss what research he had done on George.

"Is that the portrait?" Drew pointed to the painting in its place above the counter. When I told her it was, she let out a low wolf whistle. "Dark and mysterious, with amber coloured eyes," she said, then looked at me encouragingly. "Researching who he was with this Rafe guy sounds like a good distraction to me," she offered, putting down her teacup.

"That's the plan." I hoped focussing on the painting would take my mind off my grief over Liam and the memories I had lost that fateful day, which were never far from the forefront of my mind.

"This mystery and the portrait aside, Liza, how're you finding being back in Lyme?" Drew asked with a concerned frown.

I was reluctant to burden Drew with my true feelings in her current state. So I tried to think of something positive to say about being back on home soil. I remembered a rather large ammonite I had found on one of my beach walks recently.

"I'd forgotten quite how much the mudslides here uncover so many fossils every year," I told her truthfully, knowing that even though I had been away for ten years, Lyme Regis was still a magical place to me. Regrettably, since the accident, my love for my hometown had been tainted with bad memories.

I pushed away a feeling of melancholy. "No wonder

there's so many visitors here now, you never know what you're going to find on the beach," I reflected.

"Yeah, sure it's a fascinating process. A great economy boost to little old Lyme Regis town." Drew was regarding me with narrowed eyes. "But really, Liza, how are you?"

I knew she was pushing me to talk about Liam, but today was not a day for discussing the past. "It was all a long time ago," I told her unconvincingly, while trying not reveal how being here where it all happened made everything seem raw again.

"Okay, well, if you're sure you'd rather not talk about it, that's fine. But you know where I am," she replied softly, gently patting a hand on my arm.

I felt guilty; Drew was only trying to help. "If you want the plain truth, it's the hardest thing I've ever done," I admitted, while struggling against the threatening tears. "But... it had to happen sometime, Drew. I couldn't keep running away from what happened," I explained, feeling the ache in my chest loosen slightly.

"I understand, and I think you've done the right thing in coming back, Liza," Drew agreed. Then she carefully steered the conversation away from the emotive subject of Liam. "What about your job?" she asked. "The teashop is lovely and all, but it's not what you want to do long-term, is it? Do you miss working at the aquarium?"

I leaned back in my chair and laughed. "So many questions, Drew. Firstly, it was time to leave the aquarium, and I wanted to move on even if Mum hadn't asked me to run the teashop. Secondly, you know what I really want to do, don't you?"

Not one day had gone by while working in Plymouth that I wasn't convinced it was the whales that I wanted to help the most. But I knew it meant I needed to travel further afield and leave the UK in search of my goal.

"Yeah, I guess I do, and are you going to do it?" Drew folded her arms across her bump and regarded me.

This was something I couldn't answer, because I'd never been able to find the courage to pursue my burning ambition. Liam was still clouding my life with grief and pulling me down into a black hole, where all my hopes and dreams for the future were being crushed.

Aware she'd hit a raw nerve, my friend shrugged and looked over at the portrait again. "It's a lovely picture to have on the wall," she observed, tilting her head as she spoke. "That man is so handsome, and he fits this place to a tee."

It was true that, in his own way, the mysterious man in the painting seemed to be helping me with my grief, because every time I looked at his enigmatic face, he lifted my spirits. And this had the effect of dragging me away from dark thoughts of Liam and easing the burden within.

After Drew had gone off to her antenatal appointment, I went back to work. But my thoughts went round and round in my head like a hamster on a wheel, and memories of my own brief pregnancy filled my mind.

Telling Chloe my news had been hard enough, because it was history repeating itself, but after I told Liam he changed. Thinking back, my heart ached as I remembered the look on his face that day. The carefree expression I had loved so much had been replaced with one of conflict and worry.

"Good morning there, Eliza!"

Pat's voice interrupted my sombre thoughts as she breezed noisily into the teashop, slamming the door behind her.

"Hello, Pat," I returned, and for once I didn't mind her loud, forthright manner. It was a welcome distraction from my dark thoughts of the past.

CHAPTER 14

MARY

*T*he tide was coming in fast. Mary looked down at her frozen hands to see they were red raw, but she had found a larger than average ammonite and, after hours of tapping with her little hammer, had almost released it from its hard rock bed.

She was drawing hard on the inner strength which fuelled her energy and enabled her to carry on digging in such treacherous conditions. With the water getting closer, she could hear the sound of the waves issuing their warning. Mary did not have long before the water would engulf the shore.

However, she did not need a warning, even though she was well aware she had slipped up when Fanny had been on the shore with her a few days before. Usually, Mary knew exactly how long she had before this happened and could count the minutes in her head to the second, before the waves overtook the shore. *Just a bit longer*, she told herself, *and then the creature would be out of its watery grave.*

Mary's relationship with nature and her understanding of what it would do at any given time, was a gift. She didn't know anyone else who knew the things she did about the weather or understood how the sea worked. Mary had never been taught it, but had grown up knowing it all in her head. It was as if she was part of the bigger picture and nature itself.

At last, with a final pull, the ammonite had been released, and Mary let out a sigh of relief before looking down at its jewel-like form in her hand. Then she quickly hauled herself upright and made her way back to the shop.

As she hurried along, Mary reflected on the fire of energy which lived inside her. It was always the same. As soon as she set eyes on a creature or a small fossil stuck fast on the rocks, she would experience a blast of energy. This energy would grow into a flame burning bright inside of her, giving her the strength to work the long hours she did.

Once, when she was quite young, she had asked her mother why she had this extra resilience. It was then that her ma had explained about the lightning strike she suffered as a baby.

"You were a sickly child," Molly Anning had told her daughter wearily. "One day a kind neighbour offered to take you out for some fresh air, to try and bring some colour to your cheeks. Lord knows you needed it, just like all my babies," she reflected sadly.

Her ma went on to tell Mary that the neighbour had also taken two 15-year-old girls with her that day. The neighbour carried Mary, who was 15 months old at the time, to a nearby field where an equestrian display was being held. Suddenly, and without warning, the rain lashed down upon the spectators with a vengeance.

"People ran for cover, and the group sheltered underneath a group of elm trees. But when lightning struck the tree, our neighbour and the two young girls were killed instantly, but somehow – and only the good Lord knows how – you survived this terrible tragedy, Mary."

Molly went on, "You were thought to be dead, too, but a doctor suggested putting you into a warm bath, and you came alive again. It be a true miracle that you were the only survivor of that little group huddled under the tree for shelter that day."

As young as she had been when her mother shared this sad tale, Mary understood why she had something extra inside of her. She firmly believed it was the lightning which had given her this energy that no-one else had, and it was a part of her.

Many people in Lyme Regis who had known Mary as a baby claimed her health changed after that fateful day. And she often wondered whether, if the lightning strike had not happened, she would have suffered the same fate as her seven brothers and sisters. Mary and her older brother Joseph were the only surviving siblings out of the nine children born to Molly and Richard.

Arriving back at the shop with the ammonite in hand, Mary's heart leapt as she spotted a letter waiting for her on the counter with George's handwriting on the envelope.

She hadn't expected any more correspondence from George, as it was only a few days since she had last heard from him, but she eagerly ripped open the envelope and read the contents.

Dear Mary,

While I wait in London a few days more for your creature to arrive at the Geological Society (much to Eleanor's disgust, I'm sure), I met up with my friend Thomas Bailey at White's Gentlemen's Club.

Thomas has been a good friend of mine for years and he writes to me regularly about the meetings at the society. As soon as I arrived at the club, he updated me on the progress of your

Plesiosaurus, and you will be pleased to hear that the creature is due to arrive tomorrow.

However, Thomas warned that the hardest thing would be to keep Ernest Holmes out of the way when the creature arrives, as he must not be allowed to get hold of the discovery. In Thomas's opinion, just because a buyer was already in place would not stop Holmes from trying to lay claim to the creature.

Thomas had heard about my confrontation with Ernest Holmes at the society, and he warned me not to make an enemy of the man. He told me that Holmes is the son of a surgeon who had become the first President of the Royal College of Surgeons, and was prominent in the Royal College and the Geological Society. Even worse, he was a friend of The Prince Regent.

Despite all this, Mary, Holmes is considered to be vain and ambitious, and it's widely believed he was not trusted within the society. However, my meeting with Thomas revealed something even more sinister about Holmes and his dirty dealings.

It seems the man has removed his deceased brother-in-law John Hadcliffe's unpublished papers from The Royal College of Surgeons, supposedly to catalogue them. But what he has actually been doing is publishing them under his own name!

I could hardly believe that even Holmes would stoop this low; it is plagiarism no less. So, Holmes is not only extremely vain and ambitious, but now a criminal as well, it seems.

Even though Holmes is her brother, it seems Annabelle Hadcliffe dare not confront him because of his ferocious temper and violent nature. After hearing this, I told Thomas how I would love to confront Holmes, but Thomas has warned me against this course of action if I value my life.

However, I have a special regard for John Hadcliffe, and I know I must do something to help his widow.

I will write again as soon as I have news of the Plesiosaurus. Stay well.

Yours truly,

George

Mary read the letter with dismay, and felt even more worried about George than before. She understood that he had a special regard for John Hadcliffe, who had been a pioneer in modern medicine. But George's friend had been clear in warning him to take no action against Holmes, as it could put him in danger of reprisal from a dangerous man. It seemed, though, that George was determined to ignore Thomas's advice.

CHAPTER 15

$\mathcal{M}$ary planned to write back to George at the earliest opportunity and reiterate his friend's advice not to get involved in Ernest Holmes's misdeeds. But the fossils were selling well in the shop, and Mary and her mother were kept busy for the next few weeks. Mary was finding and preparing the fossils, and her mother was selling them to visitors and visiting geologists.

Mary was also studying some new scientific papers which had recently been released in the geological world, and spent most evenings working hard on those. When two more letters arrived from George, Mary realised that she had not found the time to reply to him to issue her warning. She set aside her work to read his correspondence.

Dear Mary,

I have spent sleepless nights thinking about the injustice of Holmes stealing John Hadcliffe's research papers and swindling John's widow out of money she badly needs. His own sister, too; it is beyond belief! It is common knowledge that Annabelle Hadcliffe was left in debt after her husband's demise, and being indebted to John Hadcliffe myself, I must do something about the situation.

His research papers saved my sister Faith's life when she was a child, so I have always held him in high esteem.

I have no idea how to help Annabelle Hadcliffe right now, but I will think of a way.

Yours truly,

George

Mary knew that George was similar to her in the way that he hated injustice of any kind, and would not be able to resist any opportunity to become involved in helping Annabelle Hadcliffe.

His next letter explained that Mary's creature had at last arrived at the Geological Society at Somerset House, in London, after much eager anticipation.

Dearest Mary,

The Plesiosaurus took ten days to arrive at the society, which meant it missed the meeting set up to discuss what exactly the creature was. Although, as we know, Holmes has already made up his mind what to call it.

When I arrived at Somerset House, it was still inside its packing box, which was ten feet long and six feet wide. It was so big that it wouldn't fit through the narrow doorway leading upstairs to the meeting room. Before I arrived, the men had been pushing and shoving the creature where it was wedged in the doorway, but it wouldn't budge.

The atmosphere was electric and was a spectacle to behold, Mary. Conybeare and Buckland were shouting instructions to everyone on how to free the creature up, but no-one could move it one way or the other.

I was squashed up against the wall of the hallway, unable to move, but I could see that Holmes had pushed his way to the front of the melee and was using brute force. I was afraid that he would damage your creature, so I stepped forward and pulled him away. Holmes was not happy and even threatened me, but as he did so in front of the other geologists, I did not take his threat seriously.

In the end, the creature had to be unpacked in the doorway of the stairs, as it was the only way to move forwards, and in the dim candlelight, the creature was examined by the Fellows.

Mary sensed that George wasn't telling her everything about his brush with Ernest Holmes, but he ended the letter by telling her he would be arriving in Lyme Regis in a few days' time for a holiday.

This time I'll be with my wife Eleanor and my son Frederick, and when time allows, I will join you on the beach, Mary.

Mary put down the letter and reflected on its contents. In the previous letter George had told her of his plans to visit John Hadcliffe's widow. It was strange how he hadn't mentioned any developments in this second letter, or what had happened since then.

CHAPTER 16

ELIZA

I stood awkwardly with about twenty other people in St Michael's church hall, in Lyme, waiting for a dance class to begin, after being persuaded to come by Drew. Nerves jumped around in my stomach as I remembered my friend's words of encouragement.

"It'll be good for you, Liza," she had said. "I'd come with you, but…" and we had both laughed as she looked downwards and tried unsuccessfully to see her feet.

She knew that I had always loved dancing, but I had lost my enthusiasm for it in the last ten years, along with most other things in life that I'd enjoyed.

Last night, a strange thing had happened. I was scrolling through Facebook, which I hadn't done for a long time, when an old memory came up. It was a photo of Liam I had taken during the summer I met him, and my heart lurched painfully as I gazed at it.

It had been a bright summer's morning and he had been waiting for the tourists to arrive for the first boat trip of the day. His job was to take tourists out on mackerel fishing trips, and to provide pleasure cruises around the coast.

As I snapped the picture, Liam had looked relaxed, with that blond hair touching his shoulders and those blue eyes of his so full of life. It was before I found out I was pregnant, and before he began to withdraw from me.

I quickly scrolled down the Facebook page to get rid of the photo, only to feel a pang of regret at my actions. So, I changed my mind and looked for it again, but it was nowhere to be seen.

Facebook usually only showed memory posts from the last two years, not ten whole years ago, so I had been surprised to see the photo come up on my newsfeed. It left me feeling very sad, and later in the night I dreamt of Liam again.

This morning when I awoke, I was determined to come to this dance class, not least because Drew had already paid for it, but mainly because I acknowledged it might help take me out of the slump I had found myself in over the past few days.

Right now, though, I was more nervous than I cared to admit and wishing I was anywhere but here. The teashop had been buzzing with customers today, and my feet hadn't touched the ground all day. An image of being cosy on the sofa with Biscuit and a good book or movie, skipped into my head, and I imagined myself turning tail and running away.

It was just at that moment that I noticed Rafe Hansom standing on the other side of the room. He saw me at the same time and nodded as our eyes met across the room. My heart did a little flip at the sight of him. He looked quite fetching with those amber coloured eyes and black tousled hair, but embarrassment at being so open with him about Liam made me feel hot and uncomfortable.

The teacher, who introduced herself as Trudy, suddenly clapped her hands together and everyone went quiet. She looked a lot like Darcey Bussell from *Strictly*, with her neat figure and fair hair severely pulled back off her face.

Trudy flitted around the room partnering us up, and my frozen stance must have drawn her attention, because her gaze fell on me. She pointed in my direction and then at Rafe, and ordered us to partner up before moving onto someone else.

"Hello, Eliza, what brings you here?" Rafe said, amusement on his face. "I was persuaded to come by my well-meaning sister." He rolled his eyes heavenwards and I glanced around for his sibling.

"Oh, she's not here tonight. She just thought it would be good for me to meet people other than fossil hunters," he explained. "It's what I've had to endure since my divorce." He tilted his head slightly to one side. "Bless her, she means well."

"Do you like dancing then?" I asked, thinking it wasn't the kind of class most men I knew would be happy to come to. "Sorry, I didn't mean that to sound rude."

Rafe laughed. "Not rude at all. I get what you're saying. It's unusual for a bloke to like dancing, but funnily enough I do," he admitted.

I was about to tell him I had also been pushed into coming along tonight, when Trudy clapped her hands again and began her dance instructions. It was time to pay attention.

"As this is a Latin dance class," she called out loudly, "we will be doing the following dances: the salsa, the rumba, and the Argentine tango." A loud cheer went up for the tango. "Today we will start with the salsa," she continued. "And don't worry if you haven't done this one before, this is a beginners/intermediate class, so just follow my instructions and you'll be fine. Gentlemen, please take your lady's left hand and place your right hand on her back."

I turned towards Rafe and took the hand he was holding out to me, immediately noticing what a strong grip he had. A shiver ran up my spine when he placed his other hand on the small of my back.

My heart was beating fast at being in such close proximity to him as I got a whiff of his aftershave. I could smell sea-salt with a hint of woody musk; it was quite intoxicating. I tried not to focus on the small jet-black chest hairs which were poking out of the top of his dark coloured t-shirt.

As the music began, Trudy instructed us to move our feet. First, the left foot forwards and then the right foot back. I was following her instructions as best as I could, and soon found the music helped me to feel more rhythmic.

Trudy told us to count the beats to the music, explaining that there were eight basic measure beats in the dance. This jogged a memory of a salsa class I had been to many years before, and I began to relax into it. Although at first, I felt stiff and uncomfortable in Rafe's arms, soon we were both moving easily around the floor, and I began to enjoy myself.

After a while, Trudy announced a ten-minute break, and I decided to go in search of the toilets. But before I headed off in that direction, Rafe caught hold of my arm.

"Eliza, I wanted to say I'm sorry I haven't been in touch. Time has been a bit short, but I did some online Google searches on George, and I found out he was a geologist. Obviously, that's really interesting for me, as it's quite close to what I do for a living."

"Wow, that's great news. A geologist, very apt," I enthused.

Rafe was looking so directly into my eyes that I was suddenly self-conscious under his gaze. "Yes, and there must be loads more to find out about him." He leaned in a little closer to me. "Shall we meet up again soon, Eliza? I mean, as soon as I have more research to discuss, that is."

His eyes looked almost golden in colour now, lighter than

I remembered them, and his designer stubble was particularly sexy today. As a lock of black hair flopped across Rafe's forehead, my fingers itched to push it back where it belonged.

Just at that moment, an image of Liam swam into my head, along with the familiar feeling of betrayal I always experienced if I found another man attractive. I swallowed hard and pushed the unwelcome sensation away.

"I'd love to meet up," I told him. At least he hadn't been put off by me talking too much about Liam, and my feelings for my fiancé, the last time we'd met.

I quickly escaped to the toilets, but when I returned it was to find Rafe looking worried. He was running his fingers through his hair in an agitated fashion, making it stand up in dark clumps around his reddened face.

"You won't believe this, but I'm going to have to go!" he said, hurriedly putting on his jacket. "My ex-wife Janine just rang to say Harry's had an accident. He's only gone and fallen out of a neighbour's tree and cut his head." He shook his head sadly. "Poor little lad."

"Oh no. I hope Harry's alright. Of course, you must go, and please don't worry about me. I'm sure Trudy will find me another partner tonight."

I watched as Rafe turned to go, then I remembered how kind he had been to me when I'd been upset. "Where's Harry now? Do you want me to come with you?" I offered, briefly wondering how that would work if his ex-wife was there, but longing to help.

Rafe shook his head. "No honestly, it's fine. But cheers, Eliza, that's very kind of you to offer. Harry's been taken to A&E, so I need to go straight to the hospital now. I'm sure he'll be alright. You know what boys are like, always getting into scrapes."

"Okay, well, if you're sure?" I said, slight had refused my offer.

"Yeah, I am. Catch up with you soon, Eliza," he He gave me a meaningful look before rushing awa leaving me standing all alone on the dance floor, wonderi how on earth I was going to stop myself from falling hook, line, and sinker, for one gorgeous guy called Rafe Hansom.

PTER 17

MARY

*E*lizabeth Philpott walked into Mary's shop, bringing a shaft of sunshine with her. "Good morning, Mary," she said, as she strolled towards the counter where Mary was sorting a small pile of ammonites and belemnites ready for display on the shelves.

"It's a beautiful day out there. How are you, my dear?" asked the older lady, as she loosened the ribbons on her bonnet and undid her cloak.

Mary returned Elizabeth's greeting. "I be with you in a moment, I'll just finish up here." She placed the fossils in neat rows behind her, and then turned back to see her friend studying her quizzically.

"You looked deep in thought just then," Elizabeth observed. "What ails you?"

Like an older sister to Mary, Elizabeth always knew if she was worried or sickening for something, which was not very often. Mary stopped what she was doing and took in a long deep sigh.

"Nothing be the matter, Elizabeth, I was thinking about

George was all. I've just got a letter from him, and he be coming to Lyme for a few days, with his family," she said.

Elizabeth nodded knowingly. "What happened about Ernest Holmes?" she asked. "Has George told you any more?"

"Nothing, as far as I know," Mary said, hoping it would stay that way. "George would be wise to forget about Holmes and his dirty dealings, in my opinion."

Elizabeth was aware of the situation with George and Holmes, which the two women had discussed at length. Mary always confided in her friend.

"Considering Holmes's reputation for having a violent temper, which is well known amongst the gentlemen geologists, that would be the best course of action," Elizabeth agreed.

Mary agreed, then retrieved her bonnet and cloak from the back room, ready for their daily walk along Black Ven cliffs. "I only hope George be alright, and comes to no harm from his confrontation with Holmes," she said.

The two women stepped outside into the sunshine of the day and strolled together towards Lyme and Charmouth beach. This was their daily walk, in search of the fossils. For Mary, those fossils were cleaned and sold in the shop, while Elizabeth's were added to her large collection displayed in a glass cabinet at her cottage in Silver Street.

Mary found such magic in the fossils after they were revealed from their rocky beds that she sometimes longed to keep them. But she had no choice but to sell them. However, before each fossil was placed onto the shelves for sale in the shop, Mary wrote about them in her journal, logging any differences in shape or colour of the creature.

If it was a new creature, something she hadn't found before, she studied the scientific research on it to find out what was known about the animal, and what exactly the creature had been in life. This was the part of her work she loved the most. It seemed to Mary she had been born with a never-ending quest to learn about the world around her, such was her lasting curiosity.

One visiting geologist had asked her once where she got her thirst for learning from. Mary had been hard pushed to answer this, until she thought about her younger self. Her education had been cut short at 12 years old after her father died, but she had attended The Dissenters Sunday school from the age of eight, where they taught religious studies and the three Rs.

In the school, the church stated that God created the universe in six days, and despite this they encouraged dissenters to study geology. This, Mary realised, was one of her first influences in the natural world around her, apart from her father's valuable teachings.

Now, as Mary and Elizabeth made their way to the cliffs, she sensed that Elizabeth was not finished with the subject of George yet. She seemed unusually quiet as they walked along.

"I might ask what ails you, too, Elizabeth? You be preoccupied today," Mary ventured.

Elizabeth stopped on the path and regarded her friend thoughtfully. "Concern for you, Mary, for I saw the way George looked at you last time he was here in Lyme," she said forthrightly.

Despite herself, Mary's face reddened. "George be nothing more than a friend," she told Elizabeth, lifting her chin a little defensively. "There could be nothing else in it because, as you know, he be already married."

Elizabeth nodded at Mary slowly and her smile wavered a little. "I am well aware of that, dear girl. But I saw the love in your eyes for him, too," she said softly, looking at Mary with a direct gaze.

Mary turned from Elizabeth and strode ahead of her.

Sometimes she wished Elizabeth was not quite so perceptive, because it meant she had no secrets from her. She was a very valuable friend and Mary didn't know what she would do without her, but she could be annoyingly accurate sometimes.

When Elizabeth caught up with Mary as she reached Black Ven, she said nothing about the younger woman's ill temper. Together, they lapsed into a companionable silence as they walked across the pebbles and began the business of fossil hunting, eyes riveted to the ground.

After a while, Elizabeth reached across and touched Mary's arm. "Please, my dear, I did not mean to offend you," she said.

Mary stopped searching the ground and regarded Elizabeth. "I know you meant well, and as usual, you be right about my feelings for George." Her stomach knotted with regret that she could never love George in the way she longed to. "But that be the way of things," she added sadly.

There had been men in the geological world in Mary's life, men who had stood on her side, but none quite like George. None so generous hearted, none who had risked anything for her or been so determined to get recognition for Mary.

She had had a dream the night before in which George took her in his arms and loved her, and this morning she had been struck by a sudden realisation. The affection she had always held for George had been replaced by a fierce love, burning brightly inside her heart.

"Mary, are you alright?" Elizabeth looked at her with concern.

Squinting against the morning sun, Mary met her gaze. "I be fine," she said. Elizabeth was a dear friend, and someone she could be honest with. "I have my pride and my dignity. I could never sacrifice these things for a man, and I could no more spend my days idle than stop breathing. Is it not enough that I am considered inferior to the male geologists as it is?"

Elizabeth agreed wholeheartedly. "I understand, Mary, we are of the same opinion," she said, giving her an affectionate smile.

This was one of the many things which bound the two women together as lifelong friends. Over the years Mary had hoped that someone would come along, a man who equalled her in intelligence. Someone who shared her passion for the earth and its treasures, still waiting to be discovered. But this had remained a dream.

Mary was an independent woman who could stand on her own two feet. Life might be hard, but she had her freedom and she answered to no man. In the deepest recesses of her heart, she knew this was the only way for her to survive.

"One day, Mary, you will get recognition from the geologists," Elizabeth said with a tilt of her head. "It will come, one day," she repeated.

Mary thought about how far she had walked this life and how hard it was at times. There were days when the wind was too cold and the work too tough, but recognition for her hard work would make it all worthwhile.

She wished she could join the men at the Geological Society and stand up and talk about her finds, to tell them everything she knew. Instead, those same men came to her little shop, bought the fossils, then claimed *they* had found them on the shores of Lyme Regis.

She understood, though, that fossil hunting was in her blood, and that she would keep searching for them until the day she died.

"I feel it, too," she answered Elizabeth with a sigh. "I

believe that recognition is coming, but it is slow, and I be running out of patience."

The burning desire to be classed as one of the geologists would never diminish; even more so because Mary knew her knowledge often exceeded the learned gentlemen.

"Finding the Plesiosaurus will make a difference," Elizabeth persisted, echoing George's words.

Mary knew Elizabeth was right. After selling the creature last year, Mary and her mother had enjoyed a comfortable winter. And she couldn't deny that things were starting to look up for her.

"Thank you, Elizabeth," she said, and for the first time ever she allowed herself to believe that appreciation and proper payment for her discoveries was on its way.

CHAPTER 18

GEORGE

*E*leanor wrinkled her nose at the smell as they passed the fish stalls on The Cobb, and George tried not to feel that niggle of annoyance at her obvious distaste. Today was a beautiful day weather-wise, and he didn't want any arguments to mar their time spent together with young Frederick.

The little boy wriggled in his arms as they walked back from The Cobb, and George's heart lifted. At barely two years old, Frederick was a delightful child, which made him very proud. George loved the child unconditionally and took comfort in spending time with him.

Eleanor hadn't liked it much when George suggested giving Maud, their young nanny, a day off. She argued that she wanted to spend time alone with George without the troublesome child getting in their way.

But this time George had been insistent, refusing to accept her argument. He wanted to spend time with his son before returning home to Christow, and to work, in a few days' time. Once back at home, he would hardly see Frederick, who was always in bed by the time George returned from the mine every evening.

He also knew that being alone with Eleanor was always a bad idea. Her possessiveness was suffocating, reminding him of the mistake he had made when she was pregnant with Frederick. George wished with all his heart he could turn the clock back, as she never let him forget the night she had found him kissing another woman.

Today his argument had been that Maud, who would normally get one half day off a week, hadn't been able to enjoy Lyme Regis since their arrival over two weeks ago. George told Eleanor that Maud deserved some time off, without her charge, before they returned home. In truth, George knew Maud had an easy life with their son, who had a gentle nature and never misbehaved. However, he'd had to say something to convince Eleanor, and it was all he could think of in the short time he had to come up with something plausible.

George wondered why Eleanor had been unusually quiet today, but he was reluctant to ask the reason, as his wife was prone to sulks.

George watched Frederick running ahead of them, laughing and giggling. As he caught the boy in his arms and tickled him mercilessly, his attention was drawn to a man up ahead, who was sitting on a wooden bench along the walkway.

His heart stopped as he recognised Ernest Holmes, and the evil look on the man's face, which was directed straight at him and his family. George suddenly remembered Thomas telling him that Holmes owned a holiday home in Lyme Regis, which explained why he was here.

Holding Frederick tighter to his body, George stared ahead as he walked along, pretending not to have noticed

Holmes, though the man could hardly be missed with his huge bulk hanging over the sides of the seat.

George could feel Holmes's eyes on him as they neared the bench, but he realised that now was not the time for confrontation. As the three of them came abreast of Holmes, the man got to his feet and puffed out his chest in an antagonistic and provocative manner.

"George Hansome!" Holmes said loudly, as George attempted to walk quickly past him with Frederick and Eleanor in tow.

George had no choice but to stop. He turned to Eleanor and hurriedly passed the child over to her. She looked surprised, and Frederick let out a wail of protest at being separated from his father, but George's instinct told him he didn't want his son anywhere near his arch-enemy.

Turning to face Holmes, George lifted his chin and stood tall. "What do you want, Holmes!" he said, pushing Eleanor and the child quickly behind him. "I've done nothing to you, so you can leave me and my family alone," he added with a glare.

Holmes pushed his face towards George. "I told you before that you would regret the day you crossed me, and you damn well will!" he said, raising his hand as if to strike George, his eyes bulging in their sockets.

George took a step back to put distance between them, and then looked pointedly around at the frightened Eleanor and the small gathering of people who were now staring at the spectacle. "I wouldn't try that, if I was you," he told Holmes, keeping his voice level. "Not with all these witnesses around."

George's words must have made the man think twice, because Holmes lowered his arm then, his eyes darting worriedly around him, and studied the small crowd gathered watching them. Holmes looked as if he wanted to escape, and

George heaved a sigh of relief that his attacker appeared slightly less sure of himself.

Eleanor clutched little Frederick tightly as she watched Holmes warily. George turned to his wife. "Eleanor, allow me to introduce you to Ernest Holmes," he said loudly enough that everyone listening had no doubt who this man was who dared to threaten him and his family in broad daylight.

Holmes said nothing but instead gave Eleanor a hard stare, then he turned and walked quickly away, all the while muttering something unintelligible under his breath. George and Eleanor stood and watched as he disappeared into the distance.

"George, why was that man threatening you?" Eleanor asked, as she handed Frederick back into his arms.

George didn't know how to explain the situation to his wife, so he simply resumed their walk as the people around them dispersed. But when she asked him again, he decided he would be frugal with the truth. He explained that he'd had a disagreement with Holmes recently, but it was nothing to worry about.

As usual, Eleanor wanted to know more. "What was the disagreement about?" she questioned, her gaze intent on his face.

On impulse, and because he wanted her to understand what a nasty character Holmes was, George found himself telling Eleanor about Annabelle Hadcliffe and her predicament. He warned her to forget about Holmes, and not to tell anyone what the man was up to, as his arch-enemy was a dangerous man to confront.

However, he had quite forgotten how Eleanor loved to socialise and, within that social circle, how she also loved to gossip.

CHAPTER 19

George's head was thumping. He wasn't prone to headaches, but he had a bad one this morning, and Eleanor's voice droning on while the maid served up their breakfast was making it worse.

He tried to shut out the noise of her constant nagging while rubbing at his throbbing temples. He had dreamt about Mary and woken up longing to see her, making him determined to escape Eleanor today to seek his friend out on the beach.

"George! You have not heard a word I have said, have you?" Eleanor glared at him accusingly. Her face was pinched and there were two spots of colour on her cheeks.

George looked up from where he had been pushing the congealed egg around his plate and frowned. "I'm sorry, my dear, what did you say?" He wished his wife would disappear in a cloud of dust and leave him alone.

"I said I saw Holmes last night at the Assembly Rooms." Eleanor took hold of a fair ringlet and curled it around her finger, then lifted one eyebrow at him in a triumphant way.

At the sound of his enemy's name, George sat up

straighter and suddenly noticed how pleased with herself Eleanor looked. "You did? I hope you didn't speak to him, as I've told you before he's a dangerous man and best avoided."

Alarm bells began ringing in George's head now, along with the thumping of the headache. What was Holmes up to now?

Eleanor slowly smiled, picked up a piece of bacon, and popped it into her mouth while George waited for her to explain. When she had finished chewing, she said, "It was such a shame you were not there, George. It was a lovely evening of much dancing and socialising."

George's irritation increased. Eleanor had asked him the night before to go dancing with her at the Assembly Rooms here in Lyme Regis, and he had wriggled out of it. Now he wondered if he should have gone after all.

"Eleanor, what happened with Holmes?" he asked directly.

She looked down her nose in a disgusted way, as if she was talking about a bad smell. "I was introduced to his wife. She was a strange one. A woman full of her own importance, she had such an air about her, and you should have seen her dress!"

George waited for his wife to elaborate and held his breath, wondering where this was leading.

"The woman was boasting about her husband and his achievements, and I couldn't help but wonder, my dear," Eleanor widened her eyes at him, "if she knew exactly what her husband had been up to recently."

George's heart beat faster, and he was dreading Eleanor's next words. "What did you say to her, Eleanor?" He hoped that she had held her tongue, because he was already worried about Holmes and his threats.

Eleanor had a gleam in her eye as if she was extremely pleased with herself. "I told his wife what Holmes has been doing with his brother-in-law's papers..." She paused, frowning, and let out a long sigh. "Unfortunately, Holmes was nearby and heard his wife deny this criminal act." She shrugged at this as if it were of no consequence, and then resumed eating her breakfast.

George's heart sank. Holmes would have even more reason to hate him, so he would have to make sure his family was safe. He wouldn't put it past Holmes to put them all in danger, from what he had heard of the man.

Eleanor leaned across the table and looked down her lashes at her husband. "I hope I didn't do the wrong thing, dear," she said simperingly. "His wife was such an annoying woman."

"Well, it's done now." George wished Eleanor had kept her mouth shut, but he could do nothing to change things. "What was his reaction after you had spoken to his wife of his misdeeds?" he probed.

Eleanor sat back in her chair and frowned. "He got very angry and denied it loudly, as you would expect, and he told me to tell my husband he would see you very soon. Holmes was quite threatening, I suppose, but I took no notice. Holmes and his wife quickly left the assembly rooms. More than likely they were scared other people had overheard our conversation."

George sighed. Eleanor's indiscretion could only be a bad thing, especially as Holmes was intent on revenge. Although George had not done anything yet to make sure the man got his just deserts for his thieving, he could only hope there would be no repercussions to him, Eleanor, or little Frederick, from the hateful Ernest Holmes.

CHAPTER 20

ELIZA

*R*afe didn't look very happy where he sat across the table from me in The Royal Standard. He was sipping his pint distractedly, and I could see that something was wrong.

"What's up? You don't seem yourself," I asked with concern. "More to the point, is Harry better now?"

Rafe sat up straighter and met my gaze. "Sorry, Eliza, I've been a bit distracted recently. Cheers for asking about Harry; I'd forgotten I hadn't updated you on what happened. When I got to the hospital, Harry looked very sorry for himself. But, thank God, he was still in one piece. Poor lad had to have his head stitched and bandaged. The consultant told us he would need to be monitored for the next twenty-four hours, in case of any concussion."

Rafe steepled his hands together and grinned. "The good news is that Harry is fine now and back at school. Sorry I had to leave halfway through the dance class the other night. I quite enjoyed it. Did you?"

"Yeah, I did, and I might even go back," I told him, trying to ignore his intense look as my heart raced at the sight of his dark hair flopping across his face. "After you left, Trudy paired me up with someone else."

"Good stuff. You know I told you before that I found out George was a geologist? I remembered you saying that he came from Devon, so I went online to a family tree website and put his name in against mine, and also the area he came from."

Rafe's face lit up as he talked about his ancestor, and I could see that discussing George was taking him out of whatever dark mood he had found himself in.

"Cool. Did you find out what relation he was to you?" I asked, beginning to feel excited that we were getting closer to discovering who George was.

"Sure did. Apparently, he was my four times great-grandfather, who was born in Exeter in the year 1800. He was the youngest of six children and the only son of a doctor, whose name was William Hansome."

"Wow. That's a lot of information in a short period of time," I quipped. "Anything else to report, sir?" I gave a mock salute and grinned at him.

Rafe laughed, and it was encouraging to see him looking less burdened now. "I'm really enjoying finding out all this stuff," he admitted, "and as my father had always wanted to know about George, I feel as if I'm doing this for him."

"Great stuff. Now, was the lovely George married, or a single man? I suppose he must have been married at some point to have been your four times great-grandfather."

"Yep. George married Eleanor Tyrell and they moved to Christow, which is about seven miles from Exeter," he continued. "Eleanor was the only daughter of Oliver and Maud Tyrell. And, interestingly enough, Eleanor's father was the owner of the South Exmouth mine where George worked as a geologist."

"Fascinating. So he married into money then? Did Eleanor and George have any children?"

"George's father, being a doctor, meant that the family would not have been poor. But marrying Eleanor would have given him wealth and status which would have allowed him, as a geologist, to join the society in London."

Rafe went on, "As for kids, they had one son called Frederick." Rafe looked thoughtful for a moment. "I know this isn't relevant, especially these days, but Eleanor was already pregnant when the couple wed. But at that time, it would have caused quite a scandal if it were known." He lifted his eyebrows at this revelation, then sat back in his chair looking pleased with himself. "That's the extent of my research so far."

"Well done you. What's the next step? And the million-dollar question, how to find out more?" I pondered.

"Well, that's something I've been thinking about." Rafe looked thoughtful. "As a palaeontologist, I'm a member of the Geological Society, and I've been thinking it would be a good idea to go there to look up more on George. That way, I'd be able to see the notes on the kind of stuff he worked on in his lifetime. Of course, I *could* look it all up online, but it's way more exciting seeing things like that in the flesh."

"Sounds like a plan to me," I enthused. I was excited about what Rafe might uncover further about George, and wished I could be more involved in it all.

"I wondered… and say no if you'd rather not, but would you like to come with me to the society in London?" Rafe asked tentatively. "It might not be the kind of thing you're into, but I thought I'd ask anyway."

"Not the kind of thing I'm into? I love history and all that stuff. And it would be so interesting uncovering more on George, as I'm super keen to find out about him and his life. I know this sounds silly, but I feel as if I know George."

When Rafe didn't answer, I ploughed on. "Does that sound daft? I mean, he died two centuries ago, but every time I look at that painting, it's as if George is still a real living person."

He nodded. "Aye well, I do know what you mean, Eliza. I used to really love that portrait while I was growing up, to the extent that I'd fight my mum to put it on the wall. Though I always lost that particular battle."

He looked sad for a moment, and for the first time since meeting him, it struck me that he loved the painting just as much as I did.

"The way I see it is this," I began, wondering if I was doing the right thing by what I was about to suggest. "The portrait means so much to you, and it really belongs in your family... so... you should have it back. After all, it'll belong to little Harry one day."

Rafe's mouth fell open at this, then he shook his head. "That wouldn't be fair, Eliza. After all, Liam bought it for you – the painting is yours now."

I shrugged. "Sure, but how about you pay me for it, then? I mean, if it'll make you feel any better about taking it back."

What was I doing trying to sell the painting to Rafe? It went against everything I'd tried to avoid doing since meeting him, but something told me he should have it back.

Rafe looked thoughtful for a moment, and I fully expected him to accept my offer. My heart was in my mouth as I waited with bated breath for his answer.

"Here's the thing, Eliza. I live in a small modern house in Bridport, and if I'm perfectly honest here, I don't think it would look right on the walls. Why don't we leave it in your tea shop for now? Especially as it looks good hanging on the wall there and fits with the new decor. I can trust you to look after it, and at least I know where it is now."

I had never been so relieved in all my life to hear his

response, although I tried not to show it. "Okay, well, if that's what you'd like to do. And I'll definitely look after the painting for you; there's no worries on that score."

"Great, that's settled then. Now, when can we visit the Geological Society together? How about me looking at when I'm free, earmarking a day to go, and letting you know? Will you have to get someone to look after the teashop for the day?"

I nodded. It would be a first for me, leaving the teashop for a whole day, but I had a feeling it would be good for me.

"As soon as I hear from you, I'll sort out cover for the teashop." I grinned. "I'm looking forward to the trip."

Although he seemed animated now, I remembered how crestfallen and concerned Rafe had been when I'd arrived at the pub, and I remembered something from our earlier conversation.

"You said earlier that you'd been distracted recently, Rafe. Is anything wrong?"

A cloud passed over his face, and once again he looked as if he had the worries of the world on his shoulders. I was pretty sure that whatever was bothering him had something to do with young Harry.

"Rafe, what is it? Is Harry really alright? You can tell me," I probed.

He shook his head. "There's nothing to worry about with Harry, Eliza, he's cool," Rafe replied. "The truth is I'm having trouble from my ex-wife. Janine can be awkward at times, which is an understatement if ever there was one."

I thought about the way Rafe had listened when I'd rambled on about Liam. "As you said to me recently, I'm a good listener if you feel like talking?" I offered. "After all, a trouble shared is a trouble halved."

Rafe frowned briefly, then seemed to come to a decision. "Harry comes to stay with me a lot at the weekends, and we have a great time together," he began. "Last weekend I took him fossil hunting and we went swimming. But as usual, he didn't want to go home when the time came." He looked across at me with a look of regret. "He never wants to go home to his mother."

"That's really hard," I sympathised, imagining how much Rafe must miss the little boy.

"Oh man, *it is hard.* Janine knows he'd rather live with me, but she won't have it, which I totally get. But she's always buying things to try and win over Harry. This time it was a puppy."

Rafe looked so forlorn, and I didn't know what to say to help his situation. "I'm sorry it's so difficult, but perhaps Harry will love the puppy."

"Sure, he'll probably love the puppy, but Janine does that kind of thing to placate him all the time."

I paused before asking warily, "Is there anything in particular you think he's unhappy about at home?"

He shrugged. "Harry doesn't tell me why he's not happy. I think he finds it hard to explain." Rafe sat back in his seat and looked thoughtful. "I think it's probably to do with Janine getting babysitters in constantly so that she can go out, which means he's short on attention from his mum. If I'm honest here, I don't think she really wants him to live with her; it's just become a battle of wills between us. She knows I would love to have him to live with me."

"Gosh, that is a difficult situation." I grimaced. "She doesn't want him, but she doesn't want you to have him." I tried to quickly think of words to make Rafe feel better.

"Hopefully Harry understands that both parents do love him, though," I soothed. Janine sounded spiteful to me, hanging onto Harry to keep him away from his father, but I didn't say that.

Rafe leaned forwards and took a sip of his beer. "No

worries on that score. Harry does know I love him. I make sure I tell him that often. What I do find tough is when he asks me constantly if he can live with me. I have to bite my tongue and *not* let him know how much I would love that to happen."

I thought hard about this. "Hypothetically speaking then, Rafe, if it were possible, *could* you have Harry to live with you?" I was wondering about the hours that he worked, and how he would actually manage to look after a child full-time.

Rafe lifted his brows in a quizzical fashion. "That's the million-dollar question, isn't it? Sure, I can't deny it would be hard holding down my job at the museum, doing my research, and having Harry around full-time. But," he sounded determined, "I would find a way if it happened."

Rafe shook his head as if to mentally clear his thoughts, then abruptly changed the subject. "Anyway, Eliza. Enough of my problems. Now we're making progress with George, let's arrange that trip to London soon, shall we?"

The trip to the Geological Society couldn't come soon enough for me, as I was eager to find out more about the handsome 19th century man in the painting, and his life as a Regency geologist.

CHAPTER 21

*I*t was a Friday morning, and Rafe and I were on the train speeding towards London Bridge, to find out more about George. Luckily, I'd managed to get cover, after Drew had offered to help Pat manage the teashop for the day. She promised me she wouldn't overdo it and would mainly sit behind the counter taking payment, rather than be on her feet all day, particularly in her condition.

"What would you normally be doing on your day off?" I asked Rafe now, genuinely interested in what he got up to when he wasn't seeing Harry.

Rafe took a deep breath and leaned towards me, and I got a whiff of his sea-salt musky scent. "Well, I always have lots of work to do on new discoveries, to make them ready for whoever will receive them," he explained. "There's cleaning and the preparing of the fossils to do, and all that is done at home in my workshop, outside of my normal working hours."

"Is that the part of the job you like doing best, or is the finding of the fossils of more interest to you?"

"Sure, I love every part of my job, if I'm honest," Rafe

replied with a gleam in his eye. "When I find the fossils, it's exciting, especially if it's one I haven't seen before. And watching the fossils come to life under my very eyes as I prep them, is quite magical. It can take several hours to do just one fossil," he explained.

"But it's worth every second. One moment, they're lumps of rock with the outline of a long-dead creature inside them; the next, the fossil is lying there exposed in my hand, looking just as it did when it was alive millions of years ago."

I smiled. "That does sound magical, like a brand-new discovery with each fossil."

"Yeah, that's it exactly. That side of palaeontology never ceases to amaze me, and when I'm doing this kind of work, the hours literally whizz by, as I'm lost in the long-ago world that I'm uncovering."

I could see how passionate Rafe was about his work, and I envied him that. Once again, I thought about my dream to help with whale conservation. I was *not* doing what I longed to do, but how could I find the courage to go to Canada in search of my ambition?

Rafe was staring at me expectantly, waiting for the next question. "And where do the fossils go, once they are the finished product?" I asked, pushing the worrisome thoughts about my own career aside for now.

"Those of scientific importance go to Lyme Museum, some go to my personal collection, and some I sell to the local shops. The other thing I have to do is to write up new papers on the fossils, for the contacts who have requested them. Sorry if this is boring you, Eliza," Rafe said with a chuckle. "You only asked what I would normally do on my day off, but I can't help going into lots of detail."

I couldn't help laughing with him. "Cool, it's not boring me, Rafe. I'm genuinely interested," I told him truthfully, again wishing I was doing something that I felt so fired up about.

"Cheers. I know it can be boring for some people. Janine always used to ask me when I was going to get a proper job." He grinned at this comment, but the humour didn't quite reach his eyes.

"That's a bit mean," I couldn't help replying. "Why does she think that palaeontology isn't a proper job?"

Rafe shrugged in an attempt to show me he didn't care. "The money's quite poor, for one thing. She can be a bit materialistic that way, and always used to go on at me about earning more money. And it's true, I could earn more working in London or for a university. My first job was at The Natural History Museum, but the thing is, I love working in Lyme Regis. It's much more hands-on, and what I love doing."

I nodded. "That's the main thing, that you enjoy your work, Rafe. You spend a lot of hours working, so it makes sense. Who gets the scientific papers once you've prepared them?"

"The Yorkshire Geological Society, The Natural History Museum, or whoever has an interest in the papers." Rafe sat back in his seat looking more relaxed. "What about you, Eliza? What do you like to do on your days off?"

"Me? Oh, I usually take long walks on the beach and try to relax," I replied, trying not to think about how everywhere I went in Lyme, there was something that reminded me of Liam and the time we had spent together.

"Nice one. Lyme Regis is great for that," Rafe enthused.

I agreed wholeheartedly, and knew that if it weren't for me trying to come to terms with Liam's death here, I would be happy to settle in Lyme Regis again.

"Yesterday, when I walked past the museum, I thought a lot about Mary Anning," I told him. "I expect you know that

Mary used to teach herself geology and about the fossils by copying out scientific papers and learning from them. She was quite a woman for her time, wasn't she?"

Rafe agreed. "Yeah, she was. Mary even taught herself French so she could study the work of an eminent geologist called Georges Cuvier. When I'm out on my fossil walks, I often imagine her walking along the shores over two hundred years ago, searching for fossils. When you think about it, Mary Anning is Lyme Regis and Lyme Regis is Mary Anning," he continued. "It was a shame she didn't get the recognition she should have had in her lifetime, but have you heard that there's to be a statue erected of her?"

I had heard and was excited that the planned statue was to be erected in the middle of Lyme. "What a great idea it is," I replied. "Apparently, it's an organisation called 'Mary Anning Rocks' who are involved. No-one deserves it more than Mary, don't you think? Harry might like to know about the new collection of 50p coins available through The Natural History Museum. I've heard they feature one of the three prehistoric reptiles that she discovered," I relayed.

"I've got one of the coins on order for him," Rafe said enthusiastically. "At last Mary is getting the recognition she deserves. They even learn about her in school now. Harry knows all about her and her achievements in life."

"So, they should," I replied. "When you think about what a pioneering woman she was, and how hard Mary's life was, what she achieved was so amazing. Not only finding the fossils, but at the same time keeping safe on these dangerous shores, where it's super easy to get cut off. It was a massive achievement."

Rafe ran a hand through his dark hair, making it stand up on end on his head. "Yep, it can't have been easy, that's for sure. It's true Mary had to earn her living from fossil hunt-ing, but I like to think she had a passion for the fossils, too. I mean, so many hours spent outdoors searching in all weathers. Isn't it amazing to think that she discovered the creatures which helped change our understanding of the earth forever? Mary was a great influence on me while I was growing up," Rafe admitted.

"Oh yeah, me too. My mum used to help me search for fossils when I was little, and she taught me all about Mary and what she did," I reflected, thinking of the many walks and searching of the beach I did with Chloe when I was young. "Of course, I hardly ever found anything," I added with a grin. "Although, the other day I did find a rather large fossil, and I wasn't *even* looking for anything at the time."

I had been lost in memories of Liam on that last trip in Old Ned's boat, and when I'd wiped the tears from my face, I'd looked down to see something lying at the bottom of the sloping wet mud of the cliffs.

Rafe was studying me intently. "You know, sometimes that's the best time to find the fossils. I mean, when you aren't even looking for them. Did it come out of its hiding place easily enough?"

"Yeah, it did," I replied, shaking the memories of Liam from my head. "I pulled it out easily, and after getting the worst of the mud off, the sea urchin was instantly recognisable."

"Cool. That's what I like to hear, when they come out a bit cleaner and more rounded That's an echinoid, also known as a sea urchin. They've lived for over 450 million years, about 200 million years before the dinosaurs appeared."

"Awesome. I'm learning so much today," I quipped.

"You are, Eliza," Rafe agreed. "Those kinds of finds are definitely the easy kind." He had a gleam in his eye as he spoke. "If you like, I'll teach you how to locate the right fossils sometime? I'm always giving Harry lessons, and I love it when he finds something of interest."

My heart flipped over at the thought of Rafe helping me to find fossils on Lyme beach. And I became aware that even though I was trying to deny it, a deep attraction was already growing between us.

In the past ten years I'd done my utmost to avoid any close relationships, feeling as if I was somehow being disloyal to Liam. He was always at the back of my mind; a dark shadow of grief, unresolved. And until I knew exactly what had happened to him on the boat that fateful day, it felt like there would be no space in my heart for another man.

"Thanks, Rafe, that's very kind of you to offer," I replied eventually. "We are lucky that out of all the places in the world, thousands of fossils are found right here in Lyme Regis every single year."

"Yep, it's the mudslides which, as you know, are the largest in Europe. Not surprising really, is it, that so many are released? I hope the work going on at the moment to save the cliffs from slipping further into the sea eventually proves successful."

"Well, something needs to be done to stop the cliffs from disappearing," I said, while thinking that Lyme Regis wouldn't be the same without the notorious Black Ven cliffs.

"Tell me about it. God. I've rescued loads of people from those cliffs. They're often fossil hunters who've come out at four o'clock in the morning," Rafe said with a quirk of his brows. "They don't realise that it's such a dangerous area, with the eroding rock landslide, and the tide that can cut you off and push you against the rocks."

"Wow, really?" I couldn't hide my surprise. "Why on earth aren't people more careful about getting cut off, and why are they fossil hunting at four in the morning?"

"Because if the weather has been awful, that is the best time to find the fossils, and they know this. But they put themselves at risk of being caught out in a landslide, in the mud, or of drowning."

Just then, an announcement came over the loudspeaker that the train was coming into London Waterloo station. "Come on, this is us," Rafe said, as he jumped up, retrieved his briefcase from the seat, and grabbed his jacket.

"By the way, Rafe, what exactly are we looking for when we get to the Geological Society?" I asked.

"That's easy," Rafe grinned. "As a Regency geologist, George would have kept journals all about his life and work. Those journals are stored at the society, where everything was recorded. This was because they had meetings about new discoveries, or new scientific evidence, just as they do today. It is what makes finding out about George all the more interesting for me, as a palaeontologist," he added enthusiastically.

As the train pulled into the station, I followed Rafe out of the carriage, and we joined thousands of other commuters on the busy platform. He took hold of my hand and steered me through the noisy crowds, and for a moment I forgot about Liam, the sadness I carried around with me daily, and about missing my vocation of whale conservation. Instead, I tried to enjoy this moment with Rafe, who looked like a modern-day version of George.

And as we headed towards the platform which would take us to Charing Cross, I let myself feel the excitement of finding out more about George Hansome and how he had lived his life.

CHAPTER 22

MARY

*I*t seemed to Mary that she had always known Elizabeth Philpot. The other woman, who was almost 20 years her elder, had moved to Lyme Regis with her sisters when Mary was young. The three women lived in a cottage at the top of Silver Street, and out of them all, it was Elizabeth who was the keen fossil hunter.

As she grew up, Mary noticed the class divide between herself and the geologists who undermined her. And she expected Elizabeth Philpot, who was middle class and from a moneyed background, to act in the same way. Despite their age and class difference, a close bond had formed between the two.

Mary soon learnt that Elizabeth, who was regarded as a prickly spinster in Lyme Regis, took no notice of their difference in standing. Her pursuit of fossils was known locally as an unladylike, dirty, and mysterious pursuit, but she did not care for others' opinion on this subject. Mary had liked and admired Elizabeth from the moment that they met.

When Mary and Joseph found the Ichthyosaur in 1811, it was Elizabeth who helped their mother Molly to find and hire the right workmen to help dig it out, taking almost two years to excavate the creature. From then on, Mary instinctively knew that Elizabeth was always on her side, and their common interest in fossil hunting ensured they got on well.

This morning, while searching on the beach with Elizabeth, Mary had been thinking about their conversation concerning George, and how he felt about her. It was as if her thoughts had conjured him up out of thin air, for when Mary glanced up, she saw him striding in her direction across the beach. *Was Elizabeth right to think that George was in love with her?* she wondered, as he neared them.

"Good morning, Miss Anning, and Miss Philpot," George greeted the two women, lifting his hat and revealing those silky black curls of his. "It's been a long time since I've seen you. How do you do today?"

Mary's voice had quite disappeared at the sight of him, he looked so handsome. She attempted to clear her head and appear composed, which was difficult with the earlier conversation about him echoing in her ears.

"Good morning, we are both well, thank you, Mr Hansome," Elizabeth replied, straightening her back. "I trust you fare well, too?" As George answered Elizabeth, Mary tried not to notice how his gaze kept darting towards her.

Elizabeth turned towards Mary. "I will be going now, my dear," she said, giving Mary a warning look before departing.

Mary was sure Elizabeth was leaving them alone, in case he needed putting straight, but she longed for her to stay and act as a buffer between them. Instead, though, she bade her friend goodbye and watched as Elizabeth strode back along the beach towards the shores of Lyme Regis and more fossil hunting.

George's gaze was now firmly fixed on Mary. "I've missed you," he said unexpectedly. His voice sounded husky, and he stepped towards her and placed a hand on her arm. "I need to talk to you on quite an urgent matter, Miss Anning," he added furtively.

Forced to look at him now, while trying to ignore the touch of his hand, Mary noticed he was quite flushed in the face. Instinctively, she shook off his hand, sensing he was going to say something she would rather not hear, and which was best avoided.

"I apologise, Mr Hansome, but I have much work to do today," she said formally, watching a pained expression come into those amber eyes.

As Mary walked towards the shoreline where she knew the fossils would be today, she could see nothing but the hurt on George's face. A moment later, when he came up behind her, she quickly pulled her hat down over her head to shield her eyes from the sunlight and hide the feelings his close proximity had brought.

She searched her mind for something to say which would ease the sudden tension which had sprung up between them. "Have you seen anything of Ernest Holmes after you confronted him the day the creature arrived at the society?" she asked, curious to know how events had unfolded in that direction.

George looked down at his feet and began kicking distractedly at a pebble. "I saw him yesterday here in Lyme Regis. He was quite threatening to me and my family," he explained. He lifted his gaze to Mary. "Thomas told me he has a holiday home here, which would explain why he was in Lyme," he added.

Mary was again fearful for George. "Please be careful, I've heard that Holmes be dangerous," she warned, trying to ignore the raw emotion in George's eyes as they resumed walking along the shore together.

"Don't worry about me, Miss Anning," George said soothingly, as she stopped in front of the cliffs. "I am quite capable of looking after myself," he declared, then he glanced around the shore as if ensuring they were alone together.

"Miss Anning, could I speak plainly to you for a moment?" he asked, pulling in his brows and shifting on his feet again.

Mary turned towards him, full of apprehension at the uneasy look on his face "What is it, Mr Hansome?" she asked a little brusquely. "You seem to be ill at ease today."

George gazed into her face, and it was then she saw the love reflected deep in his beautiful eyes. Quite suddenly, she was powerless to move, as Elizabeth's words of warning echoed in her head.

He stepped towards her, and the smell of his citrus scented cologne wafted in the air, making her heart race. All of a sudden, George was so close that she could feel his warm breath on her cheek.

"George! I mean… Mr Hansome," she heard the emotion in her voice, and was torn between putting space between them and yearning for them to be close.

Then before she knew what was happening, George's lips came down on hers, and the world and Mary's resolve slipped away, lost on the salty sea air. Her heart was hammering fiercely in her chest as George kissed her hungrily.

The sound of an overhead gull broke the spell, and Mary managed to tear her lips from his. She stared at him accusingly. "George, what be you doing?" she demanded, rubbing at her mouth as if to erase that wonderful, tender kiss they had just shared.

"Oh, my dear, Mary, whyever not?" he whispered, running his hands agitatedly through his hair and reaching his arms out towards her again.

Mary planted her feet and held up her hand to George, warning him to keep away. She was feeling stronger now he was at a distance from her, even if it were only a few feet. "You be married," she stated simply. *What else could she say?* This was the truth, although it wasn't the only reason they couldn't be together in this class divided world.

George shook his head sadly. "That I cannot deny, but I have realised, dear Mary, in the periods I haven't seen you, how very much I love you." The look on his face made her heart flutter. "Could you not find it in your heart to love me, too?" he pleaded.

Mary's legs were weak, but she stood firm. "You may think you do love me, George, but that don't change anything. If only it were that simple."

Hearing George declaring his love for her was like a dream come true, but she knew as well as he did that they were trapped between two worlds. He leaned towards her and stared longingly into her eyes, and in doing so almost loosened Mary's resolve.

"There is a way, Mary. You could become my mistress. Please... I can see you don't like the idea of this, but think about it. At least we could be together," he declared, as he touched his breastbone, as if this was where he loved her the most.

For a moment Mary didn't know what to think or what to feel, and then she was just plain angry with him. "How dare you suggest that, George Hansome!" she yelled, stumbling over the words as they left her mouth in such a hurry.

She jabbed a hand towards his chest. "You be offering me nothing of value," she told him, wondering why he could not see the plainness of this, in his selfishness.

George seemed to have been struck dumb and continued to gape at her as if she had given him a hard slap in the face, while Mary tried to find the words to make him understand that she could never consider such a thing. *If only he had asked her to marry him years ago,* she thought regretfully, *she*

135

would have accepted. However, it would never have happened, not between the two of them.

"Mr Hansome…" she began, reverting to formality again. "What do you think I would do as your mistress?" When he didn't answer this question, she carried on. "I'll tell you what I would do, absolutely nothing!"

"Oh, Mary, why can't you see? You would have fine clothes and a nice house to live in, and I would visit you whenever I could." He glanced across the shore towards Cockmoile Square. "Your mother would be provided for, too," he added, as if this would ensure Mary agreed to his offer. Then he stared back at her with wide eyes, hopeful that this was the solution to the problem of their love.

The flame inside Mary ignited and her anger at last exploded. "How can you not see that I would be like a beautiful bird in a gilded cage?" she raged. "Something to be owned and shown off like a prize, to be paraded, for all to see! Why can you not see the humiliation of it?"

Mary was frustrated, but she had the feeling she wasn't handling this situation very well. She had hoped Elizabeth had been wrong when she suggested that George would proposition her, but today had proved her right. Now she had to get away from him before she did something she would regret.

Turning her head away from his miserable gaze, she started heading towards Lyme beach where she knew Elizabeth would still be searching for fossils. Once she was with her friend, she reasoned, she would be on safer ground away from George.

"As I told you afore, George, I have work to do," she insisted over her shoulder.

Mary had to escape that look on his face and hide her own vulnerability before he tried to wear her down again.

She walked quickly away, her anger burning out now, leaving her love for George lying exposed and raw in her heart.

A moment later she found her breath was short from hurrying too quickly along the shore. She stopped and breathed in, before glancing back from where she'd come, and saw George staring bleakly in her direction.

CHAPTER 23

*M*ary was ignoring George whenever he happened upon Lyme Regis or Charmouth beach, where she worked daily. She was still angry about his proposition, and it made her heart ache. Especially as there was something she was dying to tell him, something he would be pleased to hear, and which was causing excitement to dance in her chest.

She had told Elizabeth the good news, but otherwise Mary was keeping it to herself for now, as her patience had run out when it came to a certain George Hansome.

He had been more than a little foolish in suggesting Mary became his mistress. She saw how it could have been the answer to their love, but it was clear he did not understand her. Not at all. Even though they had known each other since they were children,

Men kept mistresses when they became bored with their wives. But it was not for Mary, even though she could see that it would make for a comfortable life for her and her mother.

There would be no more cold days spent scrabbling on

the rocks looking for fossils, and no more working outside in all weathers. But there would be boredom, and what would happen to her precious work?

How could she study the eminent gentlemen's scientific papers and learn about the latest finds in the geological world, if she wasn't searching out and discovering the fossils every day?

Elizabeth had not been at all surprised when Mary told her later that George had propositioned her. Now, as the two women worked along the shore, Elizabeth said, "You know he's over there watching us, don't you?"

Mary lifted her gaze from the pebbles where she had been pretending to search for fossils. In truth, she saw nothing but George's hurt expression from across the other side of the beach.

"I do know, Elizabeth," she answered sadly.

Mary had seen him earlier in the day on the beach, more than likely searching for her. Maybe even intending to apologise to her before returning home with his family. But she couldn't bring herself to speak to him, such was the anger still burning inside her at his blunder.

"It won't do him no good. He might as well go home," she added dismally, glancing across at her friend.

Elizabeth nodded in a resigned way, then they both looked around at the sound of George's retreating footsteps. Mary had a pang of regret that she had snubbed George so badly, but she would only get angry with him if she attempted to speak to him, so it was better this way. He should go back to his wife and his privileged life and leave her be.

"Forget George for now, as today is a day to celebrate, is it not?" Elizabeth's eyes sparkled as she regarded Mary. "I told you it was coming, and I was right," she added, placing a hand on Mary's arm.

Mary tore her gaze away from George's disappearing figure. "Thank you, Elizabeth, it came as quite a surprise, but it will make all the difference to what I earn from the fossil hunting."

For the first time in a long time, she felt excited and hopeful for the future now. "Ma be very pleased, and that doesn't happen often," Mary said with an ironic smile. Her mother was not given to smiling, and was often unwell with a constant cough, but her face had lit up when she'd heard the news this morning.

It seemed that Mary's discovery of the Plesiosaurus had made her more well-known, and a letter had arrived that morning from a London agent. The man was a dealer in natural curiosities and was offering to sell Mary's fossils, for 20 percent commission, which was a huge surprise.

As the two women resumed their fossil hunting, Mary became aware of a dark figure hiding behind some rocks, near to where George had just been watching them. She stopped and squinted across the beach to see who was there.

"There be someone loitering over there, Elizabeth," she told her friend, staring across at the man who was barely showing himself, but who seemed to be peering in their direction.

Elizabeth straightened her back and looked at where Mary was pointing. "He looks like he's hiding from someone," she said with a frown.

Before the women could investigate further, George reappeared on the footpath above the rocks and was now confronting the man. He seemed to be angry, and she couldn't make out what he was saying. But suddenly the man began running away, his long black cloak trailing behind him as he disappeared into the distance. When Mary looked up at the footpath again, George had also gone.

CHAPTER 24

ELIZA

I waited on the steps next to Rafe as he announced into the intercom, to the side of the large wooden doors of the society, that we had arrived. The words *Geological Society* were embossed in big gold letters along the top of the doors. It all looked rather formal, but exciting at the same time.

The short walk to Piccadilly from the train station hadn't taken us long, and once we arrived, Rafe explained that he had been required to make an appointment before arriving here at Burlington House.

"When I rang to let them know we were coming, the first thing they asked me was what material I needed to source in the library. I gave them what little I knew about George, which means they'll be able to help if I can't find his journal," he told me.

"There's so much information here, as you can imagine, that if you didn't know how to locate something, it could take you weeks to find what you're looking for. We should be okay, as I know this library well."

Once inside the building we were greeted warmly by the

receptionist, and then Rafe signed us both in. "The library is just up those stairs," he explained, "so we will start there, but before we do, would you like to have a look around the society?"

"Yes, that would be great," I enthused, eager to take in as much as I could while I was here.

Rafe led the way into a large room which had a horse-shoe-shaped, polished wooden table which ran the whole length of the room.

"This is the meeting room, which is also called the council room, and is where geologists and palaeontologists like me come when there are new finds to discuss. Or if we want to review new scientific research," he said.

"Right. George would have come here then?" I asked.

Rafe shook his head. "Nope, not here in this building. In George's time, the society was located in Bedford Street, which is now the club for Acts and Actors."

I glanced around the room to see several portraits of famous geologists, but one painting in particular was bigger than the rest. It depicted eight men, seven of them standing around a table and one man sitting. They were studying a cluster of human skulls which were laid out on the large table.

The picture was entitled 'Discussion on the Piltdown Skull', and told the story of the supposed human remains first published in the society's Quarterly Journal, which were later exposed as a fraud in the field of archaeology.

"Are you ready to move on? Next stop is the map room," Rafe announced. I could see he was enjoying showing me around rooms which were obviously so familiar to him. "Be prepared to see lots of maps," he quipped on the way there.

When we arrived at the map room, Rafe greeted the two people who were quietly working in the corner, and I imme-diately saw what he meant about the maps. The room consisted of floor-to-ceiling shelving, every available square inch of which was rammed full of box files and folders. In the middle of the room was a large square table with several maps spread out across its surface, and a large world globe.

"Here you go, Eliza." Rafe swept his arms to encompass the room. "Maps are still used today for geologists' and palaeontologists' work," he explained. "And I have access to all this as a fellow of the society, of course."

"Awesome. What kind of maps would George have used then?" I was looking around with interest, while thinking that this room looked like something out of a Harry Potter movie.

"George would have used William Smith maps for his work," Rafe related, then he glanced around before taking a rolled-up map down from a shelf and spreading it out across the table. The map had large areas shaded out in different colours, which was to show the different minerals in rocks and land in certain areas of the country, Rafe told me.

After looking at a few more maps, I was told that there was one more place to visit. "The lecture room is last, Eliza, then we'll go into the library," he explained, leading me towards a door a short way along the corridor.

The first thing I noticed was that the room looked completely out of context to the rest of the society; it looked quite modern in comparison.

The room had rows and rows of blue seats, all lined up to face a massive whiteboard screen and a podium, with two large speakers on either side. This was obviously for delivering lectures about the latest finds or anything of scientific interest. The wall was adorned with several old William Smith-type maps.

"Looks a bit Sixties," I remarked, glancing around.

Rafe nodded. "Yeah, I suppose it does, with its modern décor... if you can call Sixties décor modern these days."

"Thanks, Rafe, I've enjoyed seeing all the different rooms," I said as he led me towards the library.

Suddenly he stopped and gave me an odd look. "God. I hope it's not too boring for you, Eliza? I do get bit carried away in my enthusiasm sometimes," he said with a resigned shrug.

"Don't be silly, I'd say if I was bored. And I might be bored ordinarily, but as this is to do with George and how he lived his life, I'm finding it interesting," I told him truthfully.

"Cool. I'm glad you're alright with it," he replied, looking relieved.

In the library, once Rafe explained to yet another receptionist what we were there for, we were quickly directed across the room to a computer.

"Right. The first thing we have to do is to log into what's known as the Lyell collection, and just to explain, that's so that we can find where in the library George's journal notes are to be found."

As Rafe made a start on this, I glanced around me. The library was stunning and was on two levels, with a beautifully carved balustrade on the second floor. The walls were covered from floor to ceiling in books and journals. Beautiful chandelier lights hung from the ceiling, and there were polished mahogany tables and chairs in the middle of the room. Today, there was only one other person in the library – a young woman who was sitting in the corner, staring intently at a computer screen.

Rafe had told me that he often travelled up to meetings of the council, and attended talks in the lecture room. And I could understand why he liked coming here. There was an almost magical oldy-world feel to the place, which again reminded me of the Harry Potter films.

"I like being with like-minded people, Eliza," Rafe had

explained. "Other people who are passionate about geology the way I am, and all that stuff."

I knew he could easily have looked up stuff about George online, from the comfort of his own home, but apparently he never passed up an opportunity to visit the society in London.

A moment later, Rafe had found the information he needed, and I watched as he logged out of the computer and then turned to me.

"The next thing we have to do is to locate George's journals," he told me. "Which shouldn't be too difficult now."

He began climbing a wooden ladder, which I could see led up to the second floor which housed a wall of files. After a few moments, I saw that he had found the right one, and he duly tucked it under his arm and descended the ladder.

"Let's sit over here and take a look," he suggested. He pointed to one of the tables nearby, and when we both sat down, he explained what he had found.

"As you can see, this journal has George's name at the top and covers the years 1821 to 1825. And judging from his date of birth, George would have been 21 in 1821, at the start of these notes." Rafe gave me a quizzical look. "I'm not sure George would have been qualified that young, but at the very least, we should be able to find out what he did at the start of his career."

As he opened the journal and flicked through some empty pages at the beginning, the first page of notes began. I had expected the notes to be handwritten, but surprisingly they were all printed, which made them easier to read.

The first page dealt with where George lived, which was the village of Christow in Devon, and how he obtained his qualification in geology. Rafe suddenly gave a loud whoop which echoed around the quiet room of the library, and was quickly shushed by the receptionist.

"Wow, Eliza," he said, more quietly now, "to think that George won a scholarship to Oxford, that's totally, like, awesome!" he exclaimed, looking quite proud of his ancestor.

"Yeah. Gosh, that is commendable," I agreed. "Especially as he wasn't born into money. And remember, this was in the Regency period, when people struggled to work in the areas they were interested in. What a legend he was."

Rafe sat back in his chair and grinned widely. "And there was me thinking it was his wife who gave George everything and he had it easy, like the money to get qualified. But it was through his own efforts that he became a practising geologist."

George's notes went on to say that after he'd finished his degree, he found work at the South Exmouth mine. The mine was 2.5 miles from Christow, and this tied in with what Rafe had already found out online. Then there was some background information on the mine. Primarily a lead mine, its licence had been granted in 1812.

Further up the document, the pages referenced the work George had been involved in at the mine. This was mainly investigating the metals and minerals in the earth and the methods needed to extract these. Another page told how George had studied earth processes in the area, such as landslides and floods, to survey the land and draw up safe building plans.

After we'd both read that information, Rafe turned over the page, and we had then arrived at the year 1824. I leaned back in my chair and let him read it first.

"This is interesting, too, Eliza," he said, immediately lifting his eyes to me. "Apparently, George visited Lyme Regis in February 1824. He was tasked with doing research into the rocks along the Lyme Regis coast, and look what he's put alongside the typed notes here." He pointed to the top of the page excitedly.

I lowered my gaze and read the words: *Attend the meeting about the Plesiosaurus and report back to Mary what conclusions are reached.* This extra note was handwritten and not typed out like the rest of the journal.

I looked up at Rafe and frowned. "Okay. What does that mean, do you think?" I asked a bit confused.

"Well, if it concerned a Plesiosaurus, then it would be a meeting held at the society in Bedford Street. This would be to establish what the creature was and whose find it was. At that time in geology, they were still learning about the fossils found, especially if only part of the creature was revealed."

"Sure, but where it says report back to Mary, would that be Mary Anning, do you think?"

Rafe nodded at this. "Oh, yeah, it's very likely he was referring to Mary Anning, and if I remember correctly, she did find a Plesiosaurus around that time."

"Wow. That's exciting. But if she found it, why would George be reporting back to her? Wouldn't she know what was going on, you know, with her own discovery?"

"Nope. Unfortunately not, as women weren't allowed to attend meetings at the society back then – strange as it may seem to us now. Perhaps if George was a friend of hers and on her side, he would have agreed to find out what was being said about the discovery of the Plesiosaurus. I guess, as it says in the journal, he would then report this back to her."

There was so much injustice against women then, I thought, letting out a long sigh. "That makes me angry on Mary's behalf, the way the men took credit for her finds. I mean I know that happened to her – it's common knowledge – but seeing here how George was trying to help her get recognition, really brings it home for me."

Rafe agreed, then turned back towards the journal. "Look at this, Eliza. Here, George records that he was back in Lyme again in November of that year, and that second trip was to investigate the effects of the Great Storm in the town."

He seemed to be thinking about this. "That's kind of strange," he said a moment later, when he turned the page and arrived at the year 1825. "The notes have completely stopped here." He pointed to a blank page. "After November 1824, there's nothing else written on George *or* his work as a geologist at the mine."

"Blimey, that is odd. Why on earth would that happen?" I asked, disappointed there was nothing further to read on George, his work, or on how he tried to help Mary. "Could he have left the profession at the end of 1824?" I wondered aloud.

"Not sure really. If he did, why would he? George sounded like he enjoyed his work and was a good geologist, and another thing, his notes were bang up-to-date until then."

Puzzled at this unusual turn of events, we both stared at the blank pages in front of us. But just as Rafe shut George's journal, a letter fell out of a pocket at the back and gently fluttered to the floor. Bending forwards, Rafe retrieved it from its resting place.

Before reading the letter, he turned it over to look on the back. "In those days, there were no envelopes, Eliza," he explained. "Letters were written on a single sheet of paper then folded up and sealed, then they were sent in the post this way. But look at this."

I nodded, reflecting on how this whole *George thing* was proving to be a history lesson in itself. "That's strange," I said, after Rafe handed me the letter.

The address on the back of the letter was to George at the mine where he worked, and handwritten along the top were the words *RETURN TO SENDER*.

Rafe took the letter back, unfolded the sheet of paper and

laid it flat on the table. As we both peered at the sloping writing, the first thing I noticed was the name and address of the recipient at the top: *Miss Mary Anning, Cockmoile Square, Lyme Regis.*

"Cool. It seems we were right, and George did know Mary Anning," I said, my interest piqued. "Which makes sense, of course, what with his trips to Lyme Regis and all. But isn't it a bit odd that this is a returned letter?"

"Yeah, it is a bit strange that it was returned to George. I wonder what happened there. Perhaps they had a falling out. It certainly shouldn't be a surprise that he knew Mary, should it? A lot of the geologists visited her when they were in Lyme. After all, she was the font of all knowledge when it came to fossil hunting."

As we settled down to read George's returned letter to Mary, I thought about how sad it was that the male geologists not only went to Mary to buy her fossils, but to obtain knowledge from her which had all been self-taught and not easily come by.

CHAPTER 25

GEORGE

*G*eorge strode quickly towards Leicester Square to visit Mrs Annabelle Hadcliffe, but he was exhausted after a restless night dreaming about Mary.

In his dream, she had raged at him for being the stupid man that he was. When he woke, he found himself hoping she would forgive him for acting like a buffoon, but he didn't hold out much hope.

Unfortunately, it was only afterwards that George realised Mary was not the kind of woman to be kept by a man. *Why had he not seen this before?* he berated himself. Mary was a woman who survived dire conditions to search for fossils, despite often freezing rain and menacing sea, and each time he saw her it seemed she only got stronger.

Self-taught when it came to her knowledge, Mary's work meant everything to her. The thought that she might want to waste away her time being George's mistress seemed more than a little ridiculous to him now. The most he could hope for would be that he hadn't lost her friendship forever, after his appalling blunder.

As soon as he could get back to Lyme Regis, George was determined that he would try and make amends with Mary. He also needed to warn her that Ernest Holmes had been spying on her. George had warned Holmes off when he saw him watching Mary and Miss Elizabeth on the beach, but he was extremely worried about the man's motives towards the two women.

Now, George knocked on the door of number twenty-eight and waited impatiently, and a moment later a young maid opened the door to him.

"Good day to you," he said to the girl. "Is Lady Hadcliffe at home?"

The maid asked his name and then ushered him inside before disappearing into the house. George waited in the dark hallway and within minutes was led into a large drawing room where Lady Hadcliffe herself greeted him warmly and offered him refreshments.

When the maid had been summoned and sent away again with her order for tea, Mrs Hadcliffe turned to George. "How may I help you today, Mr Hansome?" she asked with a lift of her brows.

George placed his hands together on his lap and regarded the woman in front of him. "I hope to be able to assist *you*, Lady Hadcliffe," he said, noticing how strained she looked. Her hair was tied back off her face, revealing a heavily lined forehead, and her eyes were ringed with dark circles.

"Assist me? How so, Mr Hansome?" she offered him a questioning gaze.

George had no idea how to reveal to Lady Hadcliffe what he had heard from Thomas, so he began to explain as best as he could.

"A friend of mine called Thomas Bailey informed me recently of a conversation you had with his wife Juliette," he said. "It was at one of your blue stocking evenings, and as soon as I heard about this, I was concerned for you, my lady."

Lady Hadcliffe's eyes widened, and she looked startled at George's words. "What I told Juliette was for her ears only," she said quickly, lowering her gaze to her lap and muttering the word 'gossip' under her breath.

George could see the lady was struggling to compose herself, but before he could speak, the maid returned to the room with the tea. He waited patiently until the girl deposited the teapot and cups on the table and left the room. Then he leaned towards Lady Hadcliffe, feeling somewhat guilty that he had only added to her distress.

"I am so sorry. Thomas did say I shouldn't say anything to anyone, but please, Lady Hadcliffe, *if it is true,* Holmes must be stopped at once!" George's anger burst out of him at the injustice the man was inflicting on his sister.

Lady Hadcliffe was now staring at George with watery eyes. "You're right, something must be done," she began hesitantly. "However, Ernest has a violent temper and I dare not confront him over this. If he even knew we were having this conversation..." she shook her head sadly, unable to finish her sentence.

It seemed Lady Hadcliffe could not even bring herself to explain to George what Holmes, her own brother, would do if he found them discussing him in this way. The situation was ludicrous.

George set his jaw. "We cannot let him get away with this. You must need the money from those papers?" he said, sitting up straighter in the armchair.

There had recently been talk that Annabelle Hadcliffe had been left in considerable debt after her husband died. George knew that if her husband's unpublished papers were published to the Royal College of Surgeons, as they should be, she would receive payment for them. He felt it was his duty to help John Hadcliffe's widow, to repay the debt he owed the man.

Lady Hadcliffe took a deep shuddering breath and lifted her gaze to his. "That is the truth, Mr Hansome," she admitted. "However, I have no idea how to stop Ernest from stealing them." Her shoulders drooped in recognition of the hopelessness of her situation.

"What happened, after John died, to lead to this situation?" he asked, trying to gain the full picture of what had previously gone on.

"The problem was that Ernest was made executor of John's will, and when John died this left him in complete control of the unpublished papers. So, removing them from the Royal College of Surgeons, under the guise of cataloguing them, was perfectly feasible."

Lady Hadcliffe paused for a moment and regarded George with a thoughtful look. "The temptation to claim them as his own must have been too great for him," she said sadly. "My brother was always greedy, even as a child, and he hasn't changed," she added.

George took in a deep breath and leaned back into his armchair. "Just as I heard then. Do you have proof of any of this?" he asked, determined to find a way of stopping Holmes from swindling his sister out of the money which was rightfully hers.

Lady Hadcliffe shook her head. "I have tried to get proof. After I heard about him releasing new papers to the society, I visited him at his house." She paused before continuing, "You must understand, Mr Hansome, that we do not see each other often, because of his bad temper, and that day he was eager for me to leave. But just before I took my leave, he left the room for a few minutes, and I took the opportunity to search for any evidence."

George's hopes were high. "Did you find anything?" he

said, while thinking how brave Annabelle Hadcliffe was if Holmes's temper was to be believed.

George shuddered as he remembered how he had seen Holmes spying on Mary the last time he was in Lyme Regis. After pursuing him, Holmes had denied everything and in truth, the man hadn't been doing anything but watching Mary and Miss Philpott. But it made George uneasy to think that because of him, Mary might be in danger from Holmes.

"Mr Hansome, are you alright?" Lady Hadcliffe leaned forwards in her chair.

"Sorry, my mind wandered there for a moment. Go on, Lady Hadcliffe," he said, pulling his thoughts back to the conversation in hand.

She gave an understanding nod. "I certainly did find something. I recognised John's work, you see, which had been copied out in Ernest's own handwriting. And Ernest had been burning the papers after copying them. I know this, because I found remnants of John's papers in the hearth, which was still warm."

She sighed deeply as if she were already resigned to her fate. "He was unaware of my discovery, but I had to leave soon afterwards without any proof of what he had been doing."

George's heart went out to Lady Hadcliffe. Her husband had been a great surgeon and a hands-on experimentalist in his exploration of human anatomy. In order to gain knowledge, he had converted this house into a lecture room. It was also the place where he carried out his research, and George knew that John Hadcliffe had worked tirelessly all his life to further medical science.

There must be some way of helping Lady Hadcliffe, George puzzled, as he racked his brains for an answer. Then he thought of something. "Which room in Ernest's house is this evidence to be found?" he asked. He stood up and paced the room agitatedly while an idea formed in his head.

"In his office, that's where he keeps all his valuable papers." Lady Hadcliffe looked worried. "Mr Hansome. Pray, what are you thinking? You cannot go searching as I did, it would be impossible..." Her voice trailed off as she stared across the room at him.

George sat down again and rested his elbows on his knees. As he regarded Lady Hadcliffe, he began to feel as if it might be possible to somehow get hold of those papers.

"Where is this office in regards to the rest of the house?" he asked, hoping she would co-operate with him.

Lady Hadcliffe clasped her hands together and bit down on her lower lip. "His office is at the back of the house, the room next to the drawing room," she revealed anxiously.

George knew what he had to do. "I could search the room when he's out, and collect some proof," he said, his mind whirling with ideas on how he would get into the house.

Lady Hadcliffe was watching him closely. "As it happens, I do have a spare key to Ernest's house," she said hesitantly.

George watched as she walked quickly over to a bureau in the corner of the room, opened one of the drawers, and drew out something. He wondered how she had come to have the key if she rarely saw her brother.

After she had returned to her seat, she looked at him thoughtfully. "I know what you're thinking," she said. "I took the key the last time I was at Ernest's house, after I saw it lying on the hallway table. I was on my way out, and I slipped it into my pocket unnoticed."

She stared into the middle distance. "I don't even know why I took it, because I had no intention of going back there. Ernest would definitely know something was up if I began visiting him frequently."

"I'll go back to the house instead of you," George said

gallantly, ignoring the warning in his head to leave well alone. "I'll be able to gather the evidence for you, and then we will go from there."

Lady Hadcliffe frowned, blinking rapidly. "I'm not sure, Mr Hansome… I don't think this is a good idea. There must be another way," she floundered.

Now he'd found the solution, though, George would not be deterred. "Please let me try, Lady Hadcliffe." He looked at her steadily. "I don't know if you're aware, but years ago your husband's research saved my sister's life."

Before she could answer, George ploughed on. "I owe your husband a huge favour, and I want to help you," he added, genuinely pleased that he could now see a way to achieve this.

Lady Hadcliffe's face brightened, and she smiled through her worries. "I do remember something about that, Mr Hansome. John told me your sister had something called croup when she was young. Remind me of what happened?"

George had no trouble remembering that fateful day when his beloved sister Faith had almost died. "Faith was only seven years old when she became seriously ill." He rubbed at a point between his brows, reliving the horrors of that terrible night.

"Faith had woken up struggling to breathe and barking like a dog, Lady Hadcliffe, and her throat had swelled to twice its size. My father, William, used his medical skills to try and help her, but she was suffocating, and it seemed there was nothing anyone could do to save her. Until my father remembered your husband's research papers on this kind of ailment, which he kept in his desk drawer."

Lady Hadcliffe was listening intently as George went on, "It was very fortunate indeed. My father read the papers, then instructed my mother to fill up the kettle and put it on the fire to heat the water. Within minutes the room was filled with dense steam, and Faith began to breathe a little easier."

"What a miracle!" Lady Hadcliffe clasped her hands together in joy.

George nodded and smiled. "It took another day before Faith looked her old self again, but she recovered soon after," he explained, feeling a pang of regret that John's research could not save Faith's life a second time.

"And how is Faith now? I trust she is well and happy, and has a family of her own?" Lady Hadcliffe enquired.

George hated to admit what had happened to Faith later in life, and he dipped his head and swallowed hard. "I'm afraid Faith passed away two years ago," he said, feeling his chest heavy with sadness, before looking up at Lady Hadcliffe sadly. "Childbirth fever," he explained sombrely.

Lady Hadcliffe's face fell at this dire news. "I'm so sorry, Mr Hansome," she said, rubbing at her forehead and looking visibly distressed.

George had to say what was in his heart. "I miss Faith every day, my lady. But if it were not for your husband's research, she would have died years before she reached adulthood. And I'm forever grateful to him for that." He sighed heavily. "She was my favourite sibling, you see," he added regretfully.

Lady Hadcliffe nodded sympathetically. "I understand, Mr Hansome. If you insist on trying to gather the evidence of my brother's misdeeds, then I won't stand in your way. But please be careful," she warned, handing him the key to Holmes's house.

George left Lady Hadcliffe a short while later, with Ernest Holmes's address written down and the key to the man's house securely in his pocket. They had gone on to discuss the best time for George to try and retrieve the papers, with Lady Hadcliffe revealing that her brother usually went out on Wednesday evenings to play bridge.

It was already Tuesday, so George decided there and then to take his courage in his hands and attempt the break-in the following evening. If he were successful, he would regain the papers for Lady Hadcliffe and at last expose Ernest Holmes for the fraud that he was.

CHAPTER 26

ELIZA

*W*hen I had begun this journey with Rafe to find out what we could about George's life, this was not what either of us had been expecting to uncover at the society. A handwritten letter from George to Mary Anning, which she had returned to him.

There was no explanation from Mary as to why she preferred not to read it, just the ominous words *RETURN TO SENDER*, written in bold capitals across the back of the page. It seemed so harsh and unfair to return his letter, but then what did we know about Mary and George's relationship, and what had gone on between them?

As my gaze lingered on George's sloped writing for the second time, I read the opening paragraph once more.

Dearest Mary,

Please forgive me for my stupidity and I hope we can put this misunderstanding behind us and still be friends.

I looked up from re-reading the letter to see Rafe looking as thoughtful about this as me. "George must have known Mary quite well," I concluded, intrigued by this interesting twist. "Do you think he was in love with her? Maybe he propositioned her, and she was offended?" I randomly guessed.

Rafe widened his amber eyes at me. "Ha. That's kind of jumping to conclusions, isn't it, Eliza?" he said, amusement on his face. "Mainly, 'cos it doesn't actually say what the misunderstanding was, does it?"

"Nope, you're right there. It doesn't," I admitted. I realised it must be me romanticising the evidence, but I had a feeling I was right. "Mary sure wasn't happy with him, though, was she?"

Rafe shook his head as he folded up the letter and replaced it in the back of George's journal just as the librarian approached us with the information that the society would be closing in 15 minutes.

A short while later, once we were settled on the train home, we resumed our conversation about Mary and George.

"In the letter, George mentioned going to see a Lady Hadcliffe about her brother, Ernest Holmes, who was also a geologist," I reflected. "George was trying to help her by exposing Holmes for plagiarism. Another good deed that George was intent on doing, it seems."

Rafe nodded. "Yeah, that's one more thing for me to investigate then. Who was this Ernest Holmes guy?" he considered. "I'd like to know what George's involvement was in *that* particular situation, too. Hopefully, it shouldn't be too hard to find out about Ernest Homes if he was a geologist of the time, like George."

As Rafe spoke, it occurred to me that our research was fast developing into something bigger than simply finding out about Rafe's ancestor. Now it was also about Mary Anning, which made it all the more interesting for me, as I'd always hero-worshipped her.

CHAPTER 27

*I*t was a warm day, the sun was streaming through my window, and I had woken up thinking about George and Mary. *An improvement on bad dreams about Liam*, I told myself. As I hadn't heard from Rafe for a few days, I texted him to ask him how the research was going.

"As it's Sunday, I've got Harry for the day," he replied. "So, you probably won't want to meet up. Sorry. I have got something to tell you about Ernest Holmes and George, though."

"Cool. I'm happy to see both you and Harry," I said truthfully, as I genuinely liked the little boy. "But no problem if you two have plans for today already."

With the teashop closed, I tried *not* to show how much I needed to see Rafe today. I was at a loose end, and it was at such times that thoughts of Liam often plagued me. To my delight, Rafe said they had no plans and that they would both love to see me. We arranged to meet for lunch in The Royal Standard, and he said he would book a table for us for lunch.

On arrival at the pub, I could see it was heaving with families, and Rafe had got the last booking, by the looks of it. Our table was squeezed into the corner of the pub garden, by the white wall and the entrance of the pub from the prom side.

Once we were seated under the umbrella in the beer garden, with drinks in hand, I was eager to discuss what we had found out at the Geological Society.

"Thanks so much for taking me to London, Rafe. I really enjoyed visiting the Geological Society," I said, feeling like an over-excited child. But before Rafe could answer me, Harry put his penny-worth in.

"Dad, Dad! Can I come next time you go to the soc... the place in London?" he asked, jumping up and down on his seat and nearly knocking his orange juice over, his brown eyes wide with enthusiasm.

We both burst out laughing. "Calm down, lad. I've already been to the society, and anyway, you were at school, darling," Rafe explained gently. "How're you ever going to be a palaeontologist, like Daddy, if you don't go to school?" he added for good measure, as he ruffled Harry's short dark hair.

"That's right, Harry," I reiterated. "You have to go to school and learn as much as you can. By the way, how's your sore head now?" I asked, changing the subject.

I watched Harry rubbing at the small red scar on his forehead. "Okay, thanks, it doesn't hurt no-more," he told me. "Are you a palaeontologist like Daddy?" he asked, with a serious expression on his young face.

"Eliza is a marine biologist, Harry," Rafe interjected. "Which means she works at helping animals in the ocean to survive," he explained patiently.

I couldn't help noticing that Rafe looked a bit down in the mouth today. He was trying to hide it, but his cheerful words didn't match his facial expression, and he had a deep frown etched between his brows.

"Is everything alright, Rafe?" I asked quietly as he glanced back at me.

"Everything's cool, Eliza, why do you ask?" he replied unconvincingly.

His smile was too bright as I met his eyes, and I saw the sadness reflected there, but perhaps now wasn't the time to discuss whatever it was that was bothering him.

I turned around to address Harry. "Well done on pronouncing the word *palaeontologist* so well." I gave him a high five and was rewarded with a wide grin.

"Dad, who was that George man again?" Harry asked excitedly, looking across at Rafe.

"Well, now, there's a question, Harry. George was the man in Eliza's portrait – you remember the picture in the teashop, the one who looks like me? He was my four times great-grandfather, and your five times great-grandfather. His son Frederick was my three times great-grandfather, and your four times great-grandfather," he explained.

Harry gave his dad a questioning gaze, obviously not quite understanding the technicalities of this. "Yeah, but what job did George do, Dad?" he persisted.

"George was a geologist, darling. They study the outer layer of the earth's crust and try to understand the history of the planet we live on. This explains when earthquakes, volcanic eruptions, and landslides might happen."

"Is it a bit like your job then, Daddy?" he asked, after a moment of contemplating this long answer.

"There's no doubt it's similar to my job, Harry, but as you know, mine is more about the study of fossilised plants and animals." Rafe was looking thoughtful himself now. "But it could've been why I chose palaeontology as a profession; it was part of my ancestry and in my blood," he added, looking across at me.

"Yeah, well, it figures that you've followed in George's

footsteps," I observed. Rafe not only looked exactly like George, but was doing almost the same job.

"It must be good to know a bit about George, after all these years," I said, relieved to see Rafe looking a bit brighter now. "It's exciting isn't it, Harry?" I looked across at the boy for confirmation.

However, Harry had become bored with the conversation, and was now fidgeting in his seat. "Dad, can I do some colouring in my new book, please?" he pleaded.

"No worries, son." Rafe retrieved Harry's Avengers and Batman colouring book from his rucksack, and quickly handed it to Harry, along with his crayons.

As I watched Harry begin carefully colouring in his book, a black cloud came from nowhere and engulfed me, despite the sun shining brightly overhead. And just as I'd done with him a moment before, Rafe noticed something wasn't right. He leaned his elbows on the table and regarded me thoughtfully.

"What on earth is it, Eliza?" he asked. He darted a glance towards Harry to make sure he wasn't listening, and then back towards me. "You look pretty down about something all of a sudden."

I swallowed hard and bit down on my lower lip, wondering how one moment I could be feeling absolutely fine, and the other it was as if the whole world was about to cave in on me. "If I'm honest, Rafe, I'm a bit lost," I began falteringly.

"What, over Liam?" he asked quietly. "Honestly, I think that with time, you'll get over him, Eliza," he reassured. "Trust me, the pain will lessen. You need to chill a bit with it."

I gazed past him at the sea and hesitated, wondering how to explain how I felt to this gorgeous man sitting in front of me. "Here's the thing. I do feel lost over Liam, you're right, but I also seem to have lost something else, my drive… not my drive, I don't mean that. I mean my purpose in life."

Rafe placed a tender hand on my arm, and I met his gaze, reflecting on how easy it was to open up to him with his kind concern. "And it's not just the Liam problem, if I'm totally honest."

"What is it then, Eliza?" Rafe was regarding me intently. "Come on, spill the beans."

I smiled at how Rafe had the ability to make life seem so much less stressful. "Okay, I'll try and explain. Being a marine biologist means I'm at the forefront of climate change," I continued. "Everything we know and love is disappearing at an alarming rate." I dipped my head and fought hard against the sadness. "The marine life that I wanted to protect is dying in front of my eyes… *all* of our eyes, Rafe."

"Dad, who is it that's dying?"

We both looked up to see Harry had stopped colouring and was now looking in our direction, looking decidedly worried.

"No worries, son. It's nothing that you need to worry about," Rafe soothed as Harry resumed his colouring. "How about we talk about this another time, Eliza?" he suggested.

"Sure, that's fine with me. I'm sorry, I got a bit carried away there." I tried to think of something we could discuss in front of Harry, as I'd seen this before. Young children who caught the conversation about what was going on with the planet, often became fearful even though they didn't understand it.

"Wasn't it a revelation that George knew Mary Anning?" I said, attempting to change the course of the conversation. "And George going to the meeting at the society in 1824 to report back to her, about what was being said about the Plesiosaurus she found the year before. One thing puzzles me, though," I said thoughtfully. "Mary obviously received that letter from George. But how on earth could she afford it? Letters cost money to receive in the Regency era. In fact, it wasn't until 1840 that it became affordable for most people to get mail."

Rafe sat back in his chair and smiled. "Wow. You certainly know your history, Eliza," he said. "Okay, well. One theory could be that George would have paid for the letters to be received by Mary. He could have done that in advance of sending them to her."

I agreed this might be the case, then I thought of something else interesting. "What would Mary's view have been, do you think, about the conservation of the planet?" I reflected. "I think, knowing the sort of person she was, Mary would have understood how important it is for us all to keep the planet healthy, especially our oceans."

Rafe agreed. "Oh, definitely. Mary would have been all for it. She was an intelligent woman who loved to keep abreast of what was going on in the natural world." He tilted his head slightly and lowered his voice. "Climate change not only affects us, but more importantly future generations like Harry," he said, throwing his son an affectionate look with a hint of concern.

The waitress appeared bearing a tray of food we had ordered earlier, and the conversation was paused as we ate our lunch. As soon as we had finished eating, Harry spotted a friend.

"Dad! Can I go and see Lucas," he said, pointing over towards the boy who had appeared at a nearby table with his family.

"Cool, Harry, but come straight back, won't you?" Rafe ordered, watching as he rushed off to see the other boy. Then he turned back towards me. "Eliza, there's something else I've been meaning to ask you. It's about Liam," he said tentatively, keeping one eye on Harry as he chatted to Lucas.

My stomach tensed at the conflicted look on his face. "What on earth is it, Rafe?" I asked with trepidation. "What's worrying you?"

"Hey, not worried, Eliza, just a bit apprehensive about mentioning Liam's name again. I know how it affects you, makes you feel bad and all. But something tells me you need to face this grief you've been supressing for ten years. So, I really hope you don't mind me mentioning the accident to you?" he asked.

The black cloud hovered nearby, but Rafe was right in that I needed to face my grief to overcome it. I nodded reluctantly. Even though every fibre of my being was screaming out at me to bury the sadness, out of sight and out of mind, I pushed it away, determined to try and come to terms with it.

Rafe was looking at me with sympathy, in a way that made me long for him to take me in his arms and hug all the damned hurt away. But, I conceded, I could not start a relationship with him, or indeed anyone, until I was healed from this past hurt.

"Okay well, here goes then," he began. "I read the report online recently from the Maritime Investigation Branch, and I saw that Liam was held responsible for the accident. This was because of safety issues on the boat, is that right, Eliza?"

I gazed across at Rafe and forced myself to swallow the lump in my throat. "Oh God. This is the hardest part for me, Rafe," I told him, feeling as if my heart were breaking all over again. "You're right. Liam was blamed for the sinking of the boat, but the truth was that I was to blame and *not* him."

"What? How do you come to that conclusion? How could you be to blame?" Rafe was incredulous. "There is no way you should be blaming yourself for something which was clearly *not* your fault."

I stared dismally down at my hands, and once again I saw the storm raging around us on that terrible, wretched day.

"Just before I blacked out," I began, "Liam told me the chilling news that he'd accidentally left the life jackets on the quay-side. All of them, that is."

I gazed up at Rafe to see him staring back at me intently. "Oh Lord. I can hardly say this out loud. But here goes. When I was rescued, I *had* a life jacket on. And because I'd lost my memory, I don't remember how the hell that came about." I heard the hitch in my voice but carried on regardless. "Maybe I was lucky, and at the last minute Liam found one for me – I just don't know the answer to this and possibly never will."

The weight of guilt on my chest was getting heavier, and as I tried to find the words to explain all this to Rafe, my throat was drying up. The noise from other people in the pub garden hummed around us, as my heart continued to ache when I thought about this terrible past event in my life.

"Oh, man. Why on earth would Liam leave life jackets behind when he was an experienced sailor and knew exactly what he was doing?" Rafe demanded, his eyes flashing with anger. "And again, Eliza. You need to explain to me, why the hell are you blaming yourself for Liam's grave mistake?"

Letting out a long sigh, I tried to make Rafe understand what had happened. "Liam had been cleaning the boat when I arrived on the quayside, and to my shame, I asked him to take time out of his chores to go out on the boat with me. Not asked; more like demanded."

"He knew I would confront him over commitment issues, and considering he'd been avoiding that conversation, Liam would have been distracted. Later on, as soon as we found ourselves in trouble, he realised his mistake. But of course, it was too late then."

Hot tears filled my eyes now and I lowered my face as they slid down my cheeks. Those dreadful memories had returned with a vengeance, and it was hard to bear.

"God, Eliza, I'm so sorry." Rafe dug deep into his pocket and retrieved one of his cotton hankies before handing it to me.

I took the hankie and sniffed into it. "Oh, Rafe, I still have the hankie you lent me last time I cried on you," I told him. "You're the only person I know who has perfectly ironed and folded handkerchiefs in their pockets."

Rafe was often dressed in old jeans and t-shirts because of his work, and even when he wasn't at work he dressed casually. And yet, he always had a clean hankie on him – it was a trait I found quite amusing.

Rafe grinned back at me with a sparkle in his eye. "We all have our little quirks," he quipped. "It's about time you gave me back the last one then, but please wash it first," he joked.

I smiled through my tears, and Rafe's expression changed to one of sympathy again. "I've been thinking, Eliza," he said thoughtfully. "I think you need a distraction while you are in Lyme Regis – apart from running the teashop and finding out about George, that is. Something you are passionate about would be good."

"What on earth do you mean, Rafe? How would I fit anything else in while running the teashop?"

Rafe folded his arms across his chest. "I don't know, but one of the things you could do would be to help with climate change, you know, right here in Lyme. Think about it, there are loads of things we can all do. And you feel so strongly about it, don't you? It might help you to come to terms with what happened with Liam. Give something back, as it were."

I could see what he meant, and perhaps he was right; it might give me more of a focus. Just then, Harry returned to his seat and resumed his colouring, and I suddenly remembered something about George.

"By the way, Rafe. What were you going to tell me about

George, and did you find out anything about that Ernest Holmes bloke?"

"Oh, I almost forgot to mention. Yes, I did do some digging into Ernest Holmes," Rafe said with a frown. "Holmes was the son of a surgeon, who was prominent in the Geological Society, and was considered to be a bit vain and ambitious. He was also a friend of the Prince Regent, but despite this, it was reported that he wasn't trusted by many in the geological circle."

"Gosh, he doesn't sound very nice, does he? And what about Holmes's sister, the one George mentioned in the letter to Mary?"

"His sister Annabel married the great surgeon John Hadcliffe, who was a pioneer in modern surgery, which helped give Holmes more influence at the time."

"That makes sense," I agreed. "And from that letter Mary returned to George, it sounded as if George suspected Holmes of plagiarism and was trying to help John Hadcliffe's widow."

"Yeah, it does. George obviously hated injustice. And another thing. As you know, George's journal came to an end abruptly in November 1824. Well, my research turned up something strange here, too. George came to Lyme that month, as we know, just after the Great Storm happened here. But what we didn't know was that he mysteriously disappeared around the same time."

Rafe leaned back in his seat and rubbed thoughtfully at his jaw, and what he said next came as a bit of a shock. "After that, George was never seen again."

CHAPTER 28

GEORGE

*I*t was now early evening on Wednesday, and George had been watching from his hiding place in the shadows outside Ernest Holmes's address in Leicester Square. He held the key to the man's house tightly in his hand, and waited patiently as Holmes closed the front door behind him and stepped into a waiting carriage.

George needed to gather his courage now and attempt to get into Holmes's house. If he were successful, he would regain the papers for Lady Hadcliffe, expose Ernest Holmes for the fraud that he was, and repay the debt George owed to John Hadcliffe.

It was a further ten minutes before he thought it was safe to move, while still checking he was not being watched. Then he walked up the steps to the front door and unlocked it quickly, glancing around him one more time at the deserted street. As quickly as he could, he let himself into the hallway of the house.

George was acutely aware he had to be hasty. What if Holmes returned for some reason, or someone had seen him enter the house? He had placed his hat far down on his head and pulled the collar up on his long, dark coat to disguise himself. But he was blatantly aware the punishment would be severe, and might even be death by the gallows, for breaking and entering Holmes's house. The risk he was taking for Lady Hadcliffe was immense, but he hoped it would be worth it in the end.

Retrieving his torch from his coat pocket, George shone it around the pitch-dark hallway, then made his way towards the back of the house. Lady Hadcliffe had given him specific instructions as to where the office was located, so he walked swiftly towards the closed door at the far end.

Pushing open the door, he shone his torch into the room. It was a small office, with a wooden desk and a high-backed chair against the wall. There were two piles of paperwork laid neatly next to each other in the middle of the desk. Perhaps this was the evidence? A shiver ran up George's spine. He hoped this was the case, as he preferred to make this a short visit.

George shone the torch onto the first pile of paperwork. The first page had 'The Royal College of Surgeons and John Hadcliffe' written across the top. He picked up the next page and the page after that, and saw they were all titled the same. Placing them back down in the position where he'd found them, he studied the second pile.

Sure enough, this was the evidence. These papers were not as deep as the first pile, and although the content was the same, they were written in different handwriting, and all had Ernest Holmes's name at the top.

Holmes must have been in the middle of copying out some of the papers before he went out. George picked up both piles, making sure they were kept separate, and placed them into a small bag he had brought with him. He was just about to leave the room when a crackle from the hearth behind him echoed through the silence and made his heart lurch.

George shone his torch into the fire, then crouched down on his knees and looked closer. The fire was low but still burning in places, and the grate was crammed with ashes. A piece of paper was sticking out of the blackened embers. Grabbing hold of the page, he gave it a quick shake and immediately saw it was one of John Hadcliffe's original papers.

Stuffing this quickly into the bag, George tried to still his racing heart, expecting at any moment to be confronted by Holmes.

Hurrying out of the room and through the hallway, he opened the front door and glanced furtively around him. Then, seeing the coast was clear, he made his way home, carrying the bag and its precious cargo under his arm.

CHAPTER 29

ELIZA

I stared dismally into my empty G&T glass. Where was Rafe? He hadn't turned up for our date, and I'd been sitting here conspicuously alone in the pub, going through all the possible scenarios in my head as to what could have happened.

Not surprisingly, Harry came into my mind. The child could have had another accident and been taken to hospital, like last time when he cut his head and had to have stitches. *Could this be the most likely explanation?* I hoped not.

Just in case there'd been a crisis with Harry, I phoned Rafe to find out what had happened. After several rings, though, it went straight to his answerphone. I listened to his dulcet tones reading out the answerphone message, and decided against leaving a voicemail.

I quickly finished my drink and walked back to the flat with an uneasy feeling working its way down my spine. As far as I could remember, everything had been okay with us last Sunday when Harry came with us for lunch at the pub.

It had been a shock hearing from Rafe that George had

disappeared in Lyme Regis just after the Great Storm hit the town. And I wondered now if George could have perished on Black Ven cliffs, just as Liam did two centuries later?

As I let myself into the flat, these dark thoughts filled my head, along with doubts about Rafe. *What else had happened the last time I saw him? Had anything changed to make him decide not to turn up for our date?*

We'd had a good discussion about George, and Rafe had filled me in on what he'd found out about Ernest Holmes, the geologist who had taken a dislike to George.

It had all been going well until Rafe mentioned reading the report online from the Maritime Investigation Branch, which stated that Liam was held responsible for the accident because of safety issues on the boat.

That had been hard for me to hear again. Especially as I still blamed myself for what happened that day. *Perhaps Rafe had lost patience with me over Liam, and really, who could blame him if he had?*

I'd been particularly looking forward to seeing Rafe today, as I'd been thinking about his suggestion of helping to raise awareness of climate change in Lyme while I run the teashop for Chloe. I could see it was a good idea and something I had been mulling over in my head.

Returning to Lyme after so long away meant it was hard to know where to start with it all. But then, it was as if fate intervened. The teashop had only been open about an hour this morning when a woman came in and asked if I could put a flyer up on the noticeboard.

"My name's Julia," she told me. "I'm part of Plastic Free Lyme Regis. We're doing a beach clean this Sunday. Would you mind displaying this for me? We need as many people as we can get," she added enthusiastically.

"Cool. Of course, I don't mind, and I'll defo join you on

the beach clean," I told her, hardly able to believe my luck, after my conflicted thoughts about how to get started with climate change efforts. "I'll put the flyer up right now," I promised.

Before she left, I explained to Julia that I actually wanted to help with climate change more, and she gave me the heads-up to follow a Facebook page dedicated to helping with the plastic problem and other environmental issues.

"It's called Zero Waste Mama, and it's run by a brilliant lady called Claire, who is totally passionate about all this climate stuff," she enthused.

"Thank you, that sounds right up my street. I'll defo have a look at that," I assured her, as Julia left with my name on her list of beach cleaners.

Now, though, it seemed that things had gone horribly wrong between Rafe and me, and I had no-one to chat to about my forthcoming endeavours. I sighed. Whatever the reason for him standing me up tonight, it was probably for the best.

Despite being attracted to him, I wasn't ready for another relationship yet. Maybe I never would be. Even so, my chest was heavy at the thought of not seeing Rafe again, or hearing about the lovely George and his life.

I sat down on the armchair, suddenly feeling weary. And, with Biscuit curled up beside me, I placed my feet up on the sofa and tried to let go of the tension building up in my head.

A short while later, I realised I must have dozed off, because the next thing I knew I was wide awake, and someone was banging on the front door. Feeling groggy, I pushed the cat off my lap and ran downstairs to find Rafe standing on the doorstep. His hair was standing up in clumps on his head, and he looked out of breath.

"Could I come in, Eliza?" he said quickly. "I've had a hell of an evening."

Despite Rafe's dishevelled look, my heart was suddenly hammering in my chest at the sight of him in his bomber jacket and tight jeans.

"Is Harry alright?" I asked urgently, hoping that my earlier fears were unfounded, as I opened the door to let him step inside.

"Yeah, he's fine, thank goodness." He rolled his eyes heavenwards then he followed me wearily upstairs to the flat, looking heavy and deflated.

"Do you want a coffee?" I asked.

Rafe sank down on the sofa, leaned his elbows onto his knees, and put his head in his hands. He looked like he had the weight of the whole world on his shoulders, and my heart turned over.

He didn't answer, but I made him a strong cup of coffee anyway, figuring he needed it. Then I placed the steaming cup on the table and sat down opposite him. "How about a shot of something stronger in that?" I joked, trying to lighten the atmosphere a little.

Rafe's head came up and he smiled weakly at me. His eyes were bloodshot and his face pale. "Nope, better not, but thanks, Eliza. Just the coffee is fine. And before I go any further, I'm really sorry about tonight," he began, running his fingers through those dark curls and making his hair stand up on end even more.

"Oh, Rafe. What on earth has happened now?" I cajoled. "I hope it's nothing too serious?"

He sipped at the coffee with his shoulders slumped, then he gazed across at me. "Oh God, where do I start?" he said, looking completely forlorn. "Janine came to see me, and she's up to her old tricks again," he added, pursing his lips.

I took a deep breath and tried to choose my words carefully. "It must be hard being divorced and having a child in the middle of it all." I was desperate to shift that sad look off his handsome face and to see those amber eyes full of life again.

Rafe nodded. "Sure, it's hell at times, Eliza. Before I forget to say, I missed your call earlier, and I'm sorry about that," he said falteringly.

"It doesn't matter about that now. Stop saying sorry. I can see you've had a problem with your ex-wife, so whatever it is, just tell me what's wrong." I leaned forward and gazed across at him expectantly.

"Yeah, you're right. The gist of it is that Janine has trust issues. Stuff she has refused to address in the past, which has affected our marriage, and is still causing trouble for me and Harry."

I tilted my head to one side. "We all have issues, Rafe. What about mine over Liam?" I thought about how long it had taken me to start facing my own problems. And even now I still wasn't finding it easy to face the grief over Liam.

Rafe quickly shook his head. "No, it's really not the same, Eliza. Your issues are only affecting you, but with Janine... well, her jealousy has all but destroyed our family." He sighed deeply and gave a small shrug as he spoke, as if resigned to the way she was.

"Hmm. That does sound bad," I said. Rafe was wrong in saying my issues had only affected me; they also affected my mother, Chloe. But I didn't correct him. "So, what happened tonight then?"

Rafe stared at me for one long moment, his expression serious. "Okay. Janine turned up without Harry and began a jealous tirade, as if we were still married," he said with wide eyes. "The worst bit was... it was all about you, Eliza."

"Me? How so?" I couldn't think why Rafe's wife would be having a rant about me.

"Yeah, well, I was confused, too. But apparently, Harry

mentioned to her about our lunch at the pub last week, and he also said how much he likes you." Rafe gave an ironic smile. "That went down like a lead balloon."

"Oh. Gosh, I'm sorry, Rafe." I was really not sure why *I* was sorry. For causing problems with his wife, perhaps? Or for the pain he was going through because of me?

"No, Eliza. It's me who should be sorry, not you. I didn't mean to drag you into all this. I've told Janine that there's nothing but friendship between you and me. That's not to say I don't wish there was more to our relationship than being friends," he added quietly, throwing me a meaningful look.

Rafe was staring at me so intently that I found it hard to tear my gaze away from those beautiful eyes. I glanced down at my lap to avoid seeing that yearning on his face any more.

"Oh, Rafe..." I murmured before looking up. And there it was again, the soft look of love reflected in that amber gaze.

As we stared at one another, I saw George's face in the painting again and the love reflected in his eyes for Mary. Those eyes, which were so like Rafe's, made my heart thump wildly. My resolve was falling away, and I tried to think of a reason *not* to love this man. "It's the Liam thing..." I began falteringly.

My words all sounded so hollow to me now. I was attracted to Rafe, and there was no doubt my feelings for him were growing. And it was blatantly obvious that he felt the same way. But now was not the time to start a new relationship, I was sure of that.

Rafe, however, was quick to reassure me. "It's cool, I understand, Eliza. And I don't want to rush you, not at all. I can wait until you're ready," he said quickly, running a hand through his hair again and letting out a long sigh.

Even though it was tempting to tell Rafe I had feelings for

him, which was true, in my heart I understood that I had to be true to myself.

"If I'm honest here, I don't know if I'll ever be ready," I replied, as unshed tears burned hot at the back of my eyes. "I'm sorry…"

Instead of my words dampening down his ardour, as I'd expected, Rafe leapt out of his seat and immediately crouched down on his knees in front of me. I could smell his sea-salt musky scent in the air, which sent my pulse racing.

"Listen, Eliza. I know you don't want to hear this, but I think I love you." His voice was husky and deep, and his face filled with emotion. "I get that you may not feel the same as me, at the moment. But I'm willing to wait as long as it takes," he added tenderly. "As long as it takes," he repeated.

Words failed me, and my voice had disappeared somewhere I couldn't find it. I was strongly attracted to Rafe, but until things came to a conclusion with Liam, I couldn't see my way forward to loving him the way that he deserved. He saw my hesitation and his face fell as he lifted himself heavily from the floor.

Guilt made my chest feel as heavy as lead. "Maybe in time things will change," I ventured. *Could this happen? Could I love this man?* I didn't know the answer to any of this. Then I suddenly thought of something else.

"Janine wasn't trying to stop you seeing Harry, was she?" I asked, eager to move the focus from our relationship to the trouble over his ex-wife. If this were the case, it would break Rafe, as he idolised the boy.

He shook his head and threw his arms up in despair. "Nope, not as such, but she's always difficult when it comes to Harry, and trying to punish me as usual," he said sadly.

"Oh, Rafe. Punishing you for what? You're a great dad to Harry from what I've seen." My words trailed off while I tried to think of good things to say about him and the way he was with his son. "What caused all this, and made Janine this way in the first place? I mean, why is she so jealous?"

Rafe had gone very still and now looked a bit shamefaced. "Oh God. This is going to sound terrible, Eliza. But I made a mistake when we were married, one she's never let me forget, and which cost us our marriage."

My mind was now whirling as to what awful thing he had done that could have had such serious consequences for them as a family. "What kind of mistake was that, Rafe?" I whispered.

He shifted on his seat awkwardly. "Well, it began one night when we had friends over for dinner, which we often did. The friends were a couple called Annie and Pete. I'd heard they were having trouble in their marriage, and was surprised to find Annie flirting outrageously with me all night."

"I tried to ignore her. But the more I tried to make light of Annie's flirting, the angrier Janine was growing. I could totally understand that. But after Annie and Pete left, the hysterics began. I got all the blame, even though at that point I hadn't done anything wrong."

"Was this something that happened a lot while you were married?" My heart went out to Harry, who must have been in the middle of this volatile relationship.

Rafe frowned and rubbed hard at a spot between his eyes. "Oh, yeah. It happened all the time, Eliza. I couldn't do anything without instigating Janine's jealousy. That day I'd really had enough of it and knew I had to get away from her, so I walked down to the pub to drown my sorrows."

I could see this was a painful memory, so I waited patiently for Rafe to go on, having a good idea where this was leading. He then explained that Annie had been in the pub alone when he got there.

"We were both upset and began drinking heavily," he

continued. "It was a huge mistake. We spent a few hours commiserating with each other, before I came to my senses and decided to go home. However, Annie had other ideas. As we were saying goodbye outside the pub, she went to hug me, and instead kissed me on the lips."

"Okay, not a good move in the circumstances," I remarked, trying to make light of the situation, and understanding why Janine had been jealous in this particular instance.

Rafe was deep in this memory and barely heard me. "Oh, man. I was shocked at first and slow to react because of the drink, but I pushed her away," he told me. "It was too late, though. Another of Janine's friends had seen us kissing. By the time I arrived home, all my belongings were in the street and Janine wouldn't let me in the house."

He slumped forwards and I wondered if he was crying, then he lifted his head and looked across at me forlornly. "I'll never forget the look on Harry's face that day. He was at his bedroom window crying, watching me pick up all my clothes from the street below. And, Eliza, it was *all* my fault."

"*Not* all your fault, Rafe," I reassured. "It sounds as if Janine drove you to it. Obviously, it *was* a silly thing to do, to drink with Annie at the pub when she'd been flirting with you previously, but not the crime of the century."

Rafe nodded at me in a determined way. "Thanks for listening, Eliza. I'm determined I won't let Janine rule my life the way she tried to when we were married," he said, then he glanced down at his watch.

"Changing the subject, I have more news about George, if you're interested. But it's getting late now. How about we meet up at the pub soon? I've just got to work some things out in my head to do with Harry, then I'll text you and arrange something. This time, come rain or shine, or any more shenanigans from Janine, I'll be there."

A smile quirked at Rafe's mouth as he spoke, and my heart melted. "Sounds like a plan to me," I replied. I was always eager to know more about George, but I was also keen for Rafe to leave now, after his uncomfortable declaration of love.

CHAPTER 30

MARY

It was early afternoon, the rain was lashing down outside Mary's shop in Cockmoile Square, and the sea was wild, with the waves almost engulfing the nearby Cobb with its fierceness.

Mary was preparing the fossils she had found the day before. She was more than happy to stay in the dry of the workshop and work on a good-sized ammonite she had uncovered.

By tomorrow the storm would have loosened the embedded fossils in the rocks which had migrated to the surface. They would then be washed clear by the turbulent sea, ready to be collected. Although, one of the dangers Mary was always on the lookout for, after a storm, was the vertical cracks in the cliff face, which warned of a landslide. She avoided those areas wherever possible.

New specimens often emerged in this never-ending process. However, a violent sea could just as easily destroy and wash away a valuable fossil, and when a large fossil was found, it could take years to excavate it.

Mary straightened her spine and stretched out the ache in

her back just as the shop door opened. Elizabeth's voice reached her ears from the workshop doorway.

"Good day to you, Mary."

Mary walked through to the shop to see her friend closing the door behind her.

"I be surprised to see you out in such weather," she said, taking in Elizabeth's long cloak dripping with water.

"I surprise myself sometimes, Mary," Elizabeth answered with a shiver, as she pulled off her hat and shook out the water. "What a day!" she said. "I needed some fresh air and thought I'd come and see how you are today. In particular, if you've heard from George?"

If anyone else had asked after George, Mary would have told them to mind their own business. But she didn't mind Elizabeth asking questions; the two women had no secrets and told each other everything.

Mary let out a long sigh. "George has stopped writing to me, and it's likely I'll never see him again." She shrugged in an attempt to show Elizabeth she cared not one bit for George.

"I'm sorry to hear this, Mary. I had hoped he would apologise for his behaviour and that you two could remain friends," she said with a lift of her eyebrows.

"To be honest, Elizabeth, I'm not sure I even want to be friends with George. Friends understand each other, they know each other well enough not to say things to upset them. To have asked me to be his mistress means George does not know me at all well."

"That is true, dear," Elizabeth admitted with a shake of her head. "But sometimes friends say the wrong thing and regret it, so let's hope that's the case here."

Mary was touched by Elizabeth's concern. It was good to have someone she could confide in, and she couldn't imagine Elizabeth ever saying anything to upset her.

"Would you like a cup of tea while you be here?" Mary asked.

"That would be lovely," Elizabeth replied, and she followed Mary back into the workshop.

A short while later, after the two women had caught up on any news about the business of fossil hunting, Elizabeth announced that she had better leave for home before the weather worsened.

After she had gone, Mary found that their conversation had brought George to the forefront of her mind again, just when she had been trying her best to forget he existed. Her heart was heavy as she resumed her work on the ammonite.

A moment later, the door pinged open again, and Mary retraced her footsteps into the shop. The post cart was just pulling away, having delivered a letter. She picked it up from the counter, and her heart sank as she recognised the writing on the envelope.

CHAPTER 31

ELIZA

*T*he sound of a seagull squawking outside my bedroom window woke me up with a jolt. I had been dreaming about Liam again, and was still in that strange place between sleep and waking.

As I sat bolt upright in bed, the memories surfaced of that day when I had known I had to confront Liam. It was September, and the nights were drawing in, but some days could be like mid-summer.

After I had met Liam, my appearance changed. Like a chameleon, I mimicked his personality, wanting to be just like him. I began wearing long flowery dresses, and let my shoulder-length auburn hair flow free around my shoulders.

Noticing this, my mother warned me to be careful. 'Don't give up on your dreams,' she had said, giving me a probing look. But I was trapped in a bubble of delusion, and her wise words passed me by as I made my way down to The Cobb, where I found Liam cleaning out Ned's boat.

At that time of year there were fewer tourists in Lyme Regis, and The Cobb was deserted, with no boat trips booked for the day. But as soon as Liam saw me, his face wore the closed look I had come to recognise.

That day, I knew it was now or never. I needed to find out what Liam intended to do, especially with the season coming to an end. He hadn't mentioned any future plans lately and was still very withdrawn.

Old Ned had told him he was selling off the business and that Liam could buy it if he wanted to stay in Lyme. But Liam had refused to broach the subject, and I felt as if he were slipping slowly through my fingers.

I watched Liam as he tidied the boat up, clearing all the stuff from inside, then scrubbing the decks. The silence between us was deafening. Before I had a chance to turn for home and forget the confrontation, I forced myself to ask him to take me out on a boat trip.

The expression on Liam's face told me he understood it was time for the truth and some tough talking. But he still looked for excuses, glancing across to Old Ned, who was not in his usual place. He told me he wasn't supposed to take anyone out on the boat unless they were tourists.

I dug my heels in and, with my heart racing, I stood firm. "Just a short trip around the bay?' I told him. "After all, it won't take long."

Liam looked uneasy, but eventually agreed, saying we couldn't be out on the sea long, as he would need to finish the cleaning on his return. I stepped onto the boat feeling as if I'd overcome the first hurdle.

The wind was high that day, but the sun was just breaking through the clouds. As we left the shore, I asked Liam what the forecast was. He told me he hadn't checked it yet that day.

As he started up the engine, I saw he was avoiding eye contact with me, and I longed to tell him he could still be free even if we stayed together. But deep down, with a baby on the way, I knew things could never be as they were before.

We'd been out in the boat for about ten minutes and had just lost sight of the shore, when the sky darkened. I tried to ignore the change in weather and forced myself to start a conversation with Liam, even though he was brooding and silent while steering the boat.

I began by asking him if he was still happy staying in Lyme Regis. He didn't answer at first, and again, he wouldn't look at me. I told him he had to tell me the truth now, because it was the only thing that mattered.

Instead of answering me, he kept looking up at the dark sky while steering the boat. At that point, I wasn't worrying too much about the weather. After all, we were still only a short distance from the shore.

I could see that my plans were going awry, and Liam was refusing to talk to me again. I stood on the deck, wondering how to get through to him, while idly looking out for the dolphins as we sailed along. Seeing those beautiful creatures swimming next to the boat always cheered me up.

It was then that I noticed the waves had grown a lot higher in the few minutes since we'd left the shore, and a sliver of alarm coursed through me. I glanced uneasily across at Liam, and tried to ignore the sick feeling growing in my stomach, which had nothing to do with my pregnancy. The weather was changing rapidly, the boat was rocking from side to side with the growing swell of the sea, and I was beginning to feel unsteady on my feet.

Liam looked worried. "We must go back, Eliza," he said urgently. "There's a storm brewing."

I could see the concern on his face, but I didn't want to go back yet when I still hadn't got him to talk to me properly. "We must discuss what's going to happen now the season is coming to an end," I yelled across the boat to him.

I knew that once we were back on dry land, things would revert to how they were before. He would bury himself in his work, and I wouldn't be able to get through to him again.

Liam refused to answer me, and instead carried on steering the boat and ignoring my pleas. All I could think of was I needed him to tell me the truth *before* we went back to shore.

Weeks of worry were coming to the surface, and frustration at trying to pin him down was eating me up and blinding me to what was happening. I shouted across the boat again, against the noise of the waves, this time telling him he had to tell me the truth.

Liam had turned his back on me and was staring mutely out to sea. I was making him clam up further, but by then I'd lost all reason. All I needed was for him to answer me, to clarify once and for all that he wanted to leave me, and then I could deal with everything along with Chloe's support.

As we stood on the boat, it began rocking violently from side to side, the waves getting bigger by the minute. Ice-cold fear clutched at me as realisation dawned, and I knew I'd made a terrible mistake in trying to pin Liam down this way. He had become distracted and taken his eye off the ball when it came to the weather, and our safety on the boat.

"Liam!" I screamed above the growing sound of the storm. "It doesn't matter now. We can discuss this another time."

I clung onto the side of the boat and looked around for the safety equipment, but couldn't see the life jackets. Suddenly, as Liam swung around and looked at me, I saw his face was ashen.

"Liam, where are the life jackets?" I screamed urgently.

"Oh my God, Izzy," he said, in a voice I could barely hear above the noise of the wind and the waves. "I've left them on the side of the quay!"

"What! Why would you do that?" I could hear my own voice stumbling over the words while I gripped onto the side of the boat, which was now swaying manically from side to side. The rain was lashing down, and I was soaked to the skin and shivering with cold.

Liam stepped towards me and almost fell over as the boat lurched to one side. "Because you were hassling me to go out in the boat…" he said. Then he added more kindly, "Don't worry, Izzy, I'll radio for help, just in case. But we'll be back on dry land in no time."

Tears were pouring down my face, because I was blaming myself for the predicament we found ourselves in. However, Liam looked more like the person I knew, in charge of everything and in control of the situation. I told myself we would be perfectly fine.

I watched as he picked up the VHF radio attached to the boat and tried to use it, but I could see he was struggling, and I didn't know why. I couldn't believe how the storm had blown up within minutes of leaving the shore, and as I looked across at the rolling waves to where land had been, I saw that it had disappeared into a blanket of murky rain and mist.

We were now being buffeted about as if the boat weighed nothing. I was petrified and holding back a scream, imagining the boat turning over at any moment and depositing us both in the violent waves beyond – and all without any life jackets.

I attempted to speak to Liam again, but he was struggling to make himself heard and still shouting into the phone. If only we hadn't left the life jackets on the side of the quay. I was filled with fear and guilt that I'd put us both in this terrible situation, and as the boat swayed from side to side, I could see raw panic in Liam's eyes.

Abruptly, he put the radio down and pointed to the shore,

and with a sigh of relief I realised we were close to the beach. In the storm, we had been buffeted towards Black Ven cliffs, where I could see a thin strip of land was visible. The beach was just about still there, meaning the tide was not completely in yet and we would be safe. I gave Liam the thumbs up.

All of a sudden, and without warning, the boat tipped dramatically to one side, and I was thrown clean off my feet and landed across the deck.

And that was the last thing I remembered of that terrifying day.

Hours later, I woke up in hospital with Chloe sitting beside my bed. She told me gently that the boat and Liam were now lost. I would never forget the sound of my own screams as I clutched at my flat stomach, finding that my baby bump had gone, too. Liam and the baby were both dead, my heart was broken, and my life left in tatters.

The following days were very traumatic, and I'll never know how I got through them. The doctor prescribed something to help keep me calm and to sleep, which helped a little, and Chloe was there constantly. She even shut the shop for a few weeks to look after me.

My mother was my rock, but even she couldn't take away the pain of that fateful day. The memories and nightmares became unbearable, and I had to escape this town with all its reminders. After recovering from the accident, I told myself I had to leave and that I never wanted to return. And somehow, during all that time, I always managed to avoid coming back.

Now, having returned, the anguish was threatening to engulf me again. Somehow, I had to come to terms with Liam's death, but how to do that, with no memory of that last hour on the boat, was beyond me. I was tormented with not knowing what really happened, why he drowned and why I survived, which left me with the heavy weight of guilt on my chest.

In the weeks following my recovery, I asked Chloe and the rescue workers from the RNLI where I had been found, and how they had received the call to say the boat was in trouble. I told them I knew Liam's VFH radio wasn't working when he tried to contact the coastguard.

The lifeguards said it had been a member of the public who alerted them about the boat being in trouble on Black Ven cliffs, and not Liam. They told me I had been found clinging to the mudslides instigated by the storm... with a life jacket on. And the official Maritime Investigation Branch report confirmed that all but one of the life jackets had been left on the side of the quay that day.

I must have been knocked out when I fell after the boat lurched to one side, but according to my rescuers, I was fully conscious when they found me.

Liam's body was found washed up on Black Ven a few days after the tragedy. Somehow, I got through the funeral and the gruelling months that followed, but I was overwhelmed with grief.

Chloe had urged me to resume my plans to do a degree the following year. But for those first awful weeks, I hid myself away from the world and simply laid on my bed in a darkened bedroom, mourning the loss of Liam and our baby.

CHAPTER 32

MARY

For a long moment, Mary stared at the letter where it sat waiting for her attention on the counter of the shop. She was feeling conflicted.

The letter was from George. It crossed her mind she could destroy it and put him and his proposal behind her forever. In doing so, she could pretend George had never existed, but in her heart she knew it would take more than that to forget him.

She imagined herself walking back through to the workshop, placing it on the fire and watching it burn, without ever reading his words, feeling satisfaction that she had put him firmly out of her life forever. The thought of becoming someone else's property went against everything Mary believed in, and George had wounded her and made her feel worthless.

Freedom of choice was limited for women, but Mary had known from an early age how she preferred to spend her days. Searching for fossils was a hard daily grind, with some days more difficult than others, but the work excited her, and her studies made her feel valuable.

Recently she had been teaching herself French so that she could read the scientific papers written by the anatomist and naturalist, Georges Cuvier. There was always so much to learn, and Mary had a never-ending curiosity about the emerging science of the world she lived in.

Many times she had asked herself what the alternative to fossil hunting was for her. In a strange way, she was trapped between two worlds: that of the men of science, whom she equalled in knowledge and ability; and the other inhabited by women of her class.

It seemed to Mary that when she freed the dragons, equally the dragons freed her. She could have been a mill worker or in service, and both of these jobs would have suffocated her. While she hunted for the fossils, she was outside, on the shores of Lyme Regis, breathing in the fresh air. Not stuck inside and at the beck and call of cruel employers.

George had understood none of this when he had asked her to become his mistress. Despite their childhood friendship, it seemed he did not know her at all.

With a sigh, Mary made a decision. She undid the red seal on the sheet of paper, unfolded it carefully, cast her eye on the sheet of paper, and began to read.

Dearest Mary,

Please forgive me for my stupidity and I hope we can put this misunderstanding behind us and still be friends.

Mary marvelled at the way Elizabeth had, once again, been right about George wanting the two of them to remain friends. But Mary wasn't so sure. *Could they be friends again after his proposal?* She longed to see George again, but she knew it would be in her best interests if they went their separate ways.

This whole scenario with George reminded her of

another geologist who had come into her life several years before and made an impression on her.

Mary had first met the handsome Colonel Birch in 1818. A well-to-do fossil collector, a retired officer in the Life Guards, he was touring the West Country in search of fossils when Mary met him, and he soon became a frequent visitor to the Anning shop. Mary got on well with him, as they had a common interest in fossil hunting.

Birch was a kind man and had become the Annings' saviour in 1819. He arrived at their shop to find the family in dire straits and selling off furniture in order to pay the rent. Mary and her brother Joseph had not found a decent fossil for a whole year, and times were hard for the family.

The Parish support which the Annings were receiving had dried up some time before, and Colonel Birch had taken it upon himself to help them out. Mary would never forget that day he had looked straight at her and held her gaze.

"You have made huge contributions to the world of scientific investigation and fossil hunting, my dear," he said with the light of love in his eyes. "I shall make sure you and your family are suitably rewarded."

Colonel Birch left that day, but later they learnt he had sold off the entire collection of fossils he had previously bought from the Annings. They were sold at Bullocks in Piccadilly at an intense three-day sale, and buyers came from far and wide to purchase the fossils. The sale brought in more than £400 for the Annings, which was not enough to pay off all their debts but helped tremendously.

Mary blushed when she thought of the rumours of a romance between her and Colonel Birch after this. But even if the class divide had not stopped a relationship developing between them, Mary had only been 21 years old at the time, and Birch 52 – far too old for her.

She had been eternally grateful for his help that year, for

he had saved her family from starvation. But despite seeing how he looked at her, Mary had not for one moment allowed herself to imagine that the colonel was in love with her.

Shaking these memories from her head, Mary read the rest of George's letter. By the time she got to the end of it, she was worried for his safety.

I visited Lady Hadcliffe, which was interesting to say the least. The lady is frightened of her own brother, is that not an awful way to go on? Holmes is despicable, and one way or another, I am determined to expose him for plagiarism.

In Mary's opinion, this was foolhardy in the extreme. It seemed George was determined to get justice for John Hadcliffe's widow, and there was nothing she could say that would persuade him otherwise.

However, she was still angry with George, despite his apology, and she didn't want to be humiliated and gossiped about the way she had been with the Colonel Birch episode.

With this in mind, Mary wrote RETURN TO SENDER on George's letter, and gave it to the post cart when it arrived the next day. But the minute the letter had gone, she regretted her actions.

CHAPTER 33

ELIZA

*F*ear clutched at my chest, and I could hardly breathe as the water heaved towards the boat. That massive wave, which was higher than the vessel itself, was deeper and wider than anything I'd ever seen in the ocean.

Our little boat would soon disappear under the water, and I tried to warn Liam, but my voice was lost in the terrible roaring of the waves.

I woke up sweating, with my heart racing like a steam train, and realised it was yet another bad dream. As I turned over, dislodging the cat, he meowed loudly in protest, and I rubbed at the pain in my lower back. The cat ran off in disgust, and my phone, which was lying on the bedside table, told me it was only 4.30am.

The dream left me with echoes of dread and the familiar feeling of helplessness I had experienced many times in the last ten years. When the accident first happened, the dreams occurred every night. My mind, it seemed, was trying to make sense of everything, but once I moved away from Lyme, the nightmares began to fade away.

Now, Liam's words from long ago echoed in my head. 'If I'm trapped, I can't breathe, Eliza,' he'd told me. 'It feels as if I'm suffocating.' The thought that Liam had been afraid to tell me how he really felt about us, had haunted me ever since.

My head was thumping from the dream, and the image of Liam's lifeless body slipping beneath the dark waves left me with a black, morbid feeling.

I adjusted the pillows and sat up in bed in the dim light, attempting to calm my racing heart. There would be no more sleep for me tonight. Maybe a walk on the beach would help. Even though it was incredibly early, I got up and dressed quickly.

Recently I had found myself being drawn back to Black Venn cliffs time and again. The cliffs seemed to be calling me towards their dangerous slopes, compelling me to follow this path, to uncover the mystery of both George and Liam's last hours on this earth.

As the memories returned, these days they were intertwined with thoughts of George and Mary, and what had happened to them all those years ago. Sometimes, I found it hard to tell where one memory began and the other one ended.

I let myself out of the flat and, using my phone torch to find my way, headed towards the beach. The sun was just rising as I stepped on the pebbles, and I hesitated and watched the beautiful colours criss-cross the waves before strolling along the beach in the semi-darkness.

After a while, I knew I was nearing Black Ven cliffs, and I could sense George and Mary close by. They were in the air around me and the pebbles underfoot. *What happened to George, and why did he disappear in Lyme?* The words swirled around in my head, blocking out everything else.

The waves were higher here and were crashing to the

shore with a fierceness I hadn't seen before. Echoes of a warning in my head told me to turn back now; in the blink of an eye, the ocean could take everything, just as it did that fateful day ten years ago.

Suddenly, I had the feeling I needed to be back on solid ground again, away from this haunting stretch of beach, away from the feeling that Black Ven cliffs had me trapped like a spider in a web.

"Hey, Eliza! What're you doing out so early?"

I jumped as the sound of Rafe's voice jolted me out of my sombre musings, and I was relieved to see him striding towards me across the beach.

"Morning, Rafe, I could ask you the same question," I asked, surprised at how calm my voice sounded while my heart was racing at the weird thoughts I'd been having.

Rafe stopped in front of me, and I noticed how awful he looked. His face was pale, and his eyes were ringed with black circles. "What on earth's the matter?" I asked.

Rafe pushed the hair back from his face with a frown. "I couldn't sleep, so I thought I'd come out and get some fresh air," he said. "Let's walk a while and I'll fill you in on everything." He walked over to a big boulder and perched on it, and I followed suit, eager to know what was wrong.

He fixed his gaze on the sea then gave a heavy sigh. "Janine took Harry to Scotland without telling me what was going on." His face reddened as he spoke, and his voice sounded shaky as he met my eyes. "I'll be seeking legal advice now, Eliza, in order to maintain visitation rights for him. There's no other way to sort this out."

"Oh, Rafe. That's just awful for you. Do you think Harry wanted to go to Scotland with his mum?"

He shook his head in a resigned way. "Nope. I don't think he did. We had all sorts of things planned for the week, as its half-term." He turned to me and frowned. "I'm concerned about Harry being in the middle of all this, Eliza, but Janine has forced my hand. Now there's nothing else I can do but take her to court."

"Sure. I'm sorry to hear that. But I think it's the right course of action and the only option left open to you now. Don't forget, though, that going to Scotland will be an adventure for Harry, so try not to worry about him." I was hoping the youngster was indeed having a good time.

"Cheers for that, Eliza. I'm sure it'll be okay in the end," Rafe said bravely, looking quite dismal. "So, what's happening with you? Is everything alright? You're out super early, too."

I quickly explained about my dream and how, once I'd woken up, I dared not go back to sleep again. Just then my phone pinged a text message, and it was Pat reminding me that she was coming into work earlier today. "Oh, Lord. I need to get back to the teashop," I told Rafe regretfully.

"Good grief. I didn't realise the time either." He glanced back the way we'd just come. "I've got a fossil walk to do this morning," he admitted, looking concerned, and then added, "I wish Harry were here with me. He always loves doing the fossil walks."

"I wish Harry were here, too," I told him sadly. "Please, let me know how the solicitor's visit goes, won't you, Rafe? What were you going to tell me about George? You said there was something else you'd found out."

Rafe jerked his head to one side and gave his thigh a slap. "Oh yeah, sorry, Eliza! I knew there was something I meant to tell you. I'd forgotten about that because of what's going on with Harry. Well, it's only a snippet of information, really."

"Go on then, a snippet of information is better than nothing."

"True enough. I came across an old newspaper cutting

about George. It was printed just after he went missing, and apparently, Mary believed that he died on Black Ven cliffs."

My heart dropped like a stone to my stomach. "What?" I croaked. "Oh, gosh. I don't know why I'm surprised, though. He would have been around that area visiting Mary, wouldn't he? But if I'm honest here, I'm a bit shocked."

I was shaking inside, and for a moment I couldn't think of anything else except that, just as I'd suspected, Liam and George had both died at the same place in Lyme Regis.

Rafe leaned forwards and gave me a tender hug, before drawing away and looking me in the eye. "It's not rocket science that you're feeling bad, Eliza. It's because of Liam, isn't it?" he said, giving me an understanding nod. "I knew the news would affect you this way, that's why I didn't tell you before."

He moved away slightly. "Listen, I'm sorry to leave you like this, but I must go now. But as soon I can, I promise, I'll do more digging on George and what happened to him." He quirked an eyebrow at me. "If I'm honest, I don't think I'll find out any more on him now, though. I reckon that the awful Holmes either killed George, or he somehow slipped on the mud on those cliffs."

"Yeah, that sounds possible," I admitted. "I mean, the weather was still so bad in Lyme at the time, and if his body was washed out to sea and never found, no-one would know what had happened to him. Would they?"

"Sure wouldn't," Rafe said, giving me an intense look. Then suddenly the atmosphere changed between us. "I don't have a clue what I'd do without you, Eliza, do you know that?" he said softly, and it felt like he was looking deep into my very soul. "Thanks so much for listening to me going on about Harry."

Instinctively, and without thinking, I reached up and kissed Rafe full on the lips. What was meant to be a quick peck turned out to be a long, lingering kiss. This, along with that musky scent of his, made my heart race and my insides turn to mush. We slowly drew apart, and for one long moment we gazed longingly at one another.

"Sorry, I didn't mean to do that," I said, pulling my eyes away and feeling breathless under his gaze. I didn't want to give Rafe false hope, and I knew I shouldn't have done that.

Rafe was still looking at me intently. "Please, don't ever be sorry, Eliza, it's fine. You know how I feel about you. And I hope one day you'll feel the same way about me."

I gave him a weak smile. There were no words to explain how conflicted I was feeling right now. I was afraid to tell him how I really felt, because if I were being truthful, I knew with a deep certainty, that despite my resistance to the contrary, I was falling deeply and madly in love with Rafe Hansom.

CHAPTER 34

GEORGE

*G*eorge held tightly onto his bag full of papers, which were tantamount to what Holmes had been up to and would expose his plagiarism to the fellows here at the Geological Society. He tried hard to focus on the meeting going on in front of him, where they were about to discuss Mary's creature.

The Plesiosaurus was laid out on the table for everyone to see, and the men had all gone very quiet, stunned it seemed by the sheer size of the enormous creature.

"Please, gentlemen, take your seats while the creature is examined properly," the geologist called William Conybeare suggested to the audience.

George shuffled in his seat nervously. The question of when and how he should reveal the evidence of Holmes's plagiarism to the society was at the forefront of his mind. He was exhausted, having tossed and turned all night long thinking about this problem.

He pulled his thoughts back to the present moment. It was now or never; this was George's chance to expose Holmes. There would never be another chance like this one.

He glanced around to see his nemesis standing towards the back of the room with a face like thunder, staring in his direction.

As all the men took their seats, George's heart was racing. Gathering his courage, he made his way to the front of the room where Conybeare and another geologist were intensely studying the creature. Before they could tell him to sit down, George positioned himself in front of the two men to address the audience.

"I have something to say which might be of interest to you all," he said above the noise of the chattering. A murmur of disapproval immediately went up as he opened his bag and took out the contents, but George quickly held up the paperwork for all to see.

"I'm sorry to interrupt the meeting, but this is a very serious matter which needs to be addressed. It won't take a moment to explain," he continued firmly.

"What the hell are you doing, Hansome?" William Conybeare demanded with a confused look in his direction.

George ignored Conybeare and lifted his chin. "Ernest Holmes has been plagiarising John Hadcliffe's work, and I have the evidence to prove it!" he announced, pointing at Holmes. A stunned silence filled the room and they all turned to look at Ernest Holmes.

Holmes did not move at first but then he found his voice. "George Hansome, you are a lying scoundrel!" he announced, his face turning bright red.

"How do you know this to be true?" one of the men stood up and asked George.

George took a deep breath and reminded himself that he had evidence right here in his hand. "I have proof that this man is robbing his sister blind," he answered the man, keeping his voice level as all eyes and ears were upon him.

Conybeare stared hard at George. "What exactly is going

on here?" he demanded glancing from George to Holmes and back at George again. "As I understand it, Ernest Holmes worked under John Hadcliffe, therefore those papers belonged to both men."

George turned to the eminent geologist and explained. "They did work together, that is true, but those notes were John Hadcliffe's *unpublished papers.* They have his name at the top, and I can show you that this is true."

Everyone in the room was listening now, and George took the opportunity to explain further. "Holmes removed them from the Royal College, under the guise of cataloguing them. Instead, he has been copying them out, burning the originals, *and* then publishing them as his own."

Most of the men in the room had known John Hadcliffe, and had voiced recently how sorry they were for his widow, particularly as she had been left with considerable debts after his death.

George could see by the looks on their faces that the geologists didn't like the thought of Holmes swindling his own sister out of money. He had hoped this would be their reaction to his announcement, and was glad that, for now at least, they seemed to be on his side.

After a moment of stunned silence, another man in the audience stood up and shouted out that this was despicable behaviour, and others soon began to follow suit. George raised his voice once again, over the noise in the room.

"If this is allowed to happen, then John's widow will not be paid for these important papers," he explained, just in case anyone had not understood the implications of Holmes's disgusting conduct.

Conybeare waved his arms around and asked the audience for quiet as he addressed the room. "The evidence Mr Hansome has here needs to be examined before we judge what has gone on," he said, looking pointedly across at Holmes.

"In the meantime, Ernest Holmes, I am suspending you from the society until this matter has been investigated and a conclusion has been reached," he declared, before collecting the paperwork from George.

All eyes turned on Holmes, who seemed to have lost his voice. He stared around the room in horror, pushed roughly through the throng of people surrounding him, and hurried quickly out of the door.

CHAPTER 35

ELIZA

*T*he teashop was busy today, but I was finding it hard to concentrate. I was distracted and thinking constantly about Rafe uncovering that George had disappeared on Black Ven cliffs.

Was George killed by Ernest Holmes, who hated him because he was on Mary's side, and because George knew all about his crimes? Or could George have accidentally fallen off those cliffs into the sea and quickly drowned?

Lyme would have still been feeling the effects of the storm when George was there, and the sea would have been wild and relentless. So, if he had ended up in the ocean, he wouldn't have had much chance of surviving.

Even though we now thought we knew what had happened to George, there were doubts in my mind about what had really gone on. We had no evidence to support our theories. Rafe had not uncovered an alternative fate for George, but I had a nagging feeling that there was something more to all this.

With these worrying thoughts came the further distraction that Jessica had now been late for work two days in a row. As a result, we had been terribly short staffed in the teashop, putting too much pressure on me and Pat.

I had tried to phone Jessica this morning, but hadn't been able to get an answer from her phone, and Pat didn't know why she hadn't come into work or where she was. The girl had often been a little lazy at work, but I could usually cajole her out of it.

The hours whizzed by and at last Jessica waltzed in the door after the rush was over. It was time for a showdown with the teenager. I asked Pat to hold the fort and pulled the young girl to one side.

"Jessica, I've noticed you keep being late into work. What's going on? If this keeps happening, I'll have to let you go," I warned her, trying to sound stern.

She looked at me from under her fringe and frowned. "Soz, Liza," she mumbled. "Just couldn't get out of bed today."

"Are you unwell?" I probed, and she shook her head in response. "That's not good enough, Jessica. Don't you like working here any more?"

Jessica shrugged her skinny shoulders at me. "I don't mind working in the teashop, but no offence, Liza, it isn't what I want to do as my forever job." She pressed her lips together mutinously and widened her blue eyes at me.

I thought about this for a moment. Jessica was still a teenager, and I'd never really asked her before if she was happy working here at the teashop.

"Okay. Tell me what you're passionate about then? What can you see yourself doing for the rest of your life, Jessica?"

The rest of Jessica's life was a long time, but it was the only way I could think of approaching this problem. When you're young, choosing a career can be hard for some people, but I wondered if Jessica knew what path she'd really like to follow.

"Looking after kids is what I'd like to do," she said, her

face immediately lighting up. "It's probably too late to do that now, though," she said, dropping her gaze and studying her fingernails forlornly.

"What do you mean, too late, Jessica? You're not even nineteen yet, of course it's not too late."

Chloe had told me that before starting work at the teashop, Jessica had abandoned her studies to be with her boyfriend. And she had only taken the teashop job under pressure from her mother to earn some money. But I'd heard recently that Jessica had broken up with the said boyfriend.

"Couldn't you go back and do the training you've missed, and then find work in a nursery or a primary school?" I suggested, giving Jessica a hard stare. To me, it seemed so simple.

"Don't know," Jessica mumbled, as if this wasn't an option she'd considered. "As I said before, I think it's too late now and I missed my chance."

It was frustrating that I wasn't getting through to the teenager, but as the teashop was filling up with customers again, I decided to call a halt on the discussion for now.

"Well, all the time you are working here, Jessica, no more lateness please. Otherwise there will be consequences. I can't have my staff just not turning up for work and leaving the rest of us to cope on our own."

Jessica promised not to be late in any more, and we got back to work. But I couldn't help thinking that I could give Jessica advice, but I couldn't make her do anything she didn't want to do.

And the irony was not lost on me that I was preaching to Jessica that she should do what she was passionate about in life, yet I still hadn't found a way – or the courage – to follow my own advice and leave the UK in search of my dream.

CHAPTER 36

MARY

*T*he sound of her heartbeat had thrashed in Mary's ears all through the night. She tried to quell the mounting panic as night turned into morning and the violent storm raging through Lyme Regis showed no sign of abating.

As she rubbed wearily at her tired eyes, having not slept a wink, she raised herself from the bed with a feeling of heavy dread weighing her down. The storm, which had started the evening before, had echoed another time, when Mary was a small child and the family had been in grave danger from the elements.

Mary had a vague recollection of events of that terrifying day when they lived in a tiny house on Bridge Street. She had been barely four years old when the sea hurled debris against the front wall of the house. Water had rushed in, and as it pulled back, the staircase was destroyed. Thankfully, the Anning family had been rescued, but the ground floor of their home had been washed away in the havoc the sea had wreaked that day.

Suddenly the bedroom door flew open, breaking into Mary's troubled memories. Ma was standing in the doorway, holding a flickering candle while cupping her shaking hand around its tiny flame.

"Mary! We 'ave to get out of this house!" she said urgently, her panic-stricken words almost drowned out by the noise of the howling wind.

Concerned they might be too late to escape before the house was swept into the angry sea, Mary shot out of bed. Thankfully, she didn't have to get dressed. They had both gone to bed fully clothed last night in preparation for a swift escape.

"I'm coming," Mary shouted back at her mother. Then she followed her slowly downstairs, desperately trying to see her way in the dim light from the single candle her mother was holding.

The storm had started the previous evening with a gale force wind. Sleep had been impossible, and even now the noise was so loud that Mary could barely hear herself think. But more worryingly, there was another sound echoing in the distance, which was growing louder by the second. This noise was a deep roaring sound coming from the direction of the sea.

The two women emerged into the small downstairs room, where the windows were rattling loudly, and the sound of angry waves crashing onto the shore echoed through the house. Mary knew the water was close by, and she was almost frozen with fear now. Why hadn't they tried to escape earlier?

She turned to look at her mother, who was gasping for breath and looked as if she might faint at any moment. Mary knew she must take charge if they were to survive this frightening situation.

Before Mary could take action, though, an even louder noise tore through the air, it drowned out the howling wind and the terrible roaring of the sea. It was the unmistakable sound of crashing masonry and glass splintering.

Mary's mother was shaking with fear as she clung onto her daughter. Then a loud rumble – a different sound she couldn't identify – began. It sounded like something huge falling from a great height, but it went on for several seconds, then suddenly they were both flung to the ground and the house was shaken to its very foundations.

Both women lay on the floor with their arms up over their heads, waiting for the roof to fall in, amid the terrible sound of anguished crying from the houses nearby.

As the noises receded, Mary tentatively stood up. Her legs were weak, and she was shaken to her very bones. She helped her mam to her feet and looked around to see that the house was still standing, but she feared others were not so lucky.

"Mam! Get your coat and boots on now," Mary ordered, grabbing hold of their outdoor clothing. Once they were ready, Mary flung open the door, which was nearly taken off its hinges with the strength of the gale force wind.

The breath was ripped from Mary's body where she stood in the doorway, and breathlessly she turned back towards her mother, taking in her pinched white face.

"Stay here for a moment," she told her, between ragged breaths. "I'll find out what damage has been done to next door," she explained. Mary tried to stay calm so Mam wouldn't see the rising panic threatening to choke her.

Mam nodded slowly at Mary, her eyes wide with fear, before slumping down onto a nearby chair. "I'll come back for you in a moment," Mary reassured her.

Briefly, Mary paused in the doorway. The wind was pulling her towards the wild sea, but she was determined to fight it. Planting her feet, she took in the truly horrifying scene around her.

Visibility was bad, with the wind gusting and the mist

swirling above Mary's head and all around her. Already her eyes were stinging from the salt water, and in the distance she could see the waves rising high into the air, covering every inch of the shore.

The Cobb was barely visible as the waves crashed around and over the top of it. Only the very tip of its dark rock could be seen. Mary's eye was caught by the image of a ship being buffeted violently from side to side in the distance.

Through the mist she could see it was the London trader ship, *The Unity.* The vessel was being driven violently to the shore from The Cobb, and was almost completely on her side in the middle of the roaring sea. Mary's heart went out to the crew on board.

The sound of the water gushing with such intensity towards the house forced Mary to address what needed to be done next. She tore her eyes from the heart-breaking scene of the ship sinking, and fought the urge to run back inside the house.

As Mary glanced down at her feet, it was a terrifying sight. The path outside the door was barely there, with only a few inches between the hungry waves and the house.

Loud shouts filled the air and seemed to be coming from next-door, where that awful noise had been heard a few minutes before. Mary looked towards their neighbour, and couldn't see anything from the doorway. Having no choice but to leave the security of their little house, she forced herself to step onto what was left of the pathway.

Clinging onto the wall for support, Mary began taking tentative steps towards the house next door. The wind whipped off her hat and pulled violently at her clothes, but she fought with everything she had to stay upright.

Mary's hand flew to her mouth as she stopped and stared at the pile of rubble where the Smiths' house had been, and the bile rose in her throat. It would be a true miracle if anyone had managed to survive such total devastation.

"Miss Anning, Miss Anning, over here!"

Mary looked up through the wind and the relentless rain to see the figure of Mr Smith standing to the side of the rubble. She could hardly believe it. But as she squinted against the force of the elements, she gradually made out the whole family standing side by side. They looked dishevelled and dirty, but they were all alive. Mother, father, and two sons had somehow survived the complete collapse of their home.

Relief coursed through Mary as she watched them all fighting to stay on their feet. "Thank the Lord you got out!" she shouted as loudly as she could, just as the awful sound of more glass breaking echoed through the air.

To Mary's horror, this time it came from her own house, where Mam was still inside waiting patiently for her return.

For a moment she couldn't move. Mary desperately wanted to go back to Mam, but was fearful of being swept out to sea. Then she saw Mr Smith making his way towards her.

"Miss Anning, we must all get to higher ground, right now!" he shouted. "Your house will be demolished next!" He gripped Mary's arm in an attempt to shake her back into action.

Mary pushed her legs back in the direction of the house. "You're right, Mr Smith, I'll fetch Mam and follow you all up the hill," she told him, not really knowing how she was going to achieve this in these appalling conditions.

"We will wait for you, but please hurry," he said urgently, as his family appeared beside Mary, clinging to each other, and whatever else they could find, to help keep themselves upright.

As Mary entered the house, Mam was standing a few feet

from the door, still staring at the broken glass of the window while the wind howled through the gap left by the shattered glass. She caught hold of her mother, pulled her outside, and tried to reassure her.

"The Smith family have survived, Mam," she told her. "They are waiting outside for us, and we must go now!"

Mary would never know how they managed to stay on their feet as they battled up the hill that fateful day. But somehow, they managed it, along with the Smith family, and all arrived safely at the assembly rooms.

Once there, Mary and her mother found many other people huddled into the building, all squashed up against each other, but safe for now. Some people were sobbing piteously, while others stared sightlessly out of the window towards the pile of rubble where their homes had once stood. A few were on their hands and knees praying, asking God to save them from the wild sea, afraid it would soon devour the whole of Lyme Regis.

The sound of the hurricane raged on around them for many hours, but more terrifying was the noise of falling bricks and mortar, as properties and anything within range were torn apart and demolished. Relief coursed through Mary that at least they had escaped the sea, although what they would find when they returned to the house, was something else entirely.

There was nothing to do but wait, so she made Mam as comfortable as possible, then found a tiny patch of floor and rested her weary body.

In those idle moments, Mary thought about George and his letter. She was still angry with him and his misjudgement of the situation. But she bitterly regretted writing RETURN TO SENDER on the letter and returning it to the post cart.

CHAPTER 37

ELIZA

$\mathcal{T}$he Royal Standard was quiet this evening, and I glanced at my phone to see that Rafe was already ten minutes late. He had rung me the night before to ask if we could meet up, and he had sounded more than a little fraught.

"There's so much I have to tell you, Eliza, but I'll explain it all when I see you," he had said urgently. Then he had rung off before saying any more.

As I waited for him to arrive, I hoped that Janine wasn't making more trouble for Rafe with Harry, and I thought about everything I had to tell him, too. Yesterday I'd helped with Julia and her friends with the beach clean on Lyme, and I'd been amazed at the rubbish we'd found, and how much could be recycled once it was all picked up.

It made me realise that education was still essential for people to understand how we all needed to help the planet. This morning, I'd left a message on the answerphone at the Women's Institute, and was waiting for them to get back to me. I was keen to give them a talk on how to help the marine life in Lyme Regis – a prospect which was exciting and terrifying at the same time.

Something else was happening to me since the beach clean. The small beginnings of hope had begun to spring up inside my chest. The hope that I could make a difference when it came to what was happening right here in my home town.

This feeling, along with the faith that Rafe had in me about helping with climate change, was propelling me forwards. I was lost in these thoughts when he came rushing into the pub.

Rafe stopped breathlessly in front of me, looking a bit red-faced and so gorgeous that my heart missed a beat at the sight of him.

"Hiya, I'm sorry to be late, Eliza…" he began. "Harry wanted a chat on FaceTime just as I was leaving the house, so I couldn't leave. You know how it is, don't you?"

His eyes sparkled as he spoke, as if he was happy from the inside out, and it was good to see him looking less burdened than he had been of late.

"No worries, Rafe. I understand Harry must come first," I told him truthfully. "Go and get yourself a drink – you look like you need one – and then you can tell me your news," I urged, before taking a sip of my G&T.

Rafe shot me a thankful look and walked quickly off towards the bar. The pub was beginning to fill up now, and I watched Rafe as he waited to be served. He cut a really attractive figure, with his long legs encased in skinny jeans, and that silky, dark hair looking a bit tousled. I forced myself to look away, not wanting to give in to the growing attraction I was feeling for him. Right now, it was all too complicated to think about.

"Take a breath, Rafe," I advised, once he sat down in front of me with his pint in his hand. "How are things?" I was wondering about the solicitor's visit and whether he'd seen Harry yet after his impromptu Scottish trip with Janine.

Rafe took a gulp of his pint and then lifted and dropped his shoulders in a bid to relax a little. "Aye well. Things have been better, Eliza," he said, with a frown etched between his dark brows. "A lot has happened, and I've got loads to tell you."

Feeling slightly alarmed, I leaned towards him. "What on earth has happened now? Is Harry okay?"

Slowly, he picked up a coaster, turned it over in his hand, and then looked at me with wide eyes. "Thankfully, everything *is* alright now, Eliza. But you wouldn't believe what I've been through. The bottom line is Harry went missing from school."

My heart was suddenly racing at the thought of little Harry out in the big wide world all alone. "Oh my God, that's awful, what happened?" I asked.

Rafe moved forwards in his chair. "Sorry, I didn't mean to scare you. I found Harry within hours, but those were the worst, and the longest, hours of my life." He ran his hand through his hair nervously. "Incredibly, Harry was on his way to see me in Lyme Regis, and was already at the train station when I located him."

"Oh, thank God for that!" I heaved a huge sigh of relief. "Was he going to travel to Lyme all on his own then, I mean… all the way from Exmouth?"

Rafe nodded, and went on to explain how Harry had previously written down in his favourite notebook how to get to Lyme, after they had made the journey by train once when the car had broken down. And despite not having a train ticket, the youngster had managed to dodge underneath the barriers and find his way onto the platform.

"When I think about it… I mean, anything could have happened to him," Rafe said, rubbing at a spot between his eyes as if he couldn't bear to think of the consequences of Harry absconding.

"Well, it sounds like it was lucky you got to him before he boarded that train."

"Yeah, I know, my thoughts exactly. Of course, I immediately drove him home to Janine. She then took Harry upstairs for a bath, while I phoned the Police to let them know we'd found him. But honestly, Eliza, God knows where he could have ended up."

He stopped and took another sip of his pint, then his face cleared, and the frown lifted. "But, hey. You'll be pleased to hear there's good news, too," Rafe explained. "When Harry came downstairs from his bath, he told me he'd be coming to live with me very soon!"

"Wow. Really? Well, that is fabulous news!" I was surprised and excited all at the same time. But one thing puzzled me. "How the hell did Janine ever agree to that?"

"Well, that's the thing. After Harry told me he would be living with me, I didn't believe him at first, as you can imagine. But Janine promised to ring me later when Harry was in bed and explain everything."

"And... did she?" I could hardly believe that Janine would allow Harry to move, given her bad behaviour towards Rafe for so long.

"Yeah, she did. Janine explained that while they were in Scotland, she'd met up with an old school friend. This *friend* was someone she went out with a long time ago. And meeting up with him again made her consider moving back to Scotland. The upshot of it is, that's exactly what she'll be doing."

This was becoming more interesting by the minute, and I had a good idea what had happened. "Okay. I'm guessing that Janine wanted to take Harry with her to live in Scotland and that's why he ran away?"

"You got it in one. Janine told Harry after they got home from the Scottish trip that he would be moving up to Edinburgh with her. She also told him he wouldn't be seeing me much in the future, and as you can imagine, the poor boy wasn't very happy about that."

Rafe rested his elbows on the table and frowned. "Oh, and apparently there was also some bullying going on at school recently, which of course hasn't helped matters."

I thought about this for a moment. "Janine doesn't usually do what Harry wants, though, does she?"

"Nope, not at all. But she was really shaken up when he ran away, and for once she thought about what Harry wanted, instead of herself. Janine asked him outright if he'd like to live with me or with her in Edinburgh, without trying to influence him one way or another."

Rafe was smiling widely now and looking very pleased with himself. "It's awesome, isn't it? Harry's coming to live with me, Eliza," he repeated. "Isn't that great news?"

"Oh, Rafe, that's brilliant and so unexpected, after all the trouble Janine's caused you." I sat back in my chair and soaked up the happiness on Rafe's face. "I can hardly believe it, but you do so deserve this."

"Cheers, it was a bit of a shock at first. But Harry running away must have jolted Janine so hard that she thought she'd lost him forever," Rafe explained. "It must have made her realise that if she didn't consider him in all this, there would be more trouble with Harry in the future."

He leaned back in his chair and regarded me. "Janine likes a quiet life and, of course, now she's met this other man, things are looking up for her in other ways. Which is ace, and takes the pressure off me."

I was genuinely pleased that things were working out for Harry and Rafe, while at the same time pushing away the thought that I'd love to be a part of their happy little family, if only I could get over Liam and what happened on the boat that fateful day.

"Of course, I haven't thought about practicalities yet," Rafe continued, breaking into my thoughts. "I've dreamt about this day coming for so long that now it's here, I feel bit overwhelmed, to be honest. One thing I do know is I'll need childcare for Harry while I'm at work, which will be hard to afford on a palaeontologist's wages, but I'll manage something. So, how are things with you?"

I filled him in on the beach clean and how I'd approached the WI about a talk with them. "I'll be doing beach cleans in conjunction with the Marine Conservation Society," I explained enthusiastically. "And I'll let people know in my talk how they can help the sea kelp, which is endangered, and about the plastic problem in Lyme, which will in turn help the wildlife here to survive."

"Wow, you're really on it, Eliza. That's awesome news. I'm sure it'll give you a focus instead of thinking about what happened with Liam quite so much."

My face must have betrayed my feelings because he quickly added, "Not that that's a bad thing, but I just think you need to move on with your life," he said, leaning in closer. "Of course, it'll take time," he added in a gentler tone.

"I know what you're saying, and you're right," I conceded. "I do need to move on, and doing this stuff for the planet is making me feel better. So, thanks for suggesting it. By the way, have we finished researching George? I mean, I know we seem to have concluded that he was killed in the area of Black Ven cliffs by Holmes, or someone hired by Holmes, but…"

My voice trailed off as I tried to ignore the nagging feeling that there was more to this than we both thought, and it would be interesting to hear Rafe's view.

"Not sure. I haven't really had time to think about it, to be honest." Rafe looked thoughtful. "But that does seem to fit the puzzle, doesn't it? I mean, Holmes hated him... Or from what we know, it could have been an accident on the notorious Black Ven cliffs. George could have got a bit too close to the edge of the cliffs when the tide was in and lost his footing."

"You don't think that there's more here than meets the eye?" I probed.

"If I'm honest, I think we're looking for further mystery when there isn't one, Eliza. Don't you? Think about it, there aren't many options. George was in Lyme after the Great Storm, presumably to do research. It was more than likely he went to check up on Mary and used the research as an excuse to come here to see her."

"Then there was the newspaper report about where he perished, although we don't know why Mary thought this, or how they came to that conclusion. The bottom line is, we can assume we've solved the mystery disappearance of my four times great-grandfather now."

I nodded, but I wasn't so sure we *had* solved George's disappearance. It seemed a bit odd that Holmes could have committed the crime and got away with it. But when I voiced my concern, Rafe had a ready answer.

"Don't forget, Eliza, this was a time before the police force came into being. Holmes was a very influential man, and also a friend of The Prince Regent. He couldn't be accused of murder without evidence anyway."

Rafe's explanation sounded quite feasible, so maybe I was the one who was reading more into this.

"Holmes sounded like a nasty piece of work, and I suppose people would have been frightened of him because of his violent temper," I conceded, attempting to push away those lingering doubts.

CHAPTER 38

GEORGE

George's head was aching from the strain of keeping still in the stifling art studio in the middle of Exeter. As the artist continued to dab paint on the canvas, in an attempt to capture his likeness, George's gaze was drawn to a gap in the green velvet curtains where sunshine streamed in, making him long to be outside.

The stiff collar of his shirt dug into his neck, and he tried not to wrinkle his nose at the strong smell of turpentine. He wished he had never agreed to this portrait session. Especially today, when he longed to be somewhere else entirely.

When Eleanor had informed him that the prestigious Thomas Bartlett was the artist she had chosen, she had spoken as if this were a status symbol. "Bartlett's reputation as a portrait painter is one of the best," she had said smugly.

However, George was feeling restless and was suffocating under the artist's watchful gaze. Desperate now to escape and go to Mary, he pulled his pocket watch out and looked at the time. Whether the portrait was finished or not, he would be leaving soon to catch the stagecoach to Lyme Regis.

Taking a deep breath, or as much as his tight collar would

allow, he moved his gaze towards the artist, who predictably rolled his eyes in frustration. Yesterday's newspaper reports that a hurricane had hit Lyme Regis was at the forefront of George's mind.

A slow trickle of sweat dripped down the middle of his chest at the thought of Mary being in amongst this devastation. As soon as he'd learnt about the storm, and on arrival at work, he had headed straight for Oliver Tyrell's office. George was blatantly aware that he needed his employer's permission for an immediate to return to Lyme Regis.

While waiting outside Tyrell's office, he had considered what he would do if he was refused permission, and decided he would go anyway. He was determined to make sure Mary was alright, and he would do all he could to help her.

Even if they were never going to be more than friends, he wanted to be there for Mary at this difficult time. If anything happened to her, he would be devastated. But he reassured himself that she had always been a woman with a huge amount of courage and fortitude, so he could only hope that would ensure she had survived this ordeal.

Thankfully, Oliver Tyrell had agreed to George's request, although he had taken some persuading at first. "What on earth do you want to go back to Lyme Regis so soon for?" he snapped. "You've only recently come back," he added, his expression stern.

George had taken a deep breath and straightened his shoulders. "You're right, sir, I have. And while I was there, I noticed many different rock formations, the Blue Lias rocks are of particular interest and are second to none. If I investigated these further, it would benefit the work done here, I am completely sure of it."

This was a sure-fire way of getting his boss's attention, because not only was Tyrell open to new ideas, but he was always eager to make more money for the company.

"Why Lyme Regis, and why now?" Tyrell had asked suspiciously, narrowing his eyes.

George had known he needed to be convincing to achieve the outcome he wanted. "Have you heard about the hurricane which hit that area a few days ago?" he asked his employer.

When Oliver said he had, George explained how much they could learn from the changes that had taken place after the storm, if he was allowed to go back for a short time.

"The Great Storm would have dislodged many new fossils, which are just waiting to be found," he went on. "There is much to be learnt from the effects of the hurricane, not only in the finding of fossils but in the uncovering of the rock formations."

George knew if there were any new discoveries in Lyme Regis, Mary would find them, but it would be better not to draw his boss's attention to that.

"Anything I discover would, of course, belong to you," he told Tyrell persuasively, and he watched his boss's eyes light up with interest.

Oliver agreed to release George for a few days to complete his studies. Then, all George had to do was to tell Eleanor of his plans without arousing her suspicions about the real reason he was returning to Lyme Regis. Unfortunately, that did not go as well as George had hoped.

The artist's voice interrupted his sombre thoughts. "Just a few more minutes, Mr Hansome, and then we will be finished for the day," Bartlett told him with a lift of his eyebrows.

George wished he were already back in Lyme Regis making sure Mary was safe, rather than being bored stiff here with this annoying artist who was taking forever to finish the portrait session.

However, after another hour of adding more brush

strokes, Bartlett finally put down his paintbrushes. George sighed with relief when at last he was told the session was at an end. Desperate to escape the confines of the studio, he quickly stood up and stretched his aching limbs.

Bartlett covered up the painting, rubbed at a paintbrush with an old cloth, and regarded George. "The painting will be sent to you when I've added the final touches," he said.

George nodded, and a few minutes later he was back on the bustling streets of Exeter, where he blinked into the sunshine and undid the necktie which had been suffocating him. It was time to catch the stagecoach to Lyme Regis and to see Mary.

CHAPTER 39

ELIZA

It was early evening, and I was just opening a bottle of beer for Rafe, with the dinner bubbling away in the background, when he arrived. We had arranged that he come to my flat tonight, even though we didn't have George to discuss any more, which made me feel as if I wasn't sure where our relationship was going now.

Rafe rushed in, looking a bit flustered. "Hiya, Eliza. I'm sorry, I can't stay late as I have Harry tomorrow, and I need to leave early in the morning to pick him up," he said, raising his eyebrows at me. "I still can't quite believe it and keep expecting Janine to change her mind," he added ruefully.

I returned his greeting with a smile. "I'm sure she won't change her mind, so try not to worry," I reassured, hoping I was right. It would break Rafe's heart to lose custody of Harry now.

Rafe paused for a moment and exhaled slowly. "Oh, Eliza. God. It's such a relief," he said, then he leaned towards me and clasped my hands in his. "I'm so happy, and a lot of this is down to you, my love."

A flush crept over my face as I met those beautiful eyes of

his and that look of adoration directed straight at me. "What do you mean? I haven't done anything," I mumbled, then I straightened my back and gazed right back at him. "You need to think more positively, and remember that the decision has been made for you regarding Harry, so there shouldn't be any problems."

"Cheers, I'll try and remember that. You've been an absolute rock, really you have," Rafe persisted, letting go of my hands and pulling his fingers through those dark, silky locks of his. "I hope Harry is not too torn about living with me. I know how much he loves his mum."

"Well, I happen to know that he also loves his dad 'to the stars and back'," I told him, recalling one of Harry's favourite sayings when it came to his dad.

Rafe grinned. "Ah well, I love him, too, and I've promised Janine that she can see him as often as she wants." He looked thoroughly content with the situation.

"Cool. I'm pleased for you both. And don't forget that you deserve this break."

As I spoke, an idea was forming in my mind. "How about giving my young waitress the job of looking after Harry? That's if Jessica agrees, and I have a feeling she would."

Rafe shook his head and frowned slightly. "Young Jessica? But doesn't she work for you? I couldn't poach your staff from you, Eliza. You're trying to be too kind. I'm sure she would prefer to be working for you in that lovely Vintage teashop of yours."

I stretched out my shoulders and paused in my laying of the table. "I can see you would think that, but I'm not being kind, Rafe. Jessica told me recently that she'd love to work with youngsters again, so I reckon she'd jump at the chance of looking after Harry."

I could see Rafe was seriously considering this. "Hmm,

but would she be qualified to look after Harry? That's the million-dollar question here."

"She would be, once she's attended college. Jessica could do that while Harry was at school. Would that work for you? From what she told me, Jessica wants to finish the childcare qualification she gave up when she met her boyfriend. And as they've since broken up, this is the ideal time for her."

"That sounds a great idea. I didn't realise she wasn't happy working in the teashop, but it means you would lose your waitress, doesn't it?"

Rafe was obviously worried about my situation, but I wasn't. "No problem. I do have someone else in mind to do Jessica's job, if she decides to leave, that is," I reassured him.

Over dinner, we chatted about George and Mary. "I've been thinking about Mary and how George could easily have been like the other geologists. You know, taken what he wanted without a care or a thought for her achievements, but instead he tried to help her," I offered.

"Yep, George was a good egg, standing up for Mary the way he did," Rafe answered ruefully. "It seemed he wanted justice for her discoveries, and not only that but he loved her, too."

Sitting at the table discussing Mary and George made me realise that whenever we chatted about the pair, we were completely at ease with each other. It almost seemed as if, in their own way, they were bringing us together.

A while later, as Rafe stood in the small kitchen helping me with the washing up, and we negotiated the tiny space, I couldn't fail to notice how the atmosphere between us had changed. We accidentally bumped into each other and both burst out laughing, but when the laughter died down, I gazed up at Rafe and found him staring straight into my eyes.

Awkwardly, I couldn't stop looking at that intense gaze. It

was sending shivers up my spine, making me aware of the thrashing of my heartbeat beating furiously in my ears.

"Rafe…" I began, trying to find the words to stop what was about to happen.

However, my words trailed off as he moved towards me, and before I knew what was happening, I found myself in his arms. And as Rafe's lips came down on mine, I was totally lost.

Rafe deepened the kiss, intensifying the pleasure coursing through my body. And that familiar scent of his, sea-salt mixed with a hint of musk, hit my senses.

"I love you, Eliza," Rafe whispered warmly, brushing his lips against my ear. "I want you," he said huskily.

As I lost myself in him, the world fell away, and I was only aware of his soft breath against my ear and that he was slowly steering me towards the bedroom. As he continued to whisper gentle words of love, I could feel him breaking down any last barriers I had managed to put up.

My body was on fire, yearning for his with a passion I had never felt before, and my head was spinning with desire for him. Somewhere in the distance, I recognised that it was too late; there was no willpower left inside me to fight this man whom I adored.

For the last ten years I had denied myself the ability to love and be loved. But now, my love for Rafe was out in the open, gloriously exposed, and staring me fair and square in the face. There was no escaping it now. It was a beating red heart of continuous, comforting love, and something that I hadn't realised that I needed until the moment Rafe's glorious body and mine became entwined.

CHAPTER 40

GEORGE

*T*he journey on the stagecoach to Lyme Regis lasted three hours, but it seemed like a lot longer to George, he was so desperate to arrive.

Had Mary and her mother survived the Great Storm? Questions spun in his head. He had read in the newspapers that some people had lost their lives during the hurricane, and he hoped to God that Mary had not been one of them.

During the interminably boring journey, George's thoughts had turned to Eleanor, and their worrying conversation earlier that morning. He had wakened early, but she was already awake and sitting up in bed.

"Her name's Mary then?" she had said with a scowl. When he didn't answer immediately, she added, "I know that's the real reason you're going back to Lyme Regis."

George couldn't trust himself to speak, but wondered how she knew. He had told her the same as he had told Oliver Tyrell, that he was going back to Lyme to investigate the Blue Lias rocks following the storm.

"What are you talking about?" he said at last, rubbing the sleep from his eyes and sitting up in bed.

Eleanor's face had reddened, and she glared angrily at him. "You talked about her in your sleep!" she yelled, pointing a finger at him accusingly.

George had to think quickly. "Mary Anning is just another geologist," he explained calmly. "I may have spoken about her, because she is fast becoming famous for her many discoveries. When we meet up, all we will be doing is exchanging knowledge."

"Huh! If she was someone you worked with, why were you declaring undying love to her then?" She folded her arms across her chest and set her jaw.

"I'm sorry, Eleanor, I do not know what you mean." George decided that denial was the best option. He swung his legs out of bed, feeling hot under Eleanor's watchful gaze, and began to dress.

His wife, however, was not giving up. "You will *not* go to Lyme Regis, George!" she ordered. "I absolutely forbid it!" Scrambling out of bed, she stood in front of him with her hands firmly on her hips. "I will make trouble for you if you do," she warned, her eyes wide with rage.

George stopped dressing and stared hard at his wife. "Mary and I are colleagues," he reiterated. "Please be sensible here, Eleanor. I won't be gone long, and should be back to you and Frederick in a few days."

Eleanor was silent for a moment as she digested this information. But as he was standing in front of the mirror adjusting his cravat, she came up behind him, her voice low and loaded with malice. "If you go to Lyme Regis, I will tell my father you are stealing from him, and he'll dismiss you from the mine!"

George's heart lurched, because the one thing Oliver Tyrell hated was dishonesty. The man was a womaniser of the worst kind, but he had always made it plain to his employees that stealing was never tolerated.

Again, George had to think carefully before answering Eleanor, and the best way was to bluff it out. "How do you propose to do that?" he asked, confident that she was issuing empty threats again.

Eleanor glared back at him, then she lifted her chin and walked quickly over to her dressing table drawer. She opened the drawer and drew out a familiar object. George immediately recognised the ornate silver letter opener belonging to Oliver Tyrell, because he had seen it on the man's desk whenever he was called into the office.

He glanced from Eleanor to the object, hardly able to believe she would stoop so low.

She turned to face him. "I will tell my father that you are going back to Lyme Regis to see Mary, and also that you stole this from him." Eleanor looked very pleased with herself.

George was feeling uneasy now, but again he had to call her bluff. "Your father is a philanderer, Eleanor. He would likely applaud me for taking a mistress such as Mary," he warned. "And he would *never* believe that I stole his letter opener."

He thought about how hard he had worked to gain his qualification in order to work at the mine. And how Eleanor's determination to make trouble could cost him everything.

Despite this realisation, in his mind he had no choice but to go to Mary. For his own peace of mind, he had to make the journey, to make sure she had survived the storm and was coping with the aftermath of the devastation.

George pulled back his shoulders and confronted his wife. "I *am* still going to Lyme Regis, Eleanor," he told her. But he had to force himself not to think of what he might find on his return as Eleanor's screams had followed him out of the door.

CHAPTER 41

MARY

*M*ary was placing a shelf back on the wall from where it had fallen during the storm, and didn't look round when she heard the shop door open. It was late in the day for customers, and she was tired after all the hard work that was needed in the shop. She hoped the customer would make his purchase quickly and go on his way.

"I'll be with you in a moment," she called out over her shoulder.

When there was no answer, Mary turned around impatiently, and her heart leapt at the sight of George standing in the open doorway of the shop. She was suddenly acutely aware of her dishevelled appearance.

Mary was wearing her outdoor clothes because it was so cold in the shop. Her cloak was covered in fine dust, and she was sure she had dirt on her face. She straightened her shoulders as a freezing draft filled the already cold space, but her face flushed with heat as George gazed across the room at her.

"Good afternoon, Mary," he said so softly that she could barely hear him.

"How do you do, George?" she said, and quickly followed it by saying, "Could you shut the door? There be a cold draft with it open." She had no idea what to say to George as she lifted a hand towards her hair, which was coming adrift from her bonnet.

It was strange that all she wanted to do was fling her arms around George, yet all she could do was refer to the cold in the room and request that he close the door.

George shivered as if the draft had only just hit him, then he immediately swung around and closed the door behind him. "I'm sorry," he said, before turning back to Mary. "The devastation… in the town, it's so bad," he began falteringly. "Oh, Mary… I was so afraid for you and your mother."

Mary gaped at him. His words didn't match the expression on his face. It seemed to her as if he was talking about how disappointed he was that they could not love each other as they both longed to do.

Unable to find the right response, Mary said the first thing that came into her head. "How did you get away from work this time, George?" But what she really wanted to say was 'I love you'.

"I went to see Oliver Tyrell and planted the idea that I needed to come back here and observe the effects of the storm on the rock formation. Luckily, he agreed to let me come, but I had an appointment to have my portrait painted, which I had to honour before making the journey."

He tilted his head slightly and laughed. "My wife Eleanor had been keen for me to have the portrait done for some time, and this time I had to agree to it.'

A rush of love for George enveloped Mary. He was so close to her that she wanted to reach out and hold him in her arms.

"Thank you for coming. It be so good to see you," she told him. And it was true, the sight of him standing in her shop felt so good that it lifted her troubled, aching heart.

George took a step towards her, and his eyes never left her face. "When I heard about the Great Storm, I was concerned for you, Mary. And, thank the Lord, you have survived it.

"The whole time I was in the artist's studio, I was thinking of you and how you had fared in these terrible circumstances." George spoke with such longing in his voice that Mary's heart turned over.

She nodded sadly. "As you can see, the storm has been devastating,' she explained. Her chin trembled as she spoke, remembering all those in Lyme who had perished or lost everything. She rubbed her cold hands together. "All the coal cellars and the coal has gone, so there be no fires this winter," she told him.

George looked dismayed at this news. "I'm sorry to hear that, Mary," he said. Then he turned towards the shelf behind him, which was miraculously still intact and full of fossils. "I will purchase these while I am here," he told her, picking up two small ammonites.

Mary knew George had a vast collection of these common fossils already, but money was money and she needed it desperately. She thanked him and dropped the coins in the till. When she turned back, he was holding a wad of notes out to her.

"This will help with the buying of the coal for the winter," he said. "Please take it," he pleaded. "It could be a loan, if you prefer?"

"That's very kind, George," Mary said, swallowing her pride and taking the money from his outstretched hand.

She was grateful to George. She and her mother had been desperately cold since the storm, and this would make a huge difference in helping them both through the long winter ahead.

"It's the least I can do, Mary, and if there's anything else you need, please let me know," George said. Then, taking in a long deep breath as if he were gathering his courage, he stepped even closer to her. "You know I love you, Mary. I think I've always loved you," he said unexpectedly.

Mary's mind whirled. *If she confessed to loving George back, how would that help their difficult situation?* No good could come of it, and she could hear Elizabeth's voice in her head telling her that. Yet she yearned to say how she really felt about George, and to let him know she had always loved him, too.

"I was deeply sorry that you decided to return my last letter, Mary," George said at length, breaking the long silence.

Mary dropped her gaze, ashamed now of her actions. "I be sorry for that," she murmured. Then she lifted her eyes to his and tried to explain.

"I was still so angry with you," she admitted. "But I did read it," she said evenly, as her love for George filled her whole body. "You said in the letter that you hoped we could still be friends…" she began, still staring into those amber eyes of his.

Suddenly Archie, the boy who was helping Mary in the shop that day, appeared from around the back. He stood by her side, looking up at the adults expectantly.

"What you want me to do next, Miss Anning?" the child asked impatiently, shuffling on his feet as his gaze flitted from her to George and back again.

Archie's appearance jolted Mary out of her thoughts, and she quickly recovered herself. "Could you pick up all the ammonites and curies that have fallen off the cabinet, please?" she instructed as sternly as she could, while at the same time pointing to the far corner of the shop.

Archie sometimes needed a bit of authority and could be wayward, but on this occasion he nodded at her and immediately ran off to do her bidding.

Mary explained to George who Archie was. "His father sent him to me to keep him out of mischief, because there be so much clearing up to do after the storm."

George nodded and looked around the shop. "It has certainly caused a lot of devastation," he said, letting out a long sigh.

Mary nodded sadly, feeling the heavy weight of loss on her shoulders. "We were among the lucky ones," she told him. "There was much that were destroyed in Lyme." Tears filled her eyes, and she dabbed at her face with her cold fingers, dipping her head to stop him seeing her distress.

"I'm sorry, Mary, I really am." George looked at her with sympathy.

Mary lifted her head and sniffed, determined not to give way to her sorrow. After all, what good would tears do now? "My brother lost a great part of his property," she explained to George. "And have you seen what's happened to The Cobb? So many people have lost their homes."

George frowned and rubbed a hand across his forehead. "The damage done is unbelievable. I saw The Cobb on my way here; it was awful. What's happened to all the ships and boats that were harboured there?"

Shivers ran up Mary's spine when she remembered the sight of what the sea had done to the ships, and all those poor souls that had been lost in a watery grave.

"The storm dragged them all out of The Cobb. One of them were *The Unity*. The raging water tossed it out to sea with the crew still clinging desperately to the rigging, but luckily, they ended up being swept ashore under Black Ven cliffs. The crew escaped with their lives, and the ship be still there, empty, and waiting to be swept out to sea."

George raised his eyebrows at this. "I shall go along and have a look at it while I carry out my studies on the rocks. I'll need to show the evidence of my research to Oliver Tyrell on my return to work. Before I do, would you like me to help with the clearing up here?"

Mary was feeling a little better now, and so grateful that George had made it to Lyme Regis to see her. "Miss Philpott be arriving shortly to help, and I have Archie here, too."

She indicated the child, who had neatly stacked all the fossils back on the cabinet just as she'd asked him to. "But thank you for the offer, George."

As he turned to go, she issued him a warning. "Please be careful out there," she said. "There be many loose rocks and debris still around, and the sea has a fierceness about it which is refusing to go away right now. You could easily get cut off when the tide comes in, which will be in about two hours' time."

George nodded. "I promise I will be careful, dear Mary," he said, then his gaze softened. "I'll come back and see you later, if that is agreeable to you?"

Mary saw that George was asking to see her alone later, with no interruptions, and this time she welcomed it. Despite not taking him up on his offer of becoming his mistress, she understood that it was time she told him how she really felt about him.

"I will be here, George," she told him, lifting her chin. "There be too much clearing up to go anywhere else," she added, giving him a weak smile.

George looked pleased. "Then I'll say good day to you, Mary." He tipped his hat. "And I will return soon," he promised, before turning towards the door.

"Wait, George!" Mary said urgently, stepping out from

behind the counter. "Don't be going near that wreck, it's dangerous. I've been searching for fossils since the storm, but only on Lyme beach. It be treacherous going near the ship on Black Ven because of its precarious position there."

"Understood. I promise I won't go near Black Ven cliffs," George reassured her with an understanding nod.

"And don't stay out too long." Mary knew she was fussing about George's safety now, but she couldn't seem to help herself. "Do you have a pocket watch with you?" she asked.

George gave her an odd look. "Don't worry, Mary, I always carry the one my sister bought for me," he said, pulling it out of his pocket to show her.

"That's good. Make sure you are not out more than an hour or so," she reminded him. "It's too dangerous on those shores to be out in the elements longer than that today."

"I'll be sure to be careful, Mary, and I'll look forward to seeing you later," George assured her, then disappeared through the door, closing it firmly behind him.

CHAPTER 42

GEORGE

*A*s George walked towards Lyme Regis beach, his heart felt light. He had known things would be tough here in Lyme after the storm, but he had been shocked at the sight that met his eyes everywhere he turned.

The stagecoach had dropped George at The Royal Lion in Broad Street, and he had gazed at the devastation that the gale had wreaked. There were many houses damaged, especially towards the bottom of Broad Street, and there was an air of grief hanging around the place.

As he had passed the assembly rooms, he could see whole families huddled together inside, obviously made homeless by the storm.

The town was a shadow of its former self and money was in short supply. He would have liked to stay and help the people rebuild Lyme Regis, but he couldn't risk being away that long, not with Eleanor's threats still ringing in his ears.

The relief to find that Mary and her mother had survived the onslaught of the elements was immense. Even so, she had been left short of essential supplies like food and coal, and her house had been damaged. It was hard to see the expression on Mary's face, too, as if she were carrying the weight of the world on her shoulders.

His heart swelled when he remembered how she had gazed at him when he had arrived in her little shop. First, her face had registered surprise, then she hadn't been able to hide how she felt about him, and he had clearly seen the light of love in her eyes.

She was obviously no longer angry with him and had forgiven him his blunder; she had even suggested that they could still be friends. That, for George, would have to do for now.

As he walked along the path towards the beach, he noticed his pocket watch was still dangling out of his waistcoat, and he replaced it to its rightful place. As he did so, the words 'Tempus Fugit', which were inscribed along the top of the watch face, caught his eye and a memory danced in his head.

This timekeeper meant so much to him because his sister Faith had given it to him for his birthday a short while before she died.

"This is for you, George," she had said in words he could barely hear. "Please remember its message, and what the Latin inscription means. I hope you love it and think of me when you look at the time."

After her death, George had looked more closely at the pocket watch and found that Faith had had his initials carved on the back, which had been a lovely surprise.

George shook the memories from his head and stopped for a moment to take in his surroundings. He had reached the beach and could see the tide was coming in. Mary had been right, and he could see that the sea was still very angry. A gust of wind was howling noisily around him even though the sun was out, and he could feel himself being buffeted along with the force of what was left of the gale.

Mary's warning rang in his head as he calculated how much time he had to study the rocks before the tide turned. It was as he was jotting down notes on the newly exposed rocks that George had the sense that someone was watching him. He stopped and gazed around, but there was no-one to be seen. It seemed he was alone.

Despite having his hessian boots on, George's feet slid from beneath him as he walked. Everywhere underfoot was wet and slippery from the storm, so he had to be extra careful. A while later, he was studying a particularly large sea urchin which had caught his eye, when he heard the sound of running footsteps behind him.

"Hey there, mister, stop!"

George turned around to see Archie looking agitated and breathless, and he bent quickly down towards the child. "Calm down, Archie, what is it?" he asked the boy.

"It's Miss Anning, she be in danger over there by the ship which got washed up on the cliffs," he said urgently, pointing over towards the Black Ven area.

George stood up and gazed into the distance. "That can't be right, Archie. She told me not to go over to the ship, so why would she go near it now?" He looked down at the child, convinced he had made a mistake.

"But she did! Miss Anning were searching for fossils and got stuck in the mud right near the ship! I followed her and saw it 'appen. She told me to come and get you. Please, mister, please! You have to rescue her afore she drowns."

The child was becoming upset, and George frowned. "Alright, Archie. You go back to the shop while I go and check if Miss Anning needs my help," he instructed.

George was sure the child had got it wrong, but if Mary was in trouble, he didn't have time to go back to her shop to check Archie's story. He did, however, have just enough time before the tide came in to have a look around the wreck for Mary.

Archie seemed reassured by this decision, and he nodded at George before running off towards Mary's shop, while George began the short walk towards Black Ven cliffs. He hadn't gone far when he realised that the beach was so slippery and full of mud that it was safer to take the footpath above the shoreline.

He could see the stricken ship in the distance, and as he came nearer to it, he stopped and looked down at the damaged vessel from the pathway above.

The ship had been smashed to smithereens. Half of it was missing, and the other half was wedged against the rocks, held fast by a bank of wet mud. Overhead the sound of a gull squawking made him glance out towards the ocean, where he saw debris from the vessel floating far out on the rough sea.

Very soon the slippery mud holding the shipwreck would give way, especially as it was now raining. And when that happened, the rest of the ship would disappear under the waves.

George was still unsure that Mary would have endangered herself by coming here, especially when she had warned him off the wreck. *Something wasn't right.* He would check she wasn't here and then return to Lyme beach via the footpath, and find out what the child Archie was up to.

"Mary, Mary! Are you here?" he shouted. He could feel his words being carried away on the strong wind which was still buffeting him where he stood.

The tide was coming in fast, and George could see it wasn't safe to be here, so he called Mary's name once again. There was no response. He decided to go back to her shop, where he would likely find her. But just as he turned towards the footpath, a strange sound reached his ears.

As he stopped and listened, it came again, and his heart lurched. Someone was crying out for help, and the sound could only have come from inside the stricken ship below him. Mary had told him that all the crew had been rescued. But maybe, as Archie had said, Mary was in danger. It just didn't make sense to George that she would have ventured inside the unstable vessel.

He knew he couldn't go back until he had checked Mary was safe. It made no sense that she was here, but he was aware she was a brave, determined person who did not always think of her own safety. Maybe she was stuck inside after trying to rescue someone who *had* been left on the ship?

He stared down at the wreck and heard again that plaintive cry ringing through the air, and tried to identify the noise. He couldn't tell for sure, but he thought it sounded like Mary's voice.

"I'm coming to help you, Mary," he shouted as loud as he could.

George would have to climb down the slippery bank and get onto the deck. *He would be alright,* he told himself, *so long as he was careful.* Against his better judgement, he began clambering down the cliffs, while trying not to slip; one false move meant he would fall to his death on the rocks far below.

As George struggled with the wet surface of Black Venn cliffs, he suddenly realised the crying had stopped. Clambering onto what was left of the deck, he felt the ship sway precariously beneath his feet, as warning bells rang in his ears.

This was too dangerous, but the thought of Mary being in peril kept him going. He stared around at the wreckage of the ship, knowing that shortly it could come completely loose from its stuck position and crash onto the rocks and sea below.

"Mary, are you here?" he shouted, desperate to get to the path above him and back onto safer ground. But no sound came back to him, except the noise of the overhead gulls and the waves crashing to shore below.

George instinctively knew he had mere minutes to get to safety before it was too late. And he became aware that someone was watching him again. He glanced around, thinking how ridiculous that was. *Who else would venture into this dangerous territory?* But the answer came back to him soon enough.

"You fell for that street urchin's story then? You stupid fool!"

The man's voice reached George's ears, followed by a boulder falling nearby, which landed next to his feet. He looked up to see a man standing above him, clinging to a large rock jutting out of the cliffs.

The manic grin on the man's face made him look almost comical, and fear clutched icily at George's heart. He was alone in this dangerous situation with a stranger who looked like a madman. *What was this man's game, and why was he looking at George like that?*

CHAPTER 43

*G*eorge's feet almost slipped as the ship moved precariously beneath him. It would not be long before *The Unity* ended up in the sea, and he could feel the force of the waves pulling viciously at the vessel.

He lifted his chin and looked up at his aggressor, trying to gather his wits. Whatever this man's game was, George must not show weakness. It could prove fatal.

"Fell for what exactly?" he called, playing for time. His thoughts were running in all directions as he tried to negotiate his escape from the man and what was left of the ship.

George tried to make out the man's features from his position on the moving deck. But he had a hat pulled down over his head, and was wearing a long black coat. Just then, the stranger threw back his head and roared with laughter, almost slipping off the cliff face as he enjoyed his own humour. George was puzzled at what was so funny.

Then the man cupped his hands to his face and made a noise that sounded just like Mary's cry for help. George then realised it was this man, not Mary, who had been making the crying sound. *But how*, he wondered, *had the man made this sound appear to come from the wreck of the ship?*

"I was on the ship a moment ago." The man seemed to guess what George was thinking, as he stared menacingly at him from his vantage point on the footpath.

The man must have climbed up the other side of the ship as George climbed down, which was a strange thing to do. George had no idea who the stranger was, or what he wanted, but the situation was becoming serious, and he had to act quickly.

Without further ado, George began clambering off the wreck, knowing that whoever this madman was, he had George at a disadvantage. His heart was beating out of control knowing that in a moment, when he reached firmer ground, he would come face-to-face with his aggressor.

George kept his gaze averted, feeling the man watching him climb back up to the pathway. At one point, his foot slipped, and he almost fell onto the cliffs below. The waves were washing up onto the rocks, becoming higher by the moment, and the wind was whistling wildly, pulling relentlessly at George's clothes as he climbed.

With the tide coming in fast and the beach now almost totally cut off, George eventually reached the pathway, just as a loud sucking noise came from below, followed by a crash that echoed through the air. Both men looked down to see the mud had released the rest of the ship, and its debris was falling plank by plank into the angry sea below.

George shivered, remembering how he had been on that deck only a moment before. He turned towards the man who was now blocking his way.

"Who the bloody hell are you?" he asked. Then, not waiting for an answer from the scoundrel, George pushed past the man before walking quickly back the way he had come.

However, the man grabbed hold of his arm and held George fast. His feet were sliding from beneath him as they struggled. Both men were perilously close to the edge of the cliffs, but George stood his ground and looked the man straight in the eye.

"What do you want?" George shouted into the wind, his face close to the man whose black eyes stared out at him menacingly.

"You been warned, but you still had to come here!" the man roared, still clutching hold of George's sleeve. "You and the Anning woman are fools!"

"What are you talking about?" George demanded. Pushing his face even further towards his assailant, he forgot for a moment what a dangerous position he was in. "Go to hell, whoever you are!" he yelled.

The man's features split into a menacing grin then he let out a cackling peal of laughter. George simply stared at him. *What was so funny? The man was mad.*

With the rain now lashing against his body, soaking through his greatcoat and down his hessian boots, George was chilled to the bone. He had had enough of this man and his games. Yanking his sleeve out of the stranger's grip, George moved to walk away, but the man wasn't letting go that easily.

It happened so quickly that George didn't see it coming. From behind him came a hard shove. Then in an instant he was rapidly falling backwards, with nothing to break his fall. As the rocks below came up to meet him, he could see the man smirking above him while he watched George plunge to his death.

CHAPTER 44

The breath was ripped from George's body as he plummeted towards the ground and the wild sea raging below him. Powerless to break his fall, he tried to cling onto the bank, but the notorious Black Ven cliffs lived up to their reputation as their dangerous wet mud slid from his grasp. His terror increased with every second that passed.

Rocks had been loosened when he fell and were tumbling around him, making a terrible rumbling sound, which echoed in his ears. Within seconds, he found himself in the sea, with silt and debris from the shipwreck floating alongside him.

Water and the relentless mud filled his mouth and nose, making him choke while struggling to breathe in the hellhole he had found himself in.

With a huge effort, he lifted a hand to push the thick mud from his eyes and forced shallow, ragged breath into his body. Heaving his head out of the water, he looked around him while fighting the strong pull of the tide to stay near to the shore.

As his gaze searched for the shoreline, he suddenly

realised it was no longer there. In the few moments it had taken him to confront his attacker, the sea had come in and the water now covered where the beach had been a short time before. Only one large rock was left standing proud of the water. *If only he could pull himself onto that rock, maybe then he could regain his strength for a moment, before attempting the difficult swim back to Lyme Regis.*

Slowly he moved his battered body towards the rock, acutely aware of his dire injuries. One arm was almost certainly broken, and he was unable to move it beneath the murky water. Other parts of his flesh had been ripped to shreds.

The excruciating pain was everywhere in his body, and blackness could close in at any moment, which would mean certain death. Eventually he managed to slide his frozen body onto the rock – a task that took every ounce of his energy to achieve. Feeling exhausted now, he waited for his ragged breath to ease.

The ice-cold water was fierce against George's legs as they dangled uselessly in the sea, and the tide was relentless in its attempts to pull him back out towards its murky depths. The ocean might want to claim him for itself, but he must fight with everything he had left. One more moment of rest was all he needed, then he would get back into the water and swim to safety.

In that interlude of calm, an image of Mary came into George's head. Those inquisitive, deep brown eyes of hers which never stopped searching for fossils, that determination which showed in the tilt of her chin, and the way she had of holding herself upright in such a proud, defiant way. Never before had he met such a remarkable young woman.

George closed his eyes in an attempt at brief respite, but he was instantly hit by a wave so powerful that it knocked him sideways. As his body hit the freezing water once again, he instinctively held his breath before he became completely submerged again.

Time stood still, and it seemed like an eternity. Holding his breath made his chest cry out in agony, but eventually he was able to pull his head free of the water and force sea air into his tormented lungs.

The safety of the rock had now disappeared, it was fully immersed in deep water, and George found himself completely adrift beneath the wild waves, with nothing but a deep dark cavern of water below him.

As he flailed around in the water, panic struck deep within his belly, and he felt himself begin to sink. He tried to force movement into his legs, but his limbs had been reduced to lumps of ice and refused to stir. Taking his courage in his hands, George pushed his body forwards and out into the dangerous open water.

In his desperation, George tried to conjure up Mary's face again in his mind. Right now, he needed some of her courage to survive this terrifying ordeal. Only Mary could give him the strength to get through this most treacherous of days.

When her image returned to his mind, he heard again her warning about watching the time and not getting into trouble on Black Ven cliffs. And he cursed himself for being fooled by the child. Archie must have been in league with the scoundrel who had pushed him off the cliffs.

While still struggling in the water, George thought about the pocket watch Faith had given him, and he longed to draw comfort from its glass face. Pushing his free hand into his pocket, George found it was empty. The watch had gone, lost forever at the bottom of the ocean.

Tearing his thoughts back to his survival, George took hold of the tiny amount of strength he had left and forced himself to keep swimming. The waves were growing higher by the second, dragging him out to sea. And the mud, which had followed the wreck into the water, was now threatening to suffocate him.

His injuries made it almost impossible to swim. George's left arm was hanging limply by his side, and his body burned painfully with every stroke of his other arm. Only the thought of seeing Mary again was keeping him going in this hell hole.

As soon as he was safely back on the shore, George was determined he would find out who had made this attempt on his life, and report him to the King's guards. The man would get his just deserts, he would make sure of that.

But George was so weakened, he began to wonder if he would survive. *He had to keep swimming,* he told himself, and as he squinted through sore, swollen eyes, he realised he had no idea where he was.

After a while, George felt himself getting nearer to where the beach would be if it wasn't covered in deep water. So he kept swimming, aiming to climb up the slippery Black Ven cliffs and once again escape the sea onto the pathway above them.

The problem was he was so tired and frozen with the cold that he had to concentrate hard not to allow his eyes to close. If he lost concentration for one second, he would be dead.

Inch by painful inch, he neared the dark cliffs, and was within an arm's length of pulling himself out of the water, when he was wrenched violently away and back down into the deep water. The massive wave had come from nowhere, and George's body was swept away from the cliffs and back into the hungry sea once more.

He was beyond panic now, struggling to move his exhausted body back to the shore and break the iron grip of the water. Despite swimming valiantly with every single ounce of strength he had left, the ocean wouldn't let him go.

It was dragging him in a dangerous frenzied circle with such ferocity that he was utterly powerless to stop it.

George didn't want to give up, but when the water came up over his head and pulled him under the waves time and time again, the breath simply left his body. Mud and silt from the cliffs filled his mouth and nostrils, and was slowly suffocating him. And worst of all, he seemed to be stuck in a whirlpool of water, which was dragging him further and further out to sea.

Making a final attempt to lift his head out of the water, George looked through blurred vision towards the shore. With utter despair, he could see that he was so far from the cliffs now that land and salvation were completely unreachable.

One last hope was a plank of wood floating on top of the water, and he tried valiantly to reach it. But the closer he got to it, the further away it floated.

Suddenly it didn't matter any more. Nothing mattered except that he wouldn't hear Mary's words of love, which he was sure she had been about to impart to him, or to see her gain the recognition she deserved for her many valuable discoveries.

George would also miss little Frederick growing up. Numbness, pain, and regret tore through him, while the penetrating sadness engulfed him at thoughts of his little son. However, he had no strength left to fight and was completely spent now. For him, this was the end.

When the last vestige of energy drained from his body, George gave up the struggle, and for the first time since being pushed off the cliff, he allowed his heavy eyes to close. Peaceful sleep beckoned him towards its dark, comforting depths.

As George began to slip silently beneath the waves, he heard a woman's voice calling his name, and somehow he lifted his head free of the water and opened his eyelids one last time. Through the water, he could just make out the figure of Mary standing on the path above the cliffs, where he had been only a moment before.

She was looking far out to sea and calling his name. If only he had the strength to keep his head above the waves and swim back to her, but he was gripped in this whirlpool of water and his voice had completely disappeared.

Mary must have come looking for him when she realised he was missing. For one brief second, just before he lost consciousness, George experienced a moment of happiness when he realised it was true: Mary did love him.

CHAPTER 45

MARY

*M*ary had been cleaning fossils in her workshop. She had just returned to the front of the shop to see that the windows were rattling with the force of the wind, and the roar of the sea was growing louder by the minute.

She was concerned for George. Over an hour had passed since he had left the shop, and she began to wish he had not gone off on his own, especially as the weather was worsening.

Mary was also dismayed to see that Archie had completely disappeared without doing the chores she had asked of him. She stared out of the window at the sight of the waves rising high into the air and made a decision.

"I'm going out, Ma, can you watch the shop?" Mary called out to her mother, who was still in the back room.

Her mother's head instantly appeared round the door to the hallway, and she peered at Mary in dismay. "What, in this weather?" she huffed. "Don't be foolish, my girl," she warned.

Mary understood that her mother had been so trauma-tised by the storm that she was afraid of going out now. But that wouldn't do for Mary. She needed a change of scene, and besides, she still needed to search for fossils or they would not eat.

Her mother had always looked on the dark side of life and rarely smiled, though Mary didn't blame her. Her ma had endured a tough life, losing seven of her children and then her husband.

However, Mary had got her resilience from her father; it was his happy disposition and gritty determination she had inherited. Despite the hardships the family faced, her pa had found joy in everything. *Perhaps*, Mary often wondered, *it was the finding of the fossils that helped his sunny disposition*. To him, they were magical. She still missed her pa, despite it being many years since his death.

Pulling on her outside shawl, Mary put on her gloves and regarded her mother. "Don't worry, Ma, I won't be long. I be going out for some fresh air," she lied, as she picked up the lamp which would help to her see her way in the developing darkness.

There was no need to worry her mother further and tell her the truth, but she needed to look for George, who had been gone for longer than he should.

The sky was full of greyish black clouds and the wind tore at Mary as she made her way towards the beach. The roar of the sea was so fierce that she shuddered, remembering the recent gale. *This weather was the aftermath of the storm, that was all*, she told herself, *it was not another Great Storm, as the last one had been*.

As she stood on the pebbles and peered across the deserted beach, Mary was surprised to see Archie standing in the distance kicking at some pebbles. She hurried towards him.

"What you be doing here, Archie?" she said, coming up behind him.

As the boy swung around to face her, she saw he had some farthings in his hand, and Mary noticed a guilty look on his face. "Where did you get that money from?" she asked, taking a step closer. She had not paid him for his work yet, and the boy came from a poor family.

Instantly, Archie pursed his lips together and, before she could stop him, he ran off across the beach in a tearing hurry, as if the devil himself was after him.

"Archie! Archie!" she called, but to no avail. The child kept on running away from her. She would have words with his father later, Mary decided.

After a while of roaming the Lyme Regis shoreline looking for George, Mary decided he was not there. The wind was so fierce she was having trouble standing up, and the waves were coming in thick and fast.

Had George gone back to his lodging house, without saying goodbye to her? This didn't sound likely, especially the way he had spoken to her before he left her shop, and the look on his face had reinforced that. *Was it her fault? Was it because Mary hadn't admitted her love for him? Or had something terrible happened to George in the short time he'd been gone?*

Fear clutched at Mary's heart as she realised that there was only one other place George could be. A dark feeling of dread washed over her, but she decided she would risk making her way towards Black Ven cliffs.

Maybe George had gone against her warning and was in peril at the site of the ship wreck. If so, she had to try and save him. With the sea coming in at such an alarming rate, there was only one way of reaching Black Ven, and that was by walking along the footpath above the cliffs.

As Mary quickly followed the path, she peered out of her bonnet to see a man hurrying towards her. "Excuse me, sir," she began, as the wind carried her voice away. But the man kept his head bent low while murmuring something unintelligible as he rushed past her.

Mary stopped for a moment and watched him disappear into the distance, his long black cloak flowing out behind him. It seemed he was in a tearing hurry, which reminded her of Archie and the way he had run away from her earlier.

A gust of wind nearly took her off her feet, reminding Mary she had limited time to get to the cliffs before the light went completely. She lifted the lamp quickly and resumed her journey.

When the cliffs at last came into view and Mary looked down on the beach below, her heart raced at the sight before her, while her limbs were frozen with dread.

The tide was now in, and the beach was completely underwater, just as she'd warned George might happen before he'd left her shop earlier. And worse still, *The Unity* was no longer stuck on Black Ven cliffs' slippery black surface, but had been washed far out to sea.

Through the fading light, Mary could see bits of debris from the ship floating on top of the wild water. She was acutely aware that if there had been anyone left on this shore not ten minutes earlier, they would have been swept out to sea and drowned very quickly.

Shivers ran up her spine, and it occurred to Mary that before turning back towards Lyme Regis, she had to make sure George was not down there somewhere, perhaps fighting for his life.

Just then the clouds parted, and light shone through onto the beach below, enabling Mary to see the sea more clearly. She stared hard at the churning water as the wind howled around her and the waves rose high into the air.

Cupping her mouth with her hands, Mary shouted as loud as she could against the elements. "George! Where are you?" she bellowed. "George, I'm here!"

Even though the wind carried away her words, she kept calling George's name. A second later, she noticed one area of the sea looked a deeper colour than the rest, and had very few breaking waves around it. The water there was not far off the shore and appeared to be circling in a fast and furious way. Mary shuddered. She had seen this kind of current before and was even more worried for George now.

Just as she turned to walk away, her gaze was caught by something in the middle of the furious swirl of water. She blinked, but when she looked again it was gone. It must have been debris from the ship which had been washed far below the waves.

As the dark clouds above her closed in again, leaving Mary standing in half-darkness, her fears for George grew. She hurried back along the path towards Lyme Regis, fervently hoping that if George had come along to these notorious cliffs, he had escaped the danger of the sea by climbing up onto the path before the water had completely closed in.

CHAPTER 46

ELIZA

It was Sunday morning, and I had been woken abruptly by the sound of thunder, lightning, and heavy rain. Taking a moment, I reflected on last night's love-making, what a considerate lover Rafe was, and my heart swelled with love for him. I reached across to pull him into my arms, only to find an empty space in the bed.

I sat up and looked at my phone to see it was only 6am. I had been in the middle of another strange dream, and this one was more vivid than any of the others.

The dream was already fading from my memory, leaving only echoes of it in my head. Images of Mary walking quickly towards Black Ven cliffs flashed in my mind; she was rushing, as if in a tearing hurry to get somewhere quickly.

My gaze searched the bedroom. It was as if Mary were in the room with me, urging me to return to Black Ven cliffs once again, to find the answer as to who had killed George. *Was it my imagination or was she telling me that, today, I would solve the final piece of the jigsaw puzzle?*

Glancing out of the window, I could see the rain was easing off and the storm had died down. I knew it was complete madness, but I had to do something. Throwing on some clothes, I grabbed my jacket, convinced that the answer to not only George, but also Liam's demise, lay amongst the pebbles and boulders of Black Ven cliffs.

I wished with all my heart that Rafe was here with me, as loneliness and fear stabbed relentlessly at my heart. But there was no time to contact him, or even to let him know where I was going. If I didn't go now, I could feel in my bones it would be too late.

It didn't take me long to get to the beach, and I quickly noticed how the storm from the night before had churned everything up. There was a sea mist, and the wind was high and tearing at my hair and clothes, but I battled on, feeling driven towards Black Ven cliffs.

As I hurried along, I tried to avoid the shoreline where the waves were lifting high into the air and crashing to shore with a frightening roar. Yesterday, while I had been here on my daily walk, the sea had been less rough. This morning, despite the early hour, there were new warning signs up on the beach.

The notices told of the high tides on this beach, made worse by the storms Lyme Regis had been experiencing recently, but I was compelled to ignore the warnings and keep going. As I neared Black Ven cliffs, I was acutely aware that this area had always been prone to landslides, and that with the sea so rough there was danger everywhere.

Stopping for a moment, I was convinced that Mary was nearby. And then it happened. I saw a woman in the distance, just as I had in the dream. She had on a long, dark dress and was walking hurriedly along the water's edge not too far ahead of me.

It was as if I was looking through a soft camera lens, making the woman look slightly blurry through the haze.

But I could still see it was Mary, from the proud tilt of her head and the straightness of her spine.

I had to watch my step, as the pebbles were wet underfoot from the rain. When I finally reached Black Ven, I had to stop and retie my trainer lace which had come undone, and when I looked up it was to find that Mary had vanished into thin air.

Finding myself completely alone now, my eyes were drawn to the dangerously slippery cliffs in front of me. I gazed at their sodden blackness, and bleakness filled my heart as the wind tore relentlessly at my face. I had a strange feeling as if something wasn't right here, apart from the atrocious weather, but I had no idea what.

As I stepped nearer to the cliffs, a small shiny object caught my eye, lodged in a crevice of one of the rocks. The breath caught in my throat, because it looked like a familiar object. Despite the water quickly getting deeper here, I pushed towards it and began wading towards the trinket, determined to retrieve it before I went home.

In an attempt to lift the object from its wedged position in the rock, I curled my fingers around it and pulled hard, but it quickly slipped from my grasp. With the water tugging at me relentlessly, I made another grab at it, and this time I succeeded.

Holding it tightly in my palm, I gazed down at what looked like the pocket watch George had been wearing in the portrait. It was recognisable because it was bronze in colour and had the distinctive words 'Tempus Fugit' on its face.

If it had been George's watch, I could hardly believe the words were still legible after two centuries of being stuck fast in this rock. How it had remained here for so long was anybody's guess. I quickly turned the watch over to see the initials *G.H.* engraved on the back. But before I had time to ponder more on the significance of this, I turned around to see a massive wave roaring towards me.

I had no idea how I had not noticed the sea coming in so quickly. But there was no time left to think of an escape route, as the water was almost upon me. Fate was closing in on me with sickening dread. I was about to be drowned here on Black Ven cliffs, just like Liam ten years earlier and George almost two centuries before him.

Before I could think about this further, the breath was ripped from my body as the freezing water hit me with such a force that it knocked me clean off my feet. I was adrift and searching valiantly for something solid to cling onto, to stop me being swept out to sea.

But my efforts proved fruitless. Every time I tried to get hold of them, the rocks merely slipped from my grasp. I was flailing around terrifyingly and uselessly in the maelstrom of water.

I had almost resigned myself to drowning when suddenly and unexpectedly some of the water receded, and I managed to haul myself up onto the side of the cliffs.

As I clung onto the freezing surface of the cliff, I noticed that the rock I had retrieved the pocket watch from a moment before was now under water. I held fast to the chain of the watch, knowing it wouldn't be long before the water returned, and it would take me with it back out to sea.

My heart was thrashing in my ears as I saw there was nothing but water now where the beach had been only minutes before. Instinctively, I reached for my mobile phone, which should have been in my pocket, but it was no longer there. It must have been lost under the water when the wave hit me moments earlier.

I was so cold that my body was shivering violently, and my teeth were chattering. It was at that moment of sheer panic that a distant memory surfaced. I saw myself again on the boat that fateful day ten years earlier, when I had just woken up groggy from the fall after the wave had hit the boat.

I saw how, in that disorientated state, I had watched Liam trying to radio for help, hardly able to stand upright because the boat was tipping precariously from side to side. The engine was dead, but worst of all, the boat was being buffeted so badly that it was completely out of control.

I had tried to control the panic rising in my chest and shaken the fuzziness from my head as I clung onto the wooden seat of the boat. The angry waves had formed themselves into a frightening swirling, never-ending circle.

As the realisation hit me that we were heading towards a rip tide and there was nothing either of us could do to avoid it, panic had taken over and I was shouting at Liam to get off the boat, all the while knowing that if we did escape and found ourselves in that whirlpool, we would both be pulled under and drowned within seconds.

I had watched all this with the understanding there were no life jackets on board the boat. But as I remembered this moment, I saw Liam telling me in an anguished voice that there *was* one life jacket left on board, and that I must put it on immediately!

Every instinct had told me not to do this, as panic along with terror vied in my head for attention. My first thought was whether we could share a life jacket. But as I fought with the agonising realisation that it would be impossible, Liam pulled the jacket from its hiding place underneath the seat and threw it at me.

I caught the life jacket and watched Liam lurch towards me, then we struggled as he tried to get it on me, and I fought against it. Meanwhile, the boat was being buffeted wildly towards the very spot where I was at this very moment, clinging dearly onto life, and slowly losing the battle for survival.

The lost memories kept coming at me like a roll of film unravelling in my head, and I could see the scene again where I was arguing with Liam and telling him that *he* should put the life jacket on.

Eventually he shoved his face towards mine, and in the midst of the panic and mayhem he yelled, 'For God's sake, Eliza. You have to live for our baby to survive, get the bloody life jacket on!'

As I continued to cling valiantly onto the cliffs now, tears streamed down my face. At last, I finally knew why I'd suffered so much guilt for the past ten years, and how I had been saved while Liam had drowned.

I understood now that Liam did love me. Maybe not in the way I wanted him to, but the love was there. I would never know whether he would have stayed with me in Lyme forever or not, but given what a free spirit he was, it was unlikely.

However, whatever Liam was, he was not a coward. And that terrible day he had been willing to give his life for mine, in the hope he would save me and our unborn baby.

More memories flooded back to me now; I hardly had time to catch them as they whizzed past me. The next was of Liam pushing me into the water and me being caught in the rip current which began dragging me under every time I attempted to swim.

I saw Liam instructing me to swim diagonally across the shore, to avoid the pull of the current. 'Once you're free of the tide, you can get to the beach,' he had shouted, the sound of his voice barely audible over the deafening noise of the wind and rain.

Even in that dire situation, though, I refused to leave Liam to certain death, and I had struggled and cried. But my protests were all to no avail, as the boat finally overturned, taking Liam with it.

I was dragged violently out to sea as water filled my mouth, my eyes, and my ears. And the current was so strong that I couldn't escape it. It was impossible to move, let alone swim, and all I could do was to try and force my head out of the water and take in deep breaths of sea air.

In amongst this terrifying chaos, I had forced myself to look behind me to see whether Liam was still alive. He was clinging to the overturned boat, and was now in the water fighting valiantly with the waves, while at the same time gesturing to me to swim diagonally across the beach. Even at that moment, while he was fighting for his life, Liam had been attempting to save me.

Eventually, after a moment I had lost sight of him. It was then that I found myself completely alone, frozen with cold, and being dragged out towards the open sea.

Self-preservation took over as I battled with the waves. I remembered what Liam had said about saving the baby, and something in my numbed brain told me that in order to survive this ordeal, I had to follow his advice. There was no other choice. Forcing movement into my arms and legs, I began to swim diagonally across the shore instead of trying to get back towards the beach.

This seemed so wrong. How could I save myself by swimming out to sea? Surely, I would be swept even further out? However, I was beyond caring by this time, and was being dragged further away from Liam and the safety of the upturned boat.

After a while of exhaustive swimming, the waves eventually released me, and the struggle became easier. That must have been the moment when I was free of the rip tide.

Seriously fatigued, I trod water for a while, at the same time desperately searching into the distance for a sighting of

Liam. But he was nowhere in sight, and the upturned boat was so far away that it was only a dot on the landscape.

Eventually, after swimming for what seemed an age, I reached the shore and dragged myself wearily up onto the wet mud. As I came to rest on that cold, slippery silt, I became aware that, despite the odds, I had survived, but my relief was mixed with the devastating heartbreak that Liam was lost somewhere under the waves.

Now, even though I had a sense of relief that the truth had finally emerged, this revelation was mixed with the blackest feeling of dread. To discover what had happened to Liam that day on the boat, at the very moment of my own death, was indeed a cruel irony.

If only I could have lived the rest of my life knowing the truth. That Liam did love me, and I was *not* to blame for his death. That knowledge would have allowed me to grieve properly for Liam, and then I would have learnt to live my life to the full once again.

Sadly, it was too late for regrets. Another wave was roaring towards me where I was still clinging desperately onto the rocks at the bottom of the cliffs, ready to sweep me out to sea and follow Liam towards a watery grave.

I was feeling drowsy, with little or no strength left. And despite wanting to live, I was almost ready to give up and let the ocean take me. I had always loved the sea, and now, I reasoned, it would be my final resting place.

My fingers were slipping from the sodden cliffs, and even though I clung on valiantly, in less than a moment I knew I would be lost forever under the waves.

"Eliza! Eliza! I'm coming. Hold on!"

The voice was faint and far away in the distance, and I could barely hear it through the rush of water drowning me. However, the sound was persistent, and somehow it was penetrating my senses. *Was I imagining that someone had come to save me? Just as I imagined seeing Mary on the shore earlier?*

With the tiny bit of strength, I had left, I forced my leaden eyes to open, and for a brief moment, I thought I could see a man swimming furiously towards me. Then there was only blackness surrounding me, and inside of me. And as my fingers finally slipped off the cliff, my body began to sink slowly into the endless darkness below.

CHAPTER 47

J was curled up with Rafe on the sofa in the tiny front room of the flat, and we were going over the frightening events of the day before.

"My God. You were so lucky that Liam found that life jacket when he did, Eliza," he said, widening his eyes at me, and touching his hand to his chest in a thankful gesture. "And you sure did have me scared yesterday. I don't even like to think of the consequences if I hadn't decided to search for you when I did."

I met his gaze and let out a long breath I hadn't realised I was holding. An ice-cold shiver ran up my spine at what could have happened if it hadn't been for this wonderful man sitting beside me.

"Oh, Rafe. What can I say? Except a big thank you for saving my life." Tears welled up in my eyes as my thoughts returned to the moment that his strong arms had grabbed hold of me, and somehow hauled me bodily out of that wild water.

At the last moment, just as all my energy had been spent and before I went under for the final time, I had seen him in the distance swimming towards me. At the time, I was convinced I was imagining it. Rafe coming to my rescue was like the image of Mary I had conjured up earlier and which had led me towards Black Ven cliffs. Perhaps it was all in my mind.

Luckily for me, he reached me just as the water completely engulfed me, filling up my mouth, my ears, and my eyes with thick, silty sludge. The waves had dragged me under with a strength I could no longer fight off.

Now, safely in the comfort of my own home, I dipped my head and let the tears fall as Rafe's arms wrapped me in a huge, comforting hug. "I'm sorry..." I sobbed, feeling an aching in my chest. "Sorry," I repeated.

Rafe tilted my head up with one finger and looked deep into my eyes. "Come on, Eliza, what on earth are you sorry for? You don't have to apologise to me. I'm just relieved that I was able to reach you in time yesterday."

The lump in my throat eased a little and I nodded before swiping away the tears. "Sorry for putting myself in that position, sorry that you had to save me, sorry for being a complete and utter burden to you."

For the second time in my life, I had been saved from drowning off the coast of Black Ven cliffs, and my heart was full of gratitude to the two men who were responsible.

"You are *not* a burden," Rafe said, standing up abruptly and pacing the room.

After a moment, he knelt down in front of me, and looked at me with a frown etched between his brows.

"Let's get this straight, Eliza, you don't have to be sorry about anything." He pursed his lips and continued to stare at me intently. "I'm not sure if you truly understand how much you mean to me, and if not, I'll spell it out for you. I LOVE YOU, Eliza Valentine, and even if you don't love me, I will continue to care for you for the rest of my life. There, is that clear?"

I had no idea why, but hysterical laughter bubbled up inside me, and I clapped my hand over my mouth to stop it erupting. Rafe's face dropped, and I realised he thought I was mocking him, even though that was the last thing I wanted to do.

He made to stand up, but I quickly grabbed hold of his arm, and for the second time in a short space of time, I embraced my feelings for him.

"I love you too, Rafe," I told him simply, and I truly meant what I said. "I really do," I repeated when he looked at me in disbelief.

It had taken me a long time to get to this point, but it was good to be here at last. I would never stop caring for Liam, and never forget what we had shared, but at last I could let go of the guilt and come to terms with his death. And now, here with Rafe, I had found a lasting love, and one in which we were equally committed to each other.

The disbelief on Rafe's face was replaced by a wide grin. "You do? Well, that's awesome news. I don't think I could have waited for you much longer!" he quipped.

When he saw the shocked look on my face, he quickly retracted, "Ha, I'm only joking. As I said before, I would have waited for you for as long as it took. Honestly."

Leaning forwards, he gave me a long lingering kiss. As we drew apart, I remembered something I'd forgotten to ask him. "How did you know I was in danger yesterday, Rafe? I mean, it was too early in the day for you to realise something was wrong."

"Well, here's the thing. It was sheer chance, really," he explained. "I accidentally left my phone at your place the night before last, and it wasn't until I was about to leave, to pick Harry up, that I realised it."

He flashed me a cheeky smile. "That's what you do to me, Eliza," he said. "I usually have my phone on me all the time and would've noticed it was missing as soon as I got home. But my mind was on other things."

My stomach fluttered and my face flushed at the memory of our lovemaking, and I took hold of Rafe's hand and held it tightly in mine as he shot me another tender look.

"As you say, yesterday morning when I did realise I had left the phone, I thought I'd chance you being awake. I wanted to collect my phone before going to pick up Harry, as I always need it with me in case Janine needs to make contact."

"When I arrived at the door to your flat and saw it was wide open, I knew something was wrong. And, when you were nowhere to be found *inside* the flat, I decided that despite the weather, you might well have gone to the beach for a walk. I've noticed recently you look a bit happier after you've been out walking."

I hadn't realised before quite how perceptive Rafe had been to my feelings, nor had I appreciated how much he had been looking out for me over the past few months.

It didn't surprise me to hear that I had left the door open; that morning my head had been full of thoughts of Mary after the strange dream I'd had. And I had been in a rush to get out of the flat.

Rafe leaned forwards and stroked the hair off my face. Then he sat back in his chair, looking confused. "Eliza, you need to tell me, what on earth made you go to Black Ven cliffs in that dreadful weather?"

It was a completely understandable question to ask, considering the danger I'd put myself in, but as I stared down at my lap, I tried to think of a way to explain.

"I had a dream... this time it was about Mary," I began. "I

only intended to have a walk on Lyme beach, but when I got there, I thought I saw her in the distant sea mist."

I looked up to see Rafe gazing at me with sympathy deep in those amber eyes. "I know it sounds daft, but she seemed to be leading me towards Black Ven cliffs."

Rafe simply stared at me, his gaze unwavering, making it impossible to know what he was thinking.

"Of course, I couldn't really have seen Mary, that's madness." I shook my head slightly. "I guess I must have been a bit confused."

I only half believed my words, because I was still convinced that Mary *had* led me to Black Ven cliffs, to find George's lost pocket watch and to understand what had happened to him. And, in doing so, had helped me answer so many questions about Liam's death.

"Who knows, Eliza?" Rafe gave me a pensive look. "I'm sure stranger things have happened, but whatever you saw on that beach, you are safe now, that's the main thing. That rip current you were caught in was pretty dangerous. They don't occur very often in Lyme, so it was sheer bad luck."

"God, it was terrifying." I shuddered and closed my eyes briefly at the memory. "And to be honest, I'd never understood before how perilous they could be, until yesterday, when I finally remembered what happened the day Liam died."

"That's why you couldn't get back to the shore, Eliza. The rip current was pulling you out further as you swam, and as Liam told you, the only way to escape it was to swim diagonally along the beach until you were completely free of it."

"Maybe that's what happened to George, too?" I sighed, feeling sad for the handsome man in my portrait, but at the same time hugely grateful to Rafe for saving my life.

He leaned back in his chair and looked thoughtfully at George's pocket watch which was lying on the small coffee table. "Finding the watch proved to us that George met his death on the cliffs." He glanced across at me. "But we still don't know who killed him."

"Don't we?" I was confused. Even though I'd had doubts that I couldn't explain that Holmes was responsible, I hadn't realised Rafe felt the same way. "I've had that feeling for a while, but surely everything points to Holmes being the culprit, doesn't it?"

Rafe didn't answer this question. Instead, he took an envelope out of his pocket and held it out to me. "I thought you'd like to read this," he said. "It's a letter from Mary, written to her friend Fanny Albright just after George disappeared. I came across it at the Dorset County Museum, and I was allowed to borrow it."

I took the letter from him and noticed it was addressed to Fanny at a London address. I wondered if after everything that had happened recently, whether this correspondence could give us the answers we needed, about what really happened to George.

My dearest Fanny,

I hope this letter finds you well and that your arm be stronger now after the weeks you spent in Lyme Regis recovering. Do you remember meeting George Hansome? He was the geologist I introduced you to when we were fossil hunting together. I be sure you must recall him, because George was not a man easily forgotten, with his dark good looks and ready smile.

Well, dear Fanny, something truly awful happened to George, so bad I can hardly bear to tell you this tale of woe. He returned to Lyme Regis a few days after the Great Storm devastated our small town, and he came back to investigate the rock formations after the storm for his employer at the South Exmouth mine. However, this explanation didn't ring true to me, because his face told me a different story when he came to see me.

You see, Fanny, the last time he was in Lyme, he made me a

proposition, in other words he asked me to be his mistress. I be
shocked at this suggestion, as you can imagine. Can you see me as
a kept woman, Fanny? There is nothing on this earth I would avoid
more than that fate. However, I fear George does not know me at
all if he thought that offer be accepted. I have to admit to being
very fond of him, I may even love him, but I have my pride to think
of and was not prepared to become a gentleman's plaything. Or to
spend my days in idle luxury doing nothing more than twiddling
my thumbs all day.

George came to see me in my shop after the storm. After we
spoke about the devastation the town had suffered, he told me he be
going for a walk.

It was then I warned him not to go near the wreck of The
Unity, *where it remained wedged in the cliffs (devoid of her crew,*
thankfully) on Black Ven cliffs. The weather was still bad, with
high winds making the sea wild, and the ship be teetering on the
edge of collapsing into the ocean at any minute. I told him it be
dangerous to be in that area, so he must avoid it.

A while later, I became worried for George when he did not
return and the weather worsened.

I shouldn't have gone out and Ma told me not to, but I went in
search of George. Along the way I found my young assistant for the
day, Archie, who had gone missing when he should 'ave been
helping me in the shop. I found the boy wasting time on the beach
and sent him packing. But as I walked the dangerous path towards
Black Ven, still looking for George, I noticed a man hurrying back
along the path from the site of the wreck.

Oh, my dear Fanny, I was soon regretting that I did not stop the
man and ask him if he had seen George. He hurried past me so
quickly, but afterwards I had a bad feeling that he had something
to do with George's disappearance.

George had made an enemy of someone called Ernest Holmes,
who was a man he knew in the Geological Society. George
exposed Holmes's dishonesty recently, and Holmes had been

suspended from the society pending an investigation into this claim.

Holmes, it seemed, hated George with a vengeance and had even threatened him once afore, earlier in the year, when he was in Lyme on holiday. George also told me that Holmes had been spying on me and Elizabeth Philpott here in Lyme recently, and warned me to be careful when I was out fossil hunting on the shore alone.

I am sorry to write such a depressing letter, but I needed to voice my suspicions to someone, as my mind has been in turmoil over George, and his fate, since the day of his disappearance.

Please write back soon, and be letting me know how your arm is and how you fare.

Sincerest regards,

Your friend,

Mary

I thought about how unfair it all was, and shook my head before gazing up at Rafe, tears in my eyes once again. It seemed I was making a habit of crying today.

"What a sad letter," I said, digging in my pocket for a tissue. "Mary warned George not to go near that shipwreck on Black Venn cliffs."

I wished with all my heart that all those years ago George had listened to Mary that day. "I think she was in love with George as much as he was with her, and I'm surer than ever now that George was murdered that day," I told Rafe. "It's obvious now that Holmes *was* responsible for his murder."

Rafe had gone very quiet as he leant back in his seat and regarded me. "Yeah, it was very sad. An old newspaper I came across of the time reported that Mary was still searching for clues as to what happened to George years later."

"What *did* local people think happened to George?" I was confused as to how this mystery had been left unsolved. "And why was Holmes never questioned about his part in George's disappearance? Especially after Mary's claim that she saw him walking away from the area at the time."

My heart went out to poor George, who had tried to help Mary gain recognition for her work, and also attempted to get justice for Annabelle Hadcliffe after her husband died.

Rafe looked at me with a pensive expression. "Mary was often not listened to, as we know now, and no-one really knew what happened to George. A little gossip went a long way in Regency Lyme Regis, where speculation must have been rife."

"Some people said he'd more than likely run off with another woman, and others thought he'd perished while looking at the wreck of *The Unity* that day."

I pursed my lips together and frowned. "Holmes *was* responsible! Surely there's no doubt about that? It was too much of a coincidence otherwise, the way Mary saw him walking back in the direction George had gone that day."

Rafe made a 'Hmmm' noise in his throat. "Okay. I know it looked that way, Eliza, but Mary didn't actually say it was Holmes who passed her when she was making her way towards Black Ven cliffs that day. From reading through George's notes and Mary's letters, *we* thought it was Holmes because no-one else had taken a dislike to George the way he had."

"What do you mean it looked that way? Are you saying there's another explanation?" I was confused.

"You could say that. I have a theory that Holmes had nothing to do with George's demise."

"Really? How do you work that one out? Everything we looked at pointed at Holmes being the culprit, and surely from her letter to Fanny, even Mary thought he responsible."

Rafe nodded. "Sure, I know, but the dates don't add up. I looked into what happened to Holmes after he was accused of plagiarism by George, and he was suspended from the society. He then disappeared for a few months. This was probably to let the dust settle while his fate at the society was being discussed. But the fact is, he wasn't even in this country when George disappeared."

"Oh my God. Wasn't he? How on earth did you come across that information?"

"In the end it was easy, I don't know why I didn't think of it before. I looked up Ernest Holmes's journal at the Geologist's Society. Online this time. Remember I told you that as a member of the society, I have access to all the journals?"

"When I found the right journal for Holmes, I made sure I was reading the right month and year – the exact time when he was under investigation for committing plagiarism, and the exact time that George went missing. Because of the investigation, Holmes had no choice but to inform the society where he was going, especially if he planned on leaving the country."

"So, where did Holmes disappear to, then?"

"It was recorded in his notes that he went to France to stay with a relative, in October 1824, and he was away for several months. The Great Storm in Lyme Regis was the same month, and it was just after that when George disappeared. The upshot of it is that Holmes would have been away at that time."

This was incredible news. I was astonished that Holmes might not be George's murderer, after everything had pointed to him. And it meant we still didn't know what had happened to George, except that he'd drowned on Black Ven cliffs, where I found his pocket watch wedged in the cliffs after almost two centuries.

Rafe echoed my thoughts. "It's surprising, but as it eliminates Holmes from the crime, this means that whoever killed George still remains a mystery."

"Could Holmes have hired someone to do the dirty deed on his behalf?" I asked, thinking on my feet. "And did Holmes get his comeuppance from the society regarding the plagiarism?"

"I thought of that, and it's possible that he could have hired someone. But, would Holmes have risked doing that when he was already under investigation for a crime? And as for his comeuppance, on his return from France a few months later, I read that Holmes was tried for plagiarism and imprisoned."

I let out a long sigh of relief. "At least that means John Hadcliffe's widow would have come into the money for John's unpublished papers, just as she should have done. That is good news, and it was all down to George exposing Holmes for the crime. What a cool guy he was. But, Rafe, who else could have had a motive to kill George?"

"Well, if I'm honest, Eliza, I don't have a clue. I mean he was well liked, so what possible motive would anyone, except Holmes, have to murder him? Maybe it was an accident."

I thought about this and couldn't deny it was a distinct possibility. "George could have slipped off the pathway above the cliffs while peering down at the wreck of *The Unity* as we discussed," I conceded. "I mean, even now, two hundred years later, it's dangerous to be in that area after a storm."

Rafe gave an understanding nod. "Yeah, exactly. Those cliffs are notoriously slippery after bad weather, and at the time George was there, it was the tail end of the gale, and there were still high winds and rough seas."

I thought about this. "I guess we'll never know for sure now. But at least we know where he died, and in a way we do have closure for George in that letter from Mary to Fanny." I took a deep breath and added quietly, "And as the memories about that day on the boat have come back to me now, I have closure for Liam at last."

Rafe smiled gently. "I hope you're feeling better about everything now?"

"Yes, thanks. Just knowing what happened on the boat during those final hours has helped my recovery, and I feel more at peace with myself. If that makes sense?" I had a warm glow inside of me that Rafe had helped me to find my way during these past difficult months.

"It does, and I'm glad." He dropped a gentle kiss on my lips. "I hope you're looking forward to your climate change talk at the WI. I think you'll be awesome."

"Thanks, Rafe. I'm a bit nervous about it, but I *am* looking forward to it," I replied. "My plan is to do the talk, and then I'm planning to approach Harry's school after that."

"I guess the talk you'll do for the WI won't be quite the same as for the primary school?"

I shook my head. "Nope it won't. When I did the beach clean, a lady called Julia told me about a Facebook page called Zero Waste Mama, which is dedicated to the plastic problem and climate change. I've been following the advice on the page ever since, as Claire who runs it is a great advisor and has been a huge influence on me."

"At Harry's school, I'll be explaining about the plastic waste on the planet, and how it's affecting the marine life in Lyme Regis," I continued, full of enthusiasm for my subject.

"I'll get their interest by talking about the white beaked dolphins who are not normally seen in Lyme, but which have been spotted off the coast here recently."

I was convinced this was the start of better things to come for me, and as soon as Chloe returned from Australia, I had made up my mind to pursue a career in marine conservation in the wild. Suddenly I realised this was something I needed to discuss in more depth with Rafe.

He was looking at me encouragingly. "That's great that you're making progress in that direction, and I can see you'll be very successful." He glanced down at his watch. "I'm sorry, but I can't stay long today, as I'm picking Harry up from Janine's house in half an hour. We're going to look at a school local to Lyme for him."

My heart lifted at this news. At last, everything was coming together for Rafe and Harry, too. "No worries, that's fine. I hope you find the right school for Harry. I'll need to get back to work soon anyway. I nearly forgot to ask you, how's Jessica getting on with Harry?"

Since my suggestion that Jessica helped out with Harry while Rafe was at work, she had been looking after him for short periods of time to see how they got on together.

Rafe smiled widely. "Harry loves Jessica, so no problem on that score. And I've been discussing her resuming her childcare course while he's at school, so that she'll be qualified to look after him during the holidays. So far, all good. Are you sure you don't mind me poaching her from you?"

I laughed out loud at this, remembering what a struggle Jessica had sometimes been in the teashop. "Oh, Rafe. No, and you're not poaching her from me. Jessica is doing what she wants to do now, looking after kids. She was never happy at the teashop. And as for staff, Drew asked me some time ago if she could work in the teashop after she had the baby, so I'm going to give her Jessica's job."

Rafe stood up and began putting on his coat.

"Before you go, there's something I want to tell you," I said, knowing it was now or never, as I might not have the courage to say what was on my mind another time.

Rafe sat back down heavily and took a deep breath. "What is it, Eliza?" he asked looking concerned.

My heart went out to him, as I was sure he wouldn't like what I was about to say. "Chloe rang me yesterday. She's coming back to Lyme soon, because she's split up with her boyfriend."

Before Rafe could answer this, I ploughed on, knowing I had to get this out in the open. "That means I won't be running the teashop for much longer," I gave him a meaningful look, "but I do have a plan in place."

Rafe crossed his arms across his chest slowly without taking his eyes off me. "Well, go on, Eliza. Spill the beans."

I leaned forwards and rested my hands on my knees. "As you know, I've always wanted to work with whale conservation. I've been making enquiries about working for a company on Vancouver Island, in Canada."

I let my words sink in and watched the emotions race across Rafe's face, feeling bad that he was now thinking the worst. "The thing is, I might be going to live and work in Canada, in the near future."

Rafe swallowed and then bit down on his bottom lip. "Oh, man. Are you trying to break up with me, Eliza? If so, I'd rather know now than later."

"No! Rafe, please don't think that. I'm definitely not breaking up with you. I'm trying to say that I want us to be together, but I also want... need, to go to Canada and follow my dream."

I paused briefly. "Do you think we could maintain a long-distance relationship? Or perhaps you and Harry could come out with me?" I was rambling now, then I stopped, held my breath, and waited for his reaction to this bombshell.

Rafe let out a long sigh and took both of my hands in his. "Phew! You gave me such a fright. To be honest, if that's what you want to do, we'll work it out, somehow. I'm not saying it'll be easy, but we'll definitely find a way around it."

What a relief it was to hear Rafe say those words. It meant that if I had the courage to go ahead, I would be able to realise my dream of helping to save the whales in Canada but *still* have Rafe, and Harry, beside me on that journey. At long last, everything I had always wanted was within my grasp.

I looked up to see Rafe staring at me with love reflected in those beautiful amber eyes of his. "Are you happy now that you've got that off your chest?" he asked with a grin.

I nodded and he leaned across to kiss me. My heart raced as desire for him chased itself around my body.

"Now, I really must go, but I'll see you later, Eliza," Rafe said breathlessly, before blowing me another kiss as he headed towards the door.

After he had gone, I sat in silence for a moment with the imprint of his lips on mine and his sea-salt musky scent hanging in the air. I was hugging this wonderful feeling to myself, knowing that I had him to thank for helping me to find my way since my return to Lyme.

He had helped me get over the grief which had threatened to overwhelm me when I first arrived here. And discovering who George was, and how he had supported and loved Mary, had also helped me to recover from the all-consuming sadness of coming to terms with Liam's death.

His suggestion that I take steps to help the environment had also paid off by giving me the confidence to think about fulfilling my ambition of working in whale conservation.

My heart was full of love for Rafe, and excitement danced in my chest about what the future held for us both. Then, as my phoned pinged, I glanced down at it to see a message from Pat, who was waiting outside the teashop to be let in.

As I hurried downstairs to work, there were echoes of George and Mary in my head. But now those thoughts were mixed with the absolute certainty that for me, Rafe, and Harry, the future looked brighter than ever before.

CHAPTER 48

1826 - MARY

The door opened, bringing with it a blast of cold air, and Mary glanced up from the counter to see a woman and a small boy had come into the shop. The child held tightly to his mother's hand, his amber coloured eyes wide with curiosity as he gazed in wonder at the fossils on display.

"Can I help you?" Mary asked with a smile, taking in the woman's full, velvet dress in a beautiful shade of dark blue, and the fair ringlets peeping out of her large bonnet.

For a moment, the woman did not speak. Instead, she met Mary's gaze and held it intently. Mary shifted uncomfortably. *Should she know this lady?* They had had a lot of visitors to the shop recently.

"So, you are the famous Mary Anning then?" the woman said at last, through pursed lips.

It was a strange question to be asking when everyone for miles around knew where Mary's new shop was. Besides, the shop had *Anning's Fossil Depot* across the top of the door. And as for famous, it was certainly true she was more well-known now, but *famous* might be stretching the truth a little.

Mary had blessed the day she had saved enough money to move her and her ma up the hill to the top of Broad Street, away from the danger of the unpredictable sea. The glass-fronted window of the shop gave her ample scope to display her larger finds, and the home they now lived in above the shop was comfortable. It was more than she could ever have hoped for in years gone by.

"That be my name." Mary lifted her chin and addressed the woman, who was still looking at her intently. "How can I help you?" she repeated, meeting her gaze.

The woman seemed flummoxed, as if she wasn't sure what she wanted in Mary's shop or why she was even there. Mary looked down at the little boy, who had pulled his hat off to reveal a head full of jet-black curls, instantly reminding her of someone she used to know. Someone who had been very dear to her.

Mary glanced towards the woman again, knowing that the best way of dealing with this type of customer was to be polite. "Would your little boy like to look at some fossils?" she enquired into the strange silence that had filled the little shop.

The woman dropped her gaze and nodded, and Mary led the child over to a shelf full of ammonites and belemnites, watching as his face lit up. "You can touch them, it's alright," she told the boy as he gazed at the fossils in absolute awe.

When she turned back to his mother, the woman had taken her gloves off and was fiddling with them agitatedly. "Were you looking for something in particular?" Mary tried again, although she was aware that they were going around in circles.

The woman took a deep breath and looked at Mary, as if gathering her courage. "I was looking for you, Mary Anning, because I believe you knew my husband," she explained shakily. "His name was George Hansome."

Mary's heart lurched as she now realised who the woman was standing in front of her. George had described his wife to her on several occasions; now here she was, Eleanor Hansome in person.

Words failed Mary as her gaze strayed to the little boy, who was running his fingers over an ammonite in the corner of the shop. So, this was Frederick, George's son.

"Did my husband speak of his family to you?"

Eleanor's voice interrupted her thoughts, and she quickly turned back to face the lady. "I did know George,' Mary admitted, avoiding answering whether George had mentioned his family to her.

"He was one of the geologists who visited me some time back," she added cautiously, not wanting to give too much away. "How be George these days?" she asked, almost dreading the answer.

A flicker of hope burned inside Mary that George had returned home that day two years ago, when it seemed to the world that he had drowned on Black Ven cliffs.

If that was the case, then it would mean that he did not love her, as he had proclaimed. But that no longer mattered to Mary. What did matter was that George was still alive and happy, and did not die that fateful day when he had gone off to look at the wreck of *The Unity*.

The look on Eleanor's face put paid to this theory, and her next words confirmed George's fate. "George perished while in Lyme Regis," she said directly. "He never returned home after he visited you," she added with a heavy sigh.

Mary's heart plummeted to her boots as her hopes were finally dashed. She had always believed George had died that day, but she had never known for sure. "I be sorry to hear that," she consoled, thinking how inadequate words were at times like these.

Eleanor nodded sadly before clutching a hand to her head shakily. Just then two things happened. The child came running up to his mother with a fossil in his hand, and Mary's mother popped her head round the door from the workroom beyond.

Mary looked from her mother to Eleanor, who had gone as white as a sheet, and made a decision. "Ma, would you mind the shop for a few minutes, and show the child some of the other fossils?" she asked. "This lady would like to see my workshop," she improvised.

Her mother readily agreed, and Mary beckoned Eleanor to follow her through the hallway, where she led the woman to a small room, next to the workshop, which was located at the back of the house.

Eleanor nodded silently, all bravado gone now, and did as Mary told her.

"Are you unwell? You looked as if you needed to sit down," Mary explained when they arrived in the room which Mary and her mother used for resting, between working in the shop or preparing the fossils.

Eleanor merely stared at Mary as they sat down opposite each other on the small seats.

"Do you feel better now?" Mary tried again, determined to find out what this visit was all about and concerned that this lady had looked as if she might faint a moment before.

"I'm fine now, thank you." Eleanor lifted her chin, a little more colour returning to her cheeks. Then to Mary's surprise, she put her head in her hands and began to weep.

Mary waited patiently for the crying to stop, wondering how to comfort Eleanor, and feeling guilty at the same time that George had loved *her* and not this woman.

"I'm sorry about George," she sympathised. "He was a nice man and a good geologist." 'And I loved him,' she wanted to add, but she kept her lips firmly closed.

At last Eleanor looked up, her eyes red and her face tear-streaked. "I didn't treat him well," she admitted sadly.

"Please, Mrs Hansome, surely, this be not my business." Mary was now feeling uncomfortable with the way the conversation was going.

Eleanor didn't seem to hear Mary and kept talking as if she hadn't spoken. "When I was growing up, I watched my father treat my mother badly," she began, staring into the middle distance. "He was a philandering cad, and it eventually killed my mother."

Mary nodded, wondering why Eleanor was telling her this, but she kept silent because the other woman was clearly lost in her memories.

"When George and I married, I told myself he was *not* like my father. However, one evening when we were at a ball, I was unable to dance because I was with child. George danced with many other women, which I tried not to mind... until I went outside for some fresh air and found him kissing one of them."

She made a wry face and dabbed at her face with a linen handkerchief. "George told me he had had too much to drink that night," she explained.

"I'm sorry," Mary whispered, understanding how that would feel like betrayal, and remembering how George had explained his mistake to her.

Eleanor sighed heavily. "Did he tell you about that?" she asked, giving Mary an intense look and holding her gaze.

It was Mary's turn not to answer. She dropped her eyes and stared down at the floor. *How could she admit to Eleanor that he had confided to her how jealous his wife had been?*

Eleanor gave a resigned shrug. "It is of no matter now," she continued. "I'm afraid that was the beginning of the end for George and myself. After that, I thought he was meeting another woman *every* time he walked out of the door."

Mary remembered George's letters, and how he had often explained how jealous Eleanor was as soon as he was out of her sight. He had told Mary that as soon as he told Eleanor he was coming back to Lyme for work reasons, the jealous rages always got worse.

One of his letters had referred to threats that Eleanor had made to George, saying she would make up lies about him stealing from her father, Oliver Tyrell, who was also George's boss, and get him into trouble if he persisted in going to Lyme Regis.

The room had gone strangely silent again.

Mary was wondering where their conversation was leading, and decided she had to be blunt. "Why you be telling me all this, Mrs Hansome?" she asked.

Eleanor's eyes suddenly widened. "I know that George was in love with you, Miss Anning," she said with a hitch in her voice. "He never admitted as much, but he often talked about you in his sleep."

Mary felt like she couldn't breathe, and forced herself to inhale. "Nothing ever happened between us," she managed after a moment, lifting her chin, and telling herself she had nothing to feel guilty about. If George had dreamt about her, that was not her fault. She had never encouraged him.

Eleanor just looked at Mary then gave a resigned nod. "As I said earlier, I drove George away, you see. So it was my fault."

Mary started to protest, but Eleanor leaned forwards in her chair and interrupted her. "I've been consumed with guilt these last two years... it's a relief to tell someone."

Was Eleanor talking about George being in love with Mary now, or something else entirely?

"Are you alright, Mrs Hansome," she asked, aware that the other woman had gone quite pale again.

Had Eleanor had something to do with George's death? Maybe she had wanted to punish him for going against her wishes, and she had arranged for him to die? Mary immediately berated herself. This demure looking woman in front of her did not look capable of murder.

"Do you have any idea what happened to George?" she asked with trepidation. She gave voice to the words, even though her gut instinct was telling her that she might not want to hear the answer to this particular question.

Eleanor's eyes look distant now, as if she were somewhere other than sitting in Mary's small back parlour. "It was my fault he died, Mary," she repeated. "My fault…"

Alarm pulsed through Mary, and she stood up abruptly, staring at the tortured look on Eleanor's face. "What do you mean?" she demanded. *How could Eleanor be responsible for her husband's death, when George had died somewhere on Black Ven cliffs?*

Eleanor's eyes flipped back to Mary, and she bit down onto her lower lip. "I was jealous… Mary," she stumbled over the words, and there were tears now streaming down her face. "And I thought he was in love with you." She clapped a hand over her mouth as if she had said too much.

"What did you do?" Mary hissed, as she peered down at the woman who was now wringing her hands agitatedly. "What happened to George?"

Just then, Frederick's cries for his mother echoed noisily through the house. And it was as if the sound of her son crying jolted Eleanor out of her stupor. She shook her head at Mary, then abruptly got up from the chair and swept past her towards the shop.

Mary hurried after her. She was not finished with this conversation yet. However, before Mary made it back to the shop floor, Eleanor had grabbed hold of Frederick, and both mother and child had disappeared out of the door, leaving her staring after them.

CHAPTER 49

2 YEARS EARLIER (1824)

*J*t had been a whole week, and George had not returned to Exeter after his visit to Mary Anning in the town of Lyme Regis. Eleanor had been sick with worry. She could barely sleep for the guilt which was eating her up from the inside out. Whatever George deserved, it wasn't this.

The scene was being played out constantly in Eleanor's head of the day on which George left, when she had threatened him with telling her father that his favourite employee was a thief. She had expected George to comply with her wishes, knowing how much he loved his job.

And it had been a shock to Eleanor to realise that he must have loved Mary Anning more than his beloved profession. It was this realisation that had made her do what she did. However, as much as she tried to justify her actions to herself, it did nothing to alleviate the pain she was feeling now. The fear that what she had intended to happen to George had gone horribly wrong, plagued her daily.

Eleanor had expected to hear from the man she had hired to give George a fright. But he had disappeared into the ether and had never been seen again. What a fool she had been to pay the man before he had done the job. It gave him no reason to return to Exeter and inform her exactly what had happened in Lyme Regis.

Her father had been constantly questioning Eleanor in the time George had been missing. He needed him back at work, he told her, and was trying to get to the bottom of where exactly George was. At first, Eleanor had told him she knew nothing, but her father knew his daughter well, and he could see there was more to the situation than met the eye. Finally, after much hand-wringing, she had admitted what she had done.

"George went against my wishes, Father," she told him with a purse of her lips, the jealousy about Mary rising up in her chest ready to choke her.

Oliver Tyrell's face reddened as he faced his daughter. "Eleanor, I gave George permission to go to Lyme Regis," he retorted, angry at her interference in his business affairs. When she didn't answer, he towered over her. "What did you do?" he roared.

Eleanor knew when she was beaten. She had no choice but to admit she had sought revenge for George not obeying her orders. "I paid a man who worked at Exeter quayside to rough him up while he was in Lyme Regis," she said, and she could hear the whine in her own voice. "George needed to be taught a lesson," she told her father, lifting her chin and glaring defiantly at him.

Oliver Tyrell merely gazed at Eleanor in disgust as she carried on telling him exactly what she had done.

"I made enquiries amongst the lower servants about who could do the job," she explained smugly, warming to her theme now. "I wanted to make sure George never went off to Lyme Regis against my wishes again."

At this, her father did something that he had never done

before, and he lifted his hand and slapped his daughter hard across the face.

"You stupid girl!' he bellowed. "George hasn't come back, which means that lout that you hired has probably killed him. Don't you understand that these types don't know the difference between roughing someone up and killing them?"

Oliver Tyrell paced the floor for a few minutes, his face red with fury. Eventually he sat down and put his head in his hands, then he looked up at Eleanor with steely determination on his face.

"You must never tell anyone what you have done, Eleanor. Otherwise you could face the gallows, along with the man who did this," he told her sombrely.

Eleanor had cried then. Not because her father had hit her for the first time, but because her jealousy over Mary had caused her to make a terrible mistake, and one which had cost George his life.

EPILOGUE

ELIZA

*T*he sun was shining down on me, and the sky was a beautiful, cloudless azure colour as the smell of freshly mown grass wafted across the graveyard. My limbs felt light on this beautiful midsummer's day, as I strolled past the large royal blue church sign and up the sloping pathway of St Michael's churchyard.

As I came abreast of Mary's final resting place, I stopped in front of the old, weathered gravestone. The inscription began with Joseph Anning, Mary's older brother, who died in 1849, aged 53 years. Underneath were the names of three of the Anning children who died in infancy, who were also buried here. Then there was Mary, whose wording read:

Also, of Mary Anning, sister of the above
Who died March 9ᵗʰ, 1847
Aged 47 years.

It didn't escape my notice that even in death Mary came second to her brother, just as she'd come second to the men in the Geological Society during her lifetime. It seemed such an ordinary inscription for such a remarkable woman, and I shaded my eyes from the sun and spoke to Mary in hushed tones.

"If I had been alive when you were, Mary," I whispered, "I reckon we would have been such good friends."

Since Rafe's research had uncovered Mary's association with George and we had learnt more about her life as a woman of consequence, I felt as if I had known her personally. I admired her and what she had achieved even more than ever, and never was a statue more deserved in the town of Lyme Regis than by this pioneering woman.

Letting out a long sigh, I left Mary and returned to the footpath, then headed towards another grave on the other side of the churchyard. Once again, I stopped and read the familiar epitaph engraved neatly. This time, I remembered the brave man who had saved my life.

Liam Sutherland

A wanderer and a free spirit.

Rest in peace.

I touched the headstone, and my fingers outlined the words *wanderer*, and I knew that's exactly what Liam had been. He was a free spirit, someone who hadn't liked to be tied down to one place or one person. Even so, it didn't mean that he hadn't loved me; that much I had learnt in the past year.

"Thank you, Liam, for giving your own life for mine that day on the boat," I whispered, feeling a lump in my throat. "And even though I thought for so long that you had no feelings for me, in the end I know you did love me... and you would've loved our baby, too."

I swallowed hard and wiped a stray tear from my face. "You'll be pleased to hear that I've found my own freedom at last. Now that my mother is returning from Australia to take over the teashop again, I'll be leaving Lyme to pursue my dream."

"I haven't been able to find the courage to do this for ten years," I admitted, "and if it wasn't for you, I wouldn't have the chance. I'm leaving for Vancouver Island soon, where I'll be helping the whales to survive in the wild, against the odds."

Saying those words sent a shiver of excitement down my spine and started my pulse racing. Liam had given up everything for me that fateful day on the boat, and it was my duty to live my life to the full now and not waste a single second of it. It was time for me to move on and to follow my dream.

As I turned to leave, a gust of wind whistled past my face, and I heard a faint whisper of sound. The words 'Goodbye, Eliza' were hardly audible on the breeze. But they were definitely there. And my mouth turned up at the corners and my heart filled with love as I saw Rafe and Harry walking up the footpath of the graveyard towards me.

AFTERWORD

If you've enjoyed this novel, do please leave a review – a few lines is all it takes. It's helpful to readers and makes authors very happy (me included)!

FREE COPY OF DELETED SCENES FROM AMETHYST

Sign up to Susan's newsletter and claim your **FREE** book.

Deleted Scenes From Amethyst is an insight into India McCarthy's life before she steps into Ruby's house for the first time, in my dual timeline novel, The Amethyst Necklace. It is exclusive content for my readers only, and a very special thank you for signing up to my newsletter.

My newsletter is sent out monthly and contains interesting historical insights into the research I have undertaken for the novels. I also send it out when there is something special to communicate – such as new book releases, special promotions or price reductions.

Go to the link below to be taken to the sign-up page. Your details will not be shared and you can unsubscribe at any time.

https://susangriffinauthor.com/subscribe-to-my-newsletter

Other Titles by this Author

Bird in a Gilded Cage (Second Edition)

The Amethyst Necklace (Book 1 of The Amethyst Series)

Scarlett's Story (Book 2 of The Amethyst Series)

A LETTER FROM SUSAN

When I began writing this book and started my research into Mary Anning, I was inspired by the life she led, in a time when women's achievements were not recognised.

Mary was born in 1799. She was a cabinet maker's daughter, was poor, uneducated, and was the wrong religion, sex and class of her time. Despite all this, at only 12 years old she unearthed the first complete fossilised skeleton of a 'fish lizard' later named as an Ichthyosaurus. This set her life pattern. However, Mary's life was not easy, instead it was a struggle against almost-impossible odds, and she became a pioneer in the emerging science of palaeontology.

In the writing of this book, I have tried to be true to Mary and portray her as the heroine that she was, I hope I have done her justice and inspired readers to learn more about her.

The real-life geologists mentioned in this book are as listed: Elizabeth Philpot, Georges Cuvier, Henry De Beche, William Buckland, William Lock and William Conybeare.

Acknowledgements:

I would like to thank my husband Shaun for his endless patience while I wrote this book. My cover designer Berni Stevens for another lovely cover, my editor Christine McPherson and my writing buddy, Suzanne Merchant, for her help in the research of this novel.

I would also like to acknowledge the late, great Claire Sumners (forever missed) for her help with the climate change details in this book. Thanks goes to palaeontologist

Paddy Howe of the Lyme Regis Museum, for the invaluable advice I gained when he took me on a fossil walk. He taught me so much about how Mary would have uncovered these long dead creatures. Also, Phil Davidson from The Charmouth Heritage Coast Centre, who took the time to point me in the right direction with my research. The Geologists Society for being so helpful when I visited them with Suzanne back in 2018, when this book was just an idea. And last but not least the Mary Anning Rocks organisation, for keeping me inspired about Mary, and acknowledging her so well in the wonderful erection of her statue in Lyme Regis. What a pioneering woman Mary was in her lifetime.

The book I used in the research for this novel was *Jurassic Mary*, by Patricia Pierce, which was recommended by Paddy Howe.

ABOUT THE AUTHOR

I live in East Sussex on the edge of the Ashdown Forest with my husband and a cat called Dave. I love writing romance with a mystery at its heart, and weaving secrets of the past with the present. I use my passion for history to research my novels, and am interested in how pioneering women in the past have managed to overcome adversity.

When I'm not writing I'm either singing with my local Rock Choir, or going for long walks in the nearby countryside.

Website:

https://susangriffinauthor.com/

Facebook:

https://www.facebook.com/susangriffinauthor

ISBN: 978-1-8382742-3-8

Printed in Great Britain
by Amazon